1994

Development in Practice

Development in Practice is the story of a major aid project: how it was origin-ated, what it was meant to achieve, and why it failed spectacularly. It challenges many of the generalizations and assumptions about development by placing them in a specific context, and provides fresh insights for anyone involved in the development process.

The authors describe events on a large Australian aid-funded rural devel-opment project, the Magarini Settlement Project in Coast Province, Kenya. While they consider why this project failed to fulfil even its minimum goals, they focus on what Magarini has in common with other development projects. They show how the Magarini is symptomatic of current practice, and they argue for a more pluralistic approach to development planning.

Accessible and lively, this book draws extensively on interviews, field diaries and file documentation, and includes numerous photographs and graphic illustrations. Its unique combination of critical theoretical and politi-cal analysis of development practice, within the context of an extended case study, will give the book a wide appeal. It will be of interest to students of geography, development studies, anthropology and economics, as well as to aid and development agency workers.

Doug Porter is Lecturer in Development Economics at the University of Western Sydney. **Bryant Allen** is Senior Research Fellow in the Department of Human Geography at the Australian National University. **Gaye Thompson** is currently working for CARE Australia on a community development pro-ject in Mozambique.

D1357782

Development In Practice

Paved with Good Intentions

Doug Porter, Bryant Allen
and Gaye Thompson

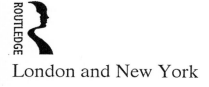

London and New York

First published 1991
by Routledge
11 New Fetter Lane, London EC4P 4EE

Simultaneously published in the USA and Canada
by Routledge
a division of Routledge, Chapman and Hall, Inc.
29 West 35th Street, New York, NY 10001

© 1991   Doug Porter, Bryant Allen and Gaye Thompson

Typeset from the authors' wordprocessing disks by
NWL Editorial Services, Langport, Somerset

**Printed and bound in Great Britain by
Biddles Ltd, Guildford and King's Lynn**

British Library Cataloguing in Publication Data
Porter, Doug *1953–*
    Development in Practice: Paved with Good Intentions
    1. Developing countries   Economic development
    I. Title   II. Allen, Bryant   III. Thompson, Gaye *1959–*
    330.91724

    ISBN 0–415–03564–3
            0–415–06626–3 (pbk)

Library of Congress Cataloging in Publication Data
Porter, Doug.
    Development in Practice: Paved with Good Intentions/Doug Porter,
    Bryant Allen, and Gaye Thompson
    p.   cm.
    Includes bibliographical references and index
    ISBN 0–415–03564–3
    ISBN 0–415–06626–3 (pbk)
    1. Rural development – Kenya – Coast Province.   2. Rural
    development projects – Kenya – Coast Province.   3. Coast Province
    (Kenya) – Economic policy   4. Economic assistance – Kenya – Coast
    Province
    I. Allen, Bryant James   II. Thompson, Gaye   III. Title
    HN793.C63P67   1991   90–39002
    307.1'412'0967623 – dc20   CIP

The road to hell is paved with good intentions

Quoted by Archbishop Trench as
'perhaps the queen of all proverbs'

All we can do is give advice. And again while giving it we say: 'This advice will be valueless if your own experience and observation do not lead you to recognise that it is worth following.'

Prince Peter Alexeivich Kropotkin
Anarchist Morality, 1892

Contents

Plates

Figures

Tables

Preface

At a recent Australian government inquiry into development assistance, a member of the inquiry board asked a development worker, 'What overall brief do you think you are working to? When you go home and talk to your wife about what you think you do, what do you say you are doing?' Without hesitation, he replied 'We talk about our disillusionment. Seriously, that is what we talk about. We talk about whether we are throwing our lives away in a futile exercise.'

During the 1980s many books on development practice have been published. A number are about 'projects' and are of the 'How to ...' genre, arguing for the reader to consider 'better' approaches, such as more comprehensive techniques of appraisal or implementation, or more effective means of monitoring and evaluating project activities. Rather like development practice itself, this literature is forward looking, and concerned with a prospectively better and more orderly future, rather than a past which is replete with distressing failures.

We believe that the failure of a great many development projects to achieve even their most fundamental objectives is due to a reluctance on the part of development practitioners to appreciate the significance of history. Projects are frequently designed as if time began with the project implementation schedule. Past lessons are seldom examined and still fewer professionals bother to enquire into the historical circumstances of the people their interventions seek to assist.

This book describes events which occurred on a large Australian aid-funded rural development project, the Magarini Settlement Project, in Coast Province, Kenya between 1976 and 1989. We have deliberately structured the book to convey the significance of history in development practice. We begin with an account of events spanning more than seventy years preceding the project, a period skipped over in project planning documents in one paragraph. We then follow the sequence in which the project unfolded. In each successive chapter we come closer to the reality of the people whom the project was designed to benefit. But when we finally reach the lived experience of these people it has become oddly too late to take them into account. Their statements parody the earnest discussion of the preceding chapters, emphasizing the irrelevance to them of the development practices we have examined.

We believe development practice cannot be critically examined independently of the social and political environment in which it occurs. Yet formal and technical project appraisal techniques are frequently taught and written about in text books in a disembodied way which gives rise to misleading conclusions about their appropriateness and the risks associated with their use. The debate about issues in development practice: sustainability, participation, land degradation are in a similar manner commonly treated in a rhetorical fashion, or informed only by highly generalized information gleaned from overviews at a national level.

Our approach requires familiarity with the case being talked about; indeed it was our familiarity with the Magarini Settlement Project that led us to consider writing this book in the first place. We have been involved with this project ourselves and it is important for readers to be informed about the extent and nature of our involvement, so they can judge the veracity of our comment and the degree of subjectivity with which we make it. Gaye Thompson grew up in Malindi, a short distance from the Magarini area. After studying anthropology in London she returned and lived for three years in Kotayo, a village on the western extremity of the project. Her prime interest here was Giriama ritual and divination. During some of this time she was supported with a grant from the Australian International Development Assistance Bureau (AIDAB), through the efforts of Susanna Price. Later, Thompson was appointed by the Kenya Freedom From Hunger Council to help formulate what became known as the Malindi NGO Programme.

Doug Porter and Bryant Allen came later to Magarini. Porter had worked for a number of years as a professional consultant before returning to postgraduate studies at the Australian National University to research the philosophical roots of the practices he had been employing in New Zealand, the Pacific and the Philippines. At Magarini he found a single project which encapsulated almost all of the development 'fashions' of the last ten years. It was one of these fashions, the involvement of non-government organizations, which first brought Porter to Magarini as an adviser to the Australian Freedom From Hunger Campaign. Later, he was a member of two Australian missions which reviewed progress of both the NGO interventions and the larger Magarini Project. Like Thompson, Porter has found this close involvement has provided a rich source of information in the writing of this book, but it has also been something of a burden. Personal biases may be limited, but can never be wholly expunged from the way events are recounted. Nevertheless, Porter's previous experience, and later partnership with Kenyan colleagues is well accounted for in the conundrums presented in the middle chapters of this volume. They illustrate some of the unintended and paradoxical effects these fashions have had on actual events outside aid agency offices or academic think-tanks.

Allen arrived at Magarini in 1987 as a member of an AIDAB review mission. Although it was his first visit to Africa, the agricultural and land use strategies adopted by the Giriama at Magarini were immediately familiar from his work with smallholder subsistence and cash crop farmers in Papua New Guinea and elsewhere in the Pacific. Like Thompson at Malindi, Allen had spent two years living in a Papua New Guinea village, observing a large Asian Development Bank (ADB)-funded project wash over the local people, leaving virtually no trace, while they made their own attempts to bring about meaningful social and economic change. But at Magarini, in an extremely fragile physical environment and a more difficult political situation, the deadly combination of forced resettlement and a failed attempt to provide water and replace a shifting cultivation system with a sedentary system had created the potential for major social and environmental upsets. As a bewildered and frustrated member of the 1987 Joint Review team he quickly accepted Porter's offer of joint authorship to try to discover how such mistakes could have been made.

It is our contention that Magarini is understandable only in terms of the many different and conflicting realities of the people who 'lived' the project. We have tried to draw upon all their accounts: the hapless beneficiaries, official and unofficial; the Australian bureaucrats who struggled to manage a growing monster in a distant country most of them had never visited; the foreign consultants who stopped by, perhaps *en route* to another project, another country; the Kenyan public servants, often unsure whether their posting offered a windfall or isolation; and those who arrived later, like the NGO staff and consultants, or the members of the final AIDAB review missions, who found the whole experience incredible and bewildering.

People we met in the course of writing this book have two things in common: they are passionate about their 'Magarini experience' and they were sincere in their wish to improve the lives of the project beneficiaries. After understandably nervous beginnings over our motives, they were all forthcoming with opinions and anecdotes. We met no-one who had not been indelibly stamped by their involvement with the Magarini Project. We began to write this book in a mood of righteous indignation that so many professionals could have made so many mistakes. We have completed it more humble than when we began and with a great deal more sympathy with those practitioners responsible for what happened at Magarini and we have attempted to express these feelings in our title. There is little doubt now that as development professionals they have failed, and some of them were disturbed to hear from us the extent of their failure. We have attempted to describe in this book how so many good intentions can yield so many poor outcomes.

As we have written, however, we have sometimes become distressed and despondent about our subject. We cannot pretend neutrality; and we believe there are few who will not share our estimation of the events recorded in these pages. Neutrality does not rest easily with development workers; we have, by definition an interest in the manipulation of social processes, in order to bring about more desirable future states of affairs. Perhaps it is this point, above all others, that at times made us wish for the disengaged position of academic scholarship. For, as we progressed, two things have focused our attention. First, it seems clear from evidence of historical trends that the outlook for people like the Giriama is one of increasing misery and dispossession of their lands, their livelihood, and the basis of their culture. We do not retain some long lost romantic image of an egalitarian and plentiful past. But neither do we see much scope in the present circumstances for the notions of 'equitable', 'environmentally sustainable', 'participatory' development futures currently popular in development literature. Second, much of this literature fails to recognize explicitly that modern development practice, in particular that which is directed towards the greater control and management of projects, is part of a broader social and political philosophy which assumes people are incapable of managing their own affairs and of making their own decisions. A less charitable view of this form of practice is that it is a deliberate attempt to make sure people do not control their own lives. The record of development practice is distressing and after 12–15 years of intellectual hegemony by the present economic orthodoxy, cracks are appearing in the facade. The 'thinking person in the street' has begun to realize that the international debt crisis and the compelling images of African famines are not accounted for by orthodox views about economic development and, to the extent that orthodox policy prescriptions are applied in practice, may actually deepen the malaise confronting us. This book is intended to encourage such questioning.

We have not been able to speak with everyone who was involved at Magarini, and some of those, and some we have spoken with, may feel we have inadequately recounted their views or their role in the project. While we have tried to represent the different realities contained within the project, as the authors of a modern history we have had to make judgements about the most likely course of events. Unfortunately, because of political circumstances in Kenya, we are not able to acknowledge by name all those Kenyan colleagues and friends who advised us during the gestation of this book. The reader will notice a liberal dotting of Australian names throughout the text, whereas Kenyan names seldom appear, and are fictitious where it has been necessary to include a name for the sake of literary style. But these people have been with us in many different ways during the writing of this book, not least in our growing awareness of the incredibly difficult circumstances in which they work and live with a commitment and perseverance that is seldom acknowledged and is frequently devalued by cynical foreigners.

In Australia, we especially acknowledge the openness of Paul McGowan, who so willingly gave of his time and accumulated experience in interviews and who attended a public workshop and answered our criticisms. Some may feel our treatment of him is unfair. In our opinion, however, he was a man with drive and vision, a larger-than-life figure for whom we have a great deal of respect. We hope that after reading this book he retains his respect for us.

Also of assistance were Dan Etherington and Peter Rohan who helped us to understand and re-assess the cost–benefit analysis which appears in Chapter Four, and Bob McCown and Brian Keating of CSIRO who spent many hours on their CERES-maize simulations under Magarini conditions, without which the analysis of Chapters Three and Four would be considerably less well-developed.

Many people went to great lengths to ensure we had access to documentary records and accurate accounts of historical events: special thanks must go to Bill Hayden, Bob Dunn and Anthony Vale in this regard. Others who freely gave of their time and their records were Maurice Bell, Denis Blight, Doug Campbell, Helen Hughes, John McGarrity, Susanna Price, Tim Reeves, Gary Simpson, Kevin Stephens and Nancy Viviani.

Most development texts are prepared to address the concerns of the policy makers and corporate interests who define development policy and increasingly set the confines of practice on the ground. Very few texts speak directly of the experiences of development practitioners, nor explain why, for the majority of them, most prescriptions are frustratingly obtuse and irrelevant to the lived experience of development practice. We hope this book will go some way towards rectifying this situation. In no small measure, our hopes for the character of this book were re-affirmed by readers of early drafts; thanks to Jean Bourke, Robin Hide, Peter Robertson, Harold Brookfield, Dean Forbes, Bob Peake and Patrick Kilby, and editor Jane Basinski.

Finally, we must acknowledge the support of Professor Harold Brookfield and the Department of Human Geography, Research School of Pacific Studies, the Australian National University who provided Visiting Fellowships to Porter and Thompson during 1989, and the able assistance of Carole McKenzie (typing), Yvonne Byron, Diane Ranck, Anne Cochrane and Barbara Banks (research assistance), Nigel Duffey (cartography) and Merv Commons (everything else), and in the United Kingdom, Viv Riley and Keishi Colour, and Alan Jarvis of Routledge.

Canberra, November 1989

Abbreviations

ACIAR	Australian Centre for International Agricultural Research
ADAA	Australian Development Assistance Agency
ADAB	Australian Development Assistance Bureau
AFFHC	Australian Freedom From Hunger Campaign
AHC	Australian High Commission
AIDAB	Australian International Development Assistance Bureau
CAA	Community Aid Abroad
CHOGM	Commonwealth Heads of Government Meeting
CP	Coast Province
CRES	Centre for Resource and Environmental Studies
CSIRO	Commonwealth Scientific and Industrial Research Organization
DC	District Commissioner
DOS	Department of Settlement
EARC	East Africa Royal Commission
EEC	European Economic Community
FAO	Food and Agriculture Organization
FRR	financial rate of return
GD	Giriama District
GDP	gross domestic product
GIS	General Investigation Station
ha	hectare
IADP	Integrated Area Development Project
IBEAC	Imperial British East Africa Company
IBRD	International Bank for Reconstruction and Development
ICVA	International Council of Voluntary Organizations
ILO	International Labour Organization
IRDP	Integrated Rural Development Project
IRR	internal rate of return
JCPA	Joint Committee of Public Accounts
K.pounds	Kenya pounds
KFI	Kilifi
KNA	Kenya National Archives

K.sh	Kenya shillings
MAL	Malindi
MGI	McGowan International Pty Ltd
MOLH	Ministry of Lands and Housing
MOLS	Ministry of Lands and Settlement
MOU	Memorandum of Understanding
MOWD	Ministry of Water Development
NGO	non-government organization
NPV	net present value
PC	Provincial Commissioner
QPR	Quarterly Progress Report
SFU	standard farm unit
SMEC	Snowy Mountains Engineering Corporation
SRDP	Special Rural Development Program
UN	United Nations
WCED	World Commission on Environment and Development
WFSCG	Water and Food Security Consultative Group

Conventions

Two organizations which underwent name changes during the course of the Magarini Project are referred to throughout this book. Paul McGowan established the consulting company G.P. McGowan & Associates Pty Ltd in 1961. In 1981, McGowan International Pty Ltd was formed. Paul McGowan retired from MGI in 1982. We refer to Paul McGowan as either 'Paul McGowan' or 'McGowan' and to the companies as 'McGowans'. The Australian government aid agency also changed names during the same period. From 1974 to 1976 it was called ADAA (Australian Development Assistance Agency). In 1976 it became ADAB (Australian Development Assistance Bureau) and in September 1987 AIDAB (Australian International Development Assistance Bureau). Throughout we refer to 'AIDAB', except in references to publications.

We have had privileged access to official documents and files. To honour agreements of confidentiality we have referred to these sources by date only, e.g. AIDAB 20 September 1989.

Plate 1 An influential Giriama elder: bystander or participant in the development imperative?

Chapter 1

A project somewhere in Africa

Seventy-five years ago, just north of the coastal town of Malindi in Kenya, the King's African Rifles spent six days sweeping either side of the Sabaki River, putting down an uprising by the Giriama people.[1] Forty-two people were killed. The colonial troops withdrew, and the Giriama stepped up their attacks. The troops returned, burning dwellings, destroying property and cultivations, and indiscriminately firing on all Giriama they met. The Giriama fled into thick bush, leaving an unknown number of dead behind. This military action was the climax to a twenty-year struggle between the British and the Giriama, the British trying to subjugate the Giriama, gain control over their lucrative trading, force them onto plantations as labourers, and with the onset of World War I, to press-gang them into a Carrier Corps. Giriama resistance eventually prompted punitive action from the British. The terms of surrender for the Giriama included onerous fines, eviction from lands granted to them by the British in 1895, and the loss of 1,000 men to the Carrier Corps. Four years later, a government inquiry re-confirmed Giriama rights to occupy the land from which they had been evicted.

After 1914, the Giriama people recovered their flourishing trade in maize and ivory by exploiting their strategic position between the coastal Arabs and Swahilis and African tribes in the hinterland. They prospered. Yet, ultimately, British taxation, restrictions on occupation of land and trade, drought and declining soil fertility, reduced Malindi District to a net importer of grains, and transformed Giriama from prosperity to chronic indebtedness.

In 1976 preliminary investigations began in this same area for what was to become Australia's largest aid project in Africa (Figure 1.1). The project aimed to settle 4,000 families on 13–ha plots within an initial acquisition area of 60,000 ha. To support settlement an extensive road network was to be provided, with groundwater reticulation taking water to within 500 m of every plot. Agricultural assistance, drawing on Australia's presumed comparative advantage in dryland farming, was to replace the bush fallowing practices with a sedentary mix of subsistence and cash crops and livestock. When implementation began however, the Magarini Settlement Project, as it became known, quickly exceeded the Kenyan government's capacity to provide the necessary

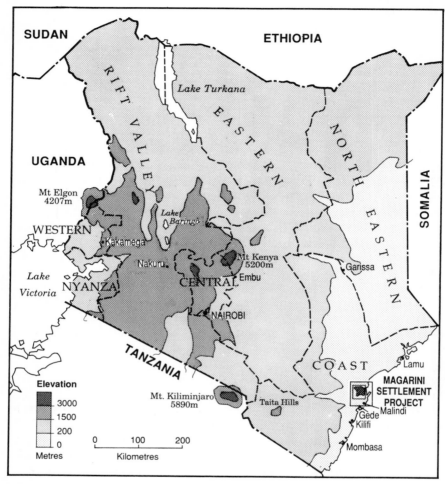

Figure 1.1 Map of Kenya and location of the Magarini Settlement Project.

staff and recurrent finance according to their agreement with the Australian International Development Assistance Bureau (AIDAB). The agricultural specialists identified the severe constraints due to the highly variable soils and rainfall patterns. Groundwater was found not to be available in the quantities first expected. Within a year of starting, this integrated rural development project had begun to unravel.

By 1980, just three years after implementation began, members of a joint Kenya–Australia review of the project privately concluded it was doomed.

Further reviews and evaluations took place, each arguing that with adjustments to the design, improved relations with the settler community, and greater political will and commitment from the Kenyan government, the project would become economically viable. But Magarini continued to flounder. Adequate supplies of food and water diminished. In 1988, the Australian government withdrew from direct involvement, leaving a small directly funded community development programme implemented by a non-governmental organization (NGO) and the rest of the project supported by the residues of unexpended monetized food-aid.

The Magarini Settlement Project is perceived by Giriama people as a continuation of their eighty-year experience with colonial and neo-colonial intervention in their affairs. While some have successfully weathered the adverse effects of resettlement on land they believed they owned, the project has contributed to their incorporation into an impoverishing and unsustainable development process which is neither in their interests nor within their power to change.

Of course this was not the intended outcome. The Giriama are not unused to interventions in their lives. Early relationships between Giriama and Arabs were marked by skirmishes. British dealings with the Giriama were characterized by blundering and ill-conceived retribution for the lack of respect shown by Giriama towards colonial institutions. Some people associated with the Magarini Project did exploit their positions of authority, diverting project resources or plot titles for their personal gain. But the critical difference between past interference in Giriama land and livelihood and the Magarini Settlement Project is that all project actions were taken on behalf of the Giriama. Settlement was said to be in *their* best interests; agricultural research was undertaken in the name of *their* food security; the extensive water reticulation was to relieve the burden on *their* women; an NGO programme was introduced to add *their* voice in an effort to bring project decisions closer to the Giriama people's interests.

The road to the Magarini Settlement Project was 'paved with good intentions'. But what occurred is a common experience for Third World people, who despite billions of dollars and immense and sincere human effort, are more frequently the victims of rural development aid projects than the beneficiaries. This book examines how these good intentions are subverted, in spite of the procedures, skills and knowledge distilled from over thirty years of development experience.

The Magarini Settlement Project is not unique. It echoes international development experience in two important respects. First, warnings of impending difficulties were not heeded. From the outset specialists in water, soils, agriculture and settlement cautioned that there were serious constraints on permanent settlement in this marginal environment of highly erodible soils and unpredictable rainfall. Also unheard was Giriama opposition to migration of outsiders onto land which they had fought and paid for in blood.

Second, the activities promoted by the project were not sustainable in economic or environmental terms. The high-cost water supply system, for example, was beyond the financial and technical resources available to either the Kenyan government or the community to operate and maintain. Moreover, simply to maintain agricultural productivity, the broader strategy of sedentary farming demanded a guarantee of water that was not available, labour that was in short supply, and agricultural inputs that were beyond most farmers' financial means. Permanent settlement at Magarini was almost certain to result in land degradation and further deterioration of the living standards of the Giriama.

It is therefore justifiable to ask how a project like the Magarini Settlement Project was begun at all, let alone sustained for fourteen years. Four recurrent themes in the Magarini experience provide an understanding. First, it is a truism that aid serves diplomatic and strategic interests. Magarini initially existed only as a desire of the Australian Whitlam Labor government for a 'project somewhere in Africa' to deflect charges by African Commonwealth leaders that Australia was a bastion of white racism. Nevertheless, diplomatic and strategic interests do not fully explain the complexities nor the paradoxes evident in the Magarini Settlement Project. These were largely determined by the prevailing fashions of the international donor community. These fashions constitute the second theme in our recovery of the Magarini experience. The definition of Magarini as a *settlement* project denotes its relationship to *the* compelling political force in Kenya, control over land. These forces were largely beyond Australian control. But Magarini was also at various times viewed in Australia as a dryland farming project, a land development scheme and an integrated rural development project. If these were the fashionable coats draped over the shoulders of Magarini, then each component of the project, the roading, the water, the agricultural packages, were the often ill-fitting undergarments that Magarini's creators and implementors thought, at various times, the people of Magarini should wear.

The metaphor of fashion imputes to Magarini a misleading sense of rapid change and lack of substance. Magarini did change, often with bewildering speed, but the most enduring feature of the project is the way early decisions tended increasingly to narrow the range of later options. This is a third theme in our understanding of the Magarini Settlement Project. Despite evaluations, reviews, appraisals and redesigns, the first patterns cut by consultants from the Snowy Mountains Engineering Corporation (SMEC) in the mid-1970s are recognizable in all the project's garments. Once running, the project appeared to gather a momentum of its own. Individual development workers who may have seen the longer term goals in the beginning, became distracted by specific problems, and often oblivious to their contribution to the project's eventual demise.

Finally, as a creature of fashion, Magarini has been influenced by what we term 'control-orientation' in development practice. This is the belief that current events and various states of land, labour, technology and capital can be manipulated according to causal relations which exist between them, to achieve a desired objective in a controlled and predictable manner. A corollary of this view is that in physical and social environments which are characterized by a great deal of uncertainty, everything must be rigorously controlled. Control-orientation carries a compelling logic, but one of our purposes is to demonstrate that such an approach is deeply flawed. Only when all relevant factors are able to be reasonably determined beforehand and controlled, such as in the construction of a dam site or an airport, does this approach have any merit. Even where a great deal is already known about a situation and where future events, like variation in rainfall, or the vagaries of government policy, are reasonably certain, such an approach cannot determine what the final outcome will be. Control-orientation also forces its proponents to make assumptions about the capacity of local institutions, and the likely behaviour of the intended beneficiaries which can only be regarded as heroic and detrimental to their interests. It is important to appreciate that events at Magarini were not isolated from international currents, in this case conservative ones, which often pre-ordain the set of options available to development workers, even where the evidence from the field clearly supports their case for a radical change in approach.

We have chosen not to write a complete description of Magarini's many facets. A full chronology of events appears in Appendix A1. Formal negotiations between Kenya and Australia began in 1974, and two Australians visited Kenya to consider a request for technical assistance for a dryland research project. The request was itself a response to repeated 'invitations' by Australian diplomats for Kenya to take advantage of Australian expertise in dryland farming. The initial proposals were politically unacceptable in Kenya. Later Australian visitors examined possible sites for projects on dryland agriculture or water conservation. In 1976 events began to move quickly. A site was chosen and approved, a project appraisal carried out, funds approved, tenders let, contracts signed and a project created. It was planned to take place in three phases. Phase I was a resource investigation and was to take place between 1977 and 1978 but was extended into 1979. In 1979 Phase II was approved.

Phase II was the implementation phase and was to have continued for two years to 1981, but by 1980 difficulties had been experienced and Phase II continued into 1982 in the absence of guaranteed continued funding from Australia and a marked reluctance on the part of Kenya to sign a new Memorandum of Understanding on Australian terms, for continuation into Phase III. This period of 'crisis' reached a climax when, in September 1983 Foreign Minister Bill Hayden refused to approve funding for Phase III. Phase III did proceed, however, in 1985 and continued to absorb considerable amounts of Australian aid funds for a further three years. The project was redesigned in 1984 and proceeded on the basis of a cost–benefit analysis which predicted economic viability for the settler farmers. An Australian NGO also became involved with a Kenyan counterpart NGO. The contract with the Australian managing agent, a very experienced agricultural consulting company, was not renewed in 1987 and in 1988 all Australian staff were withdrawn from the project. A relatively small amount of money to directly support continued NGO activity at Magarini was being supplied by Australia in 1989, and other project activities were being funded by money realized by the sale of Australian wheat in Kenya by the Kenyan government.

Magarini has a complex and circular history. Paradoxically, we find that the first recommendations of the 1974 Mission, politically unacceptable at the time, were unknowingly repeated by the last substantial mission in 1987. In between, there is a wide fourteen-year arc of events which took the participants away from any prospect of sustainable interventions, permanent settlement and secure water and food. During this time we see many smaller eddies in which the same problems circulate without resolution.

We believe the lessons of the Magarini Project are critically relevant to future development practice. It is increasingly likely development workers will find themselves in semi-arid, marginal environments, in areas of heightened political tension, with rapidly growing populations, shortages of arable lands, faced with the urgent scramble for assets by alienated and apprehensive African people. The outlook is not good. Debt, poverty and environmental degradation interlock in a perplexing spiral that defies easy answers.

In particular, four aspects of development addressed in this book are likely to have prominence over the next decade. First, the urgent need to enhance food security in environments marked by highly variable soils and climates, intense pressure from ecologically unsustainable farming practices by marginal smallholders, and conflicting, often irresponsible interventions by distant authorities. Chapter Three examines this issue in some detail.

Second, the necessity for improved techniques for the appraisal of development activities, both to reduce the uncertainties of investment outcomes and to limit the appalling tendency for intended beneficiaries to be detrimentally affected by the interventions. Chapter Four reviews the use of cost–benefit analysis in the 1984 Appraisal of Magarini and begins to assemble the essential features of the control-oriented approach.

Third, the recent popularity of NGOs can be attributed to northern governments' desires to by-pass what they perceive as inefficient recipient governments, and a desire to directly incorporate intended beneficiaries into their development designs. 'Participation' is seen as essential to the fine-tuning of design, the mobilization of local people's resources, and to the long-term sustainability of the interventions. With the projected demise of debt-ridden African states, and the current popularity of economic and political privatization strategies amongst official donor agencies, NGOs are likely to gain increased prominence. Chapter Five examines the experience and impact of NGOs in the Magarini Project and raises broader issues regarding their strategy and comparative advantage.

Fourth, the unsustainability and inappropriateness of much rural development assistance has prompted a re-evaluation of the relevance of indigenous knowledge and institutions for coping with uncertain physical and social circumstances. Chapter Six contrasts the ways Giriama people deal with uncertainty with the approaches taken by the development agents employed on the Magarini Project.

APPENDIX 1   MAGARINI SETTLEMENT PROJECT: MAIN EVENTS 1972–89

1972
December FAO recommends to Australian High Commissioner (AHC), Nairobi, that Australia provide Kenya with an expert in dryland agriculture.

1973
At Ottowa Commonwealth Heads of Government Conference (CHOGM) Australian Foreign Minister offers Kenyan Vice-President technical assistance in dryland agriculture.
   Senator Willesee, Minister Assisting the Foreign Minister, visits seven black African countries, including Kenya, the first Australian minister to have done so.
July AHC, Nairobi, proposes to Kenyan Vice-President that Australia provide to Kenya a chief irrigation engineer or an arid zone agronomist.
September A.I. McCutchan, First Assistant Secretary, Australian Department of Environment and Conservation, visits Kenya and suggests to AHC and FAO Nairobi that a two person Australian team be sent to Kenya to study marginal areas northeast of Nairobi.
   AHC Nairobi communicates several times with Kenya Ministry of Agriculture, offering a dry zone project, but receives no reply.

1974
January AHC Nairobi recommends to Australian Department of Foreign Affairs (DFA) that a small study team visit Kenya, although the Government of Kenya (GOK) will make no commitment to further work at this point.
March Australia receives draft application for technical assistance for a Dryland Research Project to be mounted in marginal areas in eastern and central provinces.
July F.H.W. Morley and H. Nix, Commonwealth Scientific and Industrial Research Organization (CSIRO) visit Kenya and report on the Kenyan request. They recommend the establishment of trial 'catchment communities' with restricted power over local area catchment land use.
August AHC Nairobi comments that Morley and Nix report will not be politically acceptable in Kenya.

1975
May GOK finds Morley and Nix proposals 'not acceptable in all aspects'. Morley and Nix respond to AIDAB that it is possible to adapt their main recommendations to Kenyan political conditions but they are not consulted further during the life of the project.
June E. Batt (AIDAB), K. Stephens, (SMEC) and D. Blight (DFA) visit Kenya as part of Australian Aid Planning Mission to Africa. They examine a number of possible sites for an Australian project in Kenya.
September AIDAB has discussions with SMEC on possibility of SMEC applying some of Morley and Nix's ideas in Kenya. SMEC agrees in principle. SMEC sets out a proposal to be carried out in a number of phases (Appraisal, Data Collection, Implementation, Agricultural Advisory). A notional budget of $10 million over 5–7 years is agreed to by AIDAB. Some concern expressed in AIDAB about SMEC's ability to manage such a project.
October AHC Nairobi reports that Morley and Nix recommendations were too complex technically and too difficult politically for the GOK. Recommends a broad survey of water resources and conservation.

December SMEC present to AIDAB plans for a Water Conservation and Development Project to be undertaken in either Taita Hills or Magarini.

1976
January GOK expresses a preference for Magarini and agrees with the Australian proposal to carry out a physical resource survey and to work up to an infrastructure and agricultural development pilot project. AIDAB has surplus funds so proposes to send H. Matthews to accompany SMEC's Stephens to examine the potential for agricultural development and with SMEC, to provide an integrated report on the complete feasibility of proposed development at Magarini.
March–April Matthews and Stephens visit Magarini and carry out project appraisal.
June Project Appraisal document presented. It recommends development of water and land resources in 2,000 ha of 'state' land to settle 400 'squatter' families as a trial. If successful the project will be replicated over 40,000 ha of similar semi-arid land in Coast Province.
September Australian Foreign Minister Peacock approves expenditure of $770,000 on Phase I of project, the Feasibility Study. Tenders called for consultants. AIDAB Technical Advisory Panel selects G.P. McGowan & Associates, an Australian agricultural consulting company with experience with the World Bank and the Food and Agriculture Organization (FAO) in Argentina and the Middle East to be appointed as managing agent.
October Kenyan Ministry of Finance and Planning approves proceeding to Phase I. Appoints Ministry of Lands and Settlement (MOLS) as executing authority.
November Memorandum of Understanding (MOU) drafted. H. Matthews (ex-AIDAB) appointed by McGowans as Project Manager. McGowans subcontract Coffey and Partners of Brisbane and SMEC to carry out water and engineering tasks.

1977
March McGowans request and receive additional contingency funds for water exploration.
May Contract with G.P. McGowan signed on 31st. (It is uncertain whether the MOU with Government of Kenya for Phase I was ever signed.)
July Interim Report on Phase I received. McGowans propose $12 million development project, cooperation with World Bank, and want to change Kenyan authority from MOLS to Department of the President because MOLS has no experience of settlement projects on 'tribal land'. McGowans also argue for no break between Phase I and Phase II.
August AIDAB agrees Phase I should have no specific cutoff date, but concern expressed that McGowans going beyond scope of services for feasibility study. AIDAB refuse to agree to Phase II proceeding on grounds of inadequate information presented in the Interim Report. Project is said to have changed from a land settlement scheme to an integrated rural development project based on land settlement.
September Australian Foreign Minister Peacock approves $630,000 eight-month extension to Phase I to allow further water exploration, and land tenure studies (not undertaken). AIDAB decides not to involve World Bank on grounds it would slow down implementation.

1978
January Government of Kenya approves funds to compensate landholders at Magarini before AIDAB has decided to proceed to Phase II.
May McGowans present Phase I report (Executive Summary, Project Report, 13 technical annexes). R. Manning visits Kenya to negotiate extent of Australian commitment to Phase II. GOK in favour of proceeding, has approved budget allocations, and is prepared to accept McGowans as managing agent.
June–July Kenyan comments received on Phase I report. Kenyans believe report is too optimistic about agriculture, water and labour, but like the integrated approach and want to speed up settlement to 15,000 ha in four years, and to bring in Kikuyu farmers to give the Giriama a lead. McGowans argue against faster phasing in case it leads to Giriama being displaced by outsiders, but groundwater is still not proven and faster settlement will create more pressure to find water.
August Australian Treasury comments on Phase I reports and is concerned that internal rate of return (IRR) has fallen from previously estimated 16 per cent to 9.5 per cent and questions economic viability.

September McGowans counter that productivity estimates in Phase I report are conservative and IRR should not be allowed to assume greater importance than political and social factors. McGowans present AIDAB with three funding options for Phase II.
October AIDAB negotiates with Government of Kenya in Nairobi about unsigned MOU for Phase I and future level of funding and timing.

1979
February Australian Foreign Minister Peacock approves submission for $900,000 for 1978. Total project budgeted at $22.4 million.
July MOU for Phase II signed.

1980
April Joint Australian–Kenyan review of project led by R.J. Staples.
July Australian members of joint review (R.J. Staples, S. Price, B. Daw) present draft report to AIDAB. Report raises serious questions about many aspects of project.

1981
April Joint Review final report presented.
October Kenya President Daniel arap Moi visits Melbourne CHOGM conference. His party is briefed by AIDAB staff and McGowans. Kenyan Minister Biwott visits Magarini.

1982
April McGowans organize seminar on water problems at Magarini at Jamison Inn, Canberra. Report recommends a combination of surface and groundwater sources and increased drilling programme.
March AIDAB submit request to Foreign Minister Street for $600,000 to extend Phase II for six months. Department of Finance agrees to request only because Australian staff are in the field and cannot be abandoned there without funds.
June Australia and Kenya disagree over draft Phase III MOU. Kenyan economy in recession but Australia wants greater Kenyan staffing and funding commitment to project.
August Project in crisis. AIDAB Africa Desk Officer A. Vale instructed to give absolute priority to redesign of project and negotiation of Phase III MOU. Regional Planner G. Gaston requested to redesign project to integrate into Malindi economy.
November G. Gaston and A. Vale visit Kenya to negotiate Phase III redesign.

1983
March First Hawke Labor Government elected. Bill Hayden becomes Foreign Minister.
April Gaston and Vale report presented but Australian Foreign Minister Hayden dissatisfied by answers from AIDAB to questions about the project and refuses further funding of project on advice from Treasury. MOU between Australia and Kenya lapses without being renegotiated. Australian funding on *ad hoc* Ministerial approval and staffing ceilings imposed on managing agent.
May McGowans present Draft Phase III project design document. AIDAB and Finance agree the cost–benefit analysis is unsatisfactory. AHC Nairobi informs AIDAB cessation of the project will damage Australia's image in Africa.
September AIDAB places final submissions for Phase III before Minister who does not approve them. AIDAB prepares plans for a phased withdrawal.
November Finance assessment of Phase III Design finds major unresolved difficulties remain, IRR will be zero. $11.8 million spent to date and $6.8 million more proposed. Foreign Minister Hayden is absolutely staggered by the history of the project.

Hayden decides to ask an independent economist of some standing to review the project. Professor Helen Hughes, head of the National Centre for Development Studies, the Australian National University is named.

AHC Nairobi advise Foreign Minister Hayden that new Kenyan Minister of Lands and Settlement Ngei has visited project and reported favourably to President Moi. Abrupt Australian withdrawal could embarrass the President and damage Kenya–Australia relations. President Moi is likely to raise matter with Prime Minister Hawke at New Delhi CHOGM. Hayden informs Prime Minister Hawke he can assure President Moi Australia will continue to provide aid to Kenya, either to a project redesigned by Hughes, or elsewhere.

1984

March Hughes visits Magarini. GOK review project independently, find existing strategies have failed and propose a new Settlement Development sequence.

May Hughes' report recommends project be redesigned and an economic analysis be undertaken on the new design.

August Phase III Appraisal Mission (S. Price and P. Rohan) visit MSP for 3 weeks and collect mainly farm production, labour, crop yields and price data for redesign.

October Phase III Appraisal Report completed. Recommends sinking all previous costs, halving block size and assumes steady increases in yields of all crops for 20 years. IRR of 15 per cent achieved. NGO involvement recommended.

1985

January Australian Foreign Minister Hayden agrees to fund project on basis of calculated IRR and Phase III MOU with Government of Kenya is signed. Recommendations of Phase III report implemented and block sizes reduced from 13 ha to 6 ha. Resurveying begins. AIDAB approaches Australian Freedom From Hunger Campaign (AFHC) to become involved at Magarini. Terms of reference for feasibility study agreed.

February–April AFFHC carries out feasibility studies.

May Phase III MOU gives official recognition of NGO role and recommends limited field activities in community organization, leadership training and water resource studies. Three NGO organizers at Magarini select nine Animators.

November NGO Phase I Design Report presented. Details participatory approach, reviews past activities, proposes NGO area include southern part of Magarini and an area south and east of Magarini. Focus to be on surface water, community training and traditional health systems.

December NGO holds orientation workshop of government staff which endorses NGO Phase I plans.

1986

January–June NGO Phase I programme begins. Identifies primary activities as water, health/nutrition and income generation. Twelve field staff, specialist training. Phase II Design Report prepared. Decision to reduce block sizes is reversed on environmental grounds.

July NGO Phase II programme; three primary activities begin, contact with 30 income-generating groups, 12 water sources groups. Health study recommends focus on water-related illnesses (bilharzia, malaria, diarrhoea).

November Australian Monitoring Review Mission visits. Supports NGO activity. NGO sponsors Water and Food Consultative Group (WFCG). Australian and Kenyan governments both introduce 'rationalization' of project funding, which raises questions about the completion and sustainability of the reticulated water supply.

1987

March Australia–Kenya Joint Review Mission. Finds settlers regularly unable to provide themselves with subsistence food requirements and reticulated water supply is not sustainable on technical, economic and health grounds. Recommends Water and Food Security Strategy in which project will concentrate on food production, surface water storages, the allocation of the remaining unallocated 2,794 blocks out of 4,000 and catchment management. NGO agrees to jointly implement catchment management strategy with the project from July for a 12-month trial period.

June McGowans leave the project. Two Australian technical assistants formerly employed by McGowans continue to advise on food production and dam construction and are administered from the Australian High Commission in Nairobi.

November Implementation Report Mission. Notes little progress with joint activities between NGO and project. Recommends further 6 months to establish working relationship. NGO expand staff capacity.

1988
March NGO Internal Review concludes NGO programme has 'lost coherence' as a result of joint activities with project. Recommends review of relationship. KFFHC informs AIDAB of decision to withdraw from joint catchment programme. Further NGO funding uncertain.
May AIDAB Review Mission. Recommends no further Australian funding of project beyond the expiry of Phase III MOU on 30 June 1988, but funding of NGO for a further 2 years with a revised programme.
June Kenyan FFHC Review and Strategy Paper. Limits NGO water activities but expands health/nutrition programme and begins community credit programme.

1989
February–March Health and Credit Evaluation. Confirms household-based Health and Nutrition Strategy. Credit activities expanded. Kenyan FFHC committed to programme beyond AIDAB funding expiry in mid-1990.

Sources: AIDAB reports and files. R. Staples, S. Price and B. Daw, (1980: 24–33); G.P. McGowan Ltd (later McGowan International Ltd) Quarterly Progress Reports; Interviews.

Chapter 2

Setting the scene

It is not uncommon to hear people who have been involved with the Magarini Settlement Project refer to the development game, but Magarini was more of a development drama than a game. Each act in the Magarini drama had a number of well-crafted scenes: feasibility studies, appraisals, designs, implementation, negotiations, redesign and economic analyses. In the early stages the cast was small and enthusiastic. On both the Kenyan and Australian sides the same actors entered for set pieces to negotiate over the details of a general plot. As the play proceeded, however, the plot became largely beyond the control of any one of the cast or the playwrights. There were, of course, many bit-part actors running on and off the stage and hustling around backstage. Desk officers in AIDAB, 'experts' in this and that, High Commissioners attempting to influence the plot with constant cables from the Mission, or a Minister ignoring the cables and stalwartly refusing to allow the play to go into the third act.

The striking thing about this play was that the people for whom it was written, the Giriama, remained towards the back of the stage, a sort of Greek chorus, commenting on the actions of the main actors, but listened to by nobody. Early in the play they wandered off, tired at being ordered about the stage and increasingly frightened that the obviously irresponsible behaviour of the actors and playwrights would set fire to the theatre and destroy them and their livelihoods.

Here we describe the backdrop against which the Magarini drama was played out and outline the overall plot. First, we examine the history of the Magarini area, and previous development interventions that have taken place there. We then touch on the politics of land in Kenya, which is critical to an understanding of the Magarini Project as well as the nature of the relationships between aid-giving and aid-receiving countries. We also look briefly at the Australian political agenda in the late 1970s in order to establish the foreign policy origins of Magarini. Finally we provide thumbnail sketches of the main players and the physical characteristics of the stage upon which the drama was played.

GIRIAMA: PEOPLE OF THE 'DISPOSSESSED TERRITORY'

The Giriama occupying Magarini in 1975 belong to the Mijikenda, a group of eight closely related peoples who trace their recent origins to nine large settlements known as *kaya*, formerly located in the Mombasa hinterland. Ancestors of the Mijikenda who now live along the Kenya coast and its hinterland between Mombasa and the Tana River, began expanding and dispersed out of their *kaya* in the early 1800s.[1] At this time the *kaya* were fortified villages located in thick forests. Linked only by narrow tracks, the *kaya* afforded protection against surprise attack, and their location between the coast and inland desert country allowed the Mijikenda to flee into vast bush and scrub refuges inland rather than submit to the will of more powerful invaders. The major threats to Giriama wellbeing since the 1800s have been Maasai warriors from inland, coastal Afro-Arabs or 'Swahili', and Arabs, Christian missionaries, the administrators of the British colony, the independent Government of Kenya and most recently the Magarini Settlement Project (Figure 2.1).

The pattern of dispersal of the Mijikenda from the Mombasa hinterland, north and east along the coast to the Malindi hinterland, was determined by the availability of water, fertile agricultural land and opportunities for trading. The Giriama were always the most prominent traders of the Mijikenda, and in their pursuit of new land to support their agricultural activities, many also sought new contacts with Sanya hunters who supplied them with ivory, the most valuable of the commodities they sold to coastal Arab traders. Ivory trading activities and the establishment of a flourishing Arab trading centre at Takaungu, near present day Kilifi, attracted groups of Giriama northwards so that by the 1880s some had reached the Sabaki River valley, northwest of Malindi.

In the Sabaki valley the Giriama took full advantage of alluvial flats and permanent water supply to develop their agriculture. Despite brief and successful skirmishes with their former Arab allies over runaway slaves, whom the Giriama allowed to live among them in return for labour, and two severe famines, their population grew and they established large villages in the valley. When the Imperial British East African Company (IBEAC) purchased a lease of part of the coastal strip from the Sultan of Zanzibar in 1887, the Company came into direct competition with the Giriama. The Company needed labour to revitalize run-down formerly Arab-owned plantations around Malindi. They saw the Giriama as a major potential source of labour, and they wanted to take over the ivory trade, then dominated by the Giriama. The Giriama steadfastly refused to offer for work, but a possible physical confrontation did not eventuate because the Company failed financially and in 1895 the British government, faced with the loss of access to its inland highland colonies, took over what it saw as the relatively worthless coastal lease.

Until 1895 the Giriama had treated the IBEAC and the British passing through their territory to the inland much like previous outsiders with whom

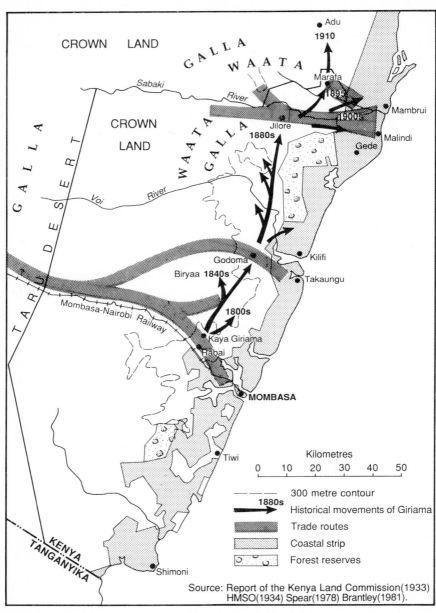

Figure 2.1 Giriama movements on the Kenya coast, 1800–1910.

they had come into contact (Brantley 1981: 46). However, when the British came into conflict with the Arab occupants of the coastal strip, and the Giriama sided with their long time Arab trading allies and provided them with grain and refuges inland, which prevented the British attacking Malindi or Mambrui from the rear, the Giriama were forced to recognize that the British were vastly more powerful than other groups they had encountered. British forces entered the Sabaki valley and captured and imprisoned a leading Giriama, Ngonyo wa Mwavuo. Ngonyo was an outstanding man from a number of points of view.

> He had accumulated wealth as an ivory trader, a producer of grain for export and as an intermittent participant in the slave trade. Over 1,200 people lived in his village, which was the largest Giriama settlement, and many of the inhabitants were slaves used as agricultural labourers. ... Ngonyo dominated his council and maintained the respect of Giriama in the surrounding area.
>
> (Brantley 1981: 47)

Ngonyo quickly decided it was pointless opposing the British and he persuaded his followers in the Sabaki likewise. One outcome was that the British thought that Ngonyo had influence over all Giriama elders, which was not the case, and that all Giriama elders held similar influence over their followers as Ngonyo did over his, which was also incorrect. Most importantly, in recognition of his loyalty, the British granted Ngonyo the right to enter and clear land on the north bank of the Sabaki River, near Marafa. Although it is likely small groups of Mijikenda and other people such as the Kauma were already cultivating land north of the Sabaki, this is the first documented instance of the Giriama being granted the land which now forms part of the Magarini Settlement Project. Previously the area had been occupied by non-agriculturalist Sanya hunters and Galla herdsmen who had suffered severely from Maasai raids, and in the 1890s from rinderpest, which killed almost all their cattle.

Evasion

The Giriama are the largest (over 300,000 people) of the Mijikenda peoples, making up over half of their total population. Of all the Mijikenda groups, however, the Giriama have been repeatedly singled out by those seeking to control the coast as perpetrators of what can only be described as an inscrutable cultural independence. The Giriama are renowned on the coast for their continued refusal, to use Goran Hyden's term, to be 'captured' by any of the outsiders who from time to time have attempted to exercise power over the east coast of Kenya. Ludwig Krapf, who opened the first Christian mission in East Africa at Rabai in 1844, was singularly unsuccessful in converting the Giriama to Christianity (1860), and 100 years later, in 1959, W.F.P. Kelly,

First encounters with the Giriama: *Plate 2* House building (top left) *Plate 3* Carpenter at work (top right) *Plate 4* Women cooking (middle right) *Plate 5* Women firing pots (bottom)

Kilifi District Commissioner, observed bitterly that if Krapf was to return to Giriama territory, he 'would see no changes in most villages'.[2] Kelly was re-iterating a widely held opinion about the noted 'conservatism' of the Mijikenda. The British in particular found the Giriama frustratingly inde-pendent, evasive, and generally lacking in cooperation and referred to them with such contradictory appelations as 'democratic', 'proud', 'recognizing no authority', 'immoral', 'apathetic' and 'obstructive anarchists'.[3]

Peasants the world over straddle both a subsistence economy in which they produce for their own consumption, and a cash economy in which they work for wages, sell commodities, or engage in small-scale business enterprise. This gains them a measure of security, and a measure of freedom from the market as well as from the government. The Giriama epitomize this ambivalence to-wards the market, and it is evident they also preciously nurse their ability to evade the dictates of government. Charles Hobley, who became Coast Prov-incial Commissioner in 1912, prided himself on his understanding of the Africans he had encountered in the up-country areas where he had previously been stationed. As we shall see, Hobley became closely and eventually violently involved with the Giriama. After this experience he wrote per-plexedly of them,

> Their psychology is perhaps the most complex of all the tribes; they knew the power of government, but always seemed to think that by the adoption of a persistent *non possumus* attitude they could wear us down so that we should become tired, thus relaxing our efforts. This policy had succeeded with the Arabs for centuries past, so why should it not succeed with us? Their reasoning was more or less sound.
>
> (Hobley 1929: 166)

The language of today's administrators echoes that of the colonialists. The majority of government extension agents remain convinced that the techno-logical and economic 'backwardness' of the Giriama, and their 'lack of incentive' (Islam 1986), is due to their cultural beliefs. Indeed the persistence of Giriama traditional beliefs is seen as 'the most difficult problem to over-come to help bring about development'.[4]

Change

Contrary to these monotonous, repeated criticisms of Giriama inability to change, the crucial experience of moving from the closely settled *kaya* to live in widely dispersed hamlets and villages throughout the hinterland and the coastal strip transformed Giriama life during the last 150 years.

Today Giriama elders claim their ancestors moved in response to popula-tion growth and the decline in fertility of agricultural land. Kaya Giriama, inland of Mombasa, was the largest in the hinterland and is estimated to have contained 20,000 people (Mutoro 1987: 100). As the Giriama spread from

Kaya Giriama, the centralized authority of the *kaya*-based ruling council of elders weakened and the powers of many institutions associated with political authority were undermined. Because not all eligible Giriama attended crucial rituals relevant to the advancement of their age-grades towards the apical status of elderhood that were held in the Kaya Giriama, the legitimate right of the elders to determine their people's lives was more and more constrained. The elders were increasingly successfully opposed by independently wealthy men who lived beyond their physical reach. Important authority among the Giriama today is invoked by divining spirit-mediums, who have in many respects taken over the traditional position once occupied by the elders. Among the northern Giriama, the majority of spirit-mediums are women.

Social organization has also radically changed since the 1840s. By 1975 Giriama lived in small homesteads composed of the patrilineal relations of a homestead head, and his wives and children. A homestead head generally had sufficient authority over his extended family to deal with most of their day-to-day problems. Elders could still be called upon in disputes which required their special knowledge, in particular as witnesses in land disputes, but spirit-medium diviners were usually sought by individuals to assist with cases of illness or misfortune that were more uncertain. Even so, the original Kaya Giriama remained a powerful symbol of a bygone authority among the Giriama in the early 1970s, for they saw it as the sacred source of their most hallowed traditions. This power was now articulated by particularly successful and influential spirit-mediums guided by the spirits of their ancestors, the leading elders. Thus the Giriama had by no means lost a strong sense of cultural identity, despite dispersion over a wide area and penetrating challenges from inside and outside their society. Although the basis and expression of their culture had shifted significantly with changes in social, economic and political circumstances, they had retained an essence of what it meant to be Giriama.

The pervasiveness of the Giriama belief system defined by its *kaya* heritage was reflected in a continued resistance to Christianity. In 1975 only 20 per cent of Giriama had converted to any of the world's major religions (Barrett 1983). A reluctance to participate in these foreign religions meant most Giriama did not attend the early mission schools, and their evasion of the colonial state and later efforts to educate them resulted in very low rates of formal education and literacy. For example, in 1979, 73 per cent of Mijikenda in Kilifi District, most of whom were Giriama, had received no formal education. Kilifi District had the highest proportion of people in Coast Province who had never been to school, and these were significantly greater numbers than the national average of 51 per cent (Central Bureau of Statistics 1980).

Allies and enemies

The Giriama have always had ambivalent relations with their neighbours, most of whom have been at some time or another both allies and enemies.

Competitive factional skirmishes among Mijikenda neighbouring groups over time, however, have been overshadowed by their significant encounters with the Arabs and Swahili on the coast, and with the colonial and independent state administrations. Giriama alliances with particular Arab and Swahili factions have been principally defined by their trading relationships, not only as middlemen but also as producers of grain for export and consumption by the inhabitants of the coastal towns. When the Giriama and Arabs came to blows it was over slaves, for although slave labour for Arab and Swahili plantations was drawn from around Lake Nyasa and Usambara via Zanzibar, some plantation owners directed raids into Mijikenda territory for slaves (Herlehey 1985: 109), jeopardizing agreements which guaranteed the safety of Swahili caravans which regularly crossed Giriama territory.

The ambivalent relationships between these groups were emphasized when families with insufficient resources to insulate themselves against the effects of famines were forced to become dependent on the patronage of coastal Arabs and Swahili. Often this took the form of labour in return for food. Consequently increasing numbers of Giriama became 'squatters' on Arab holdings on the coastal strip. Most of the privately owned land on the strip was the property of Arab and Swahili landowners who had run plantations, largely using slave labour. After the abolition of slavery removed the major sources of labour from these plantations many Arab landowners could see no economic future in plantations which had to employ wage labour. They were now little interested in prohibiting its occupation by Giriama and some encouraged Giriama to use the land in exchange for a nominal rent (Herlehy 1985: 293–4). Increasing numbers of Giriama moved onto this more fertile and better watered land and they returned less often to the hinterland.

Labour and land

In the 1900s the new element around Malindi was British plantations attempting to produce cotton, rubber and copra. The plantation owners, who were largely absentees and employed local managers, formed a planters' association and lobbied the colonial and imperial governments continuously over the question of the provision of plantation labour in Coast Province. The Giriama were again cited as the obvious source of the required labour and their refusal to work was viewed as a form of passive resistance. When Charles Hobley, who had previously strongly supported African rights, was confronted with the choice of either forcing the Giriama to work or accepting a posting to the back blocks of Uganda he chose the former (Brantley 1981: 77).

As Coast Province Provincial Commissioner, Hobley first attempted to administer the Giriama through the elders acting as village councils, but as a result of earlier confusion over Giriama leadership, he failed to realize how little real authority the elders held over younger men of labouring age. He sent Assistant District Commissioner Arthur Champion inland to Jilore on the south bank of the Sabaki River to set up a station, take a census and collect taxes. Champion met stiff resistance from the Giriama there. They went to extremes to avoid paying taxes, leaders agreed to cooperate but did nothing, and people moved away from Jilore to avoid contact with him. At first they earned his respect and sympathy. He proposed an irrigation system for the Sabaki valley to develop the potential which Giriama agriculture had demonstrated (Brantley 1981: 81). Hobley, under increasing pressure to provide labour for the plantations, did not accept this advice and became determined to impose a tax and a labour scheme. In June 1913 he threatened the Giriama with a military patrol and with the loss of their land north of the Sabaki. In the same month the East African Coast Planters Association was formed in London to cooperate with the local Coast Planters Association at Malindi. The Associations sent a letter to the Secretary of State for Colonies in August 1913 complaining about the lack of government effort in supplying labour to the coast plantations (Brantley 1981: 92).

Pressure to provide labour began to tell on Hobley and Champion. By October 1913 Arthur Champion had changed his mind about the Giriama and decided they needed to be punished for their resistance. Despite all the evidence of Giriama agricultural productivity he justified himself with these words,

> The loss of their fertile plain of Madunguni and that of Garashi would be punishment certainly felt by the most unmanageable section of the tribe and one that would not be forgotten for a long time to come. At present it is a crying shame to see the rich black cotton soil of the valleys overgrown with rank grass and tangled with reeds and grass, where enough rice could be grown to suffice half the wants of the coast if in the hands of intelligent people.

However, he revealed the real reasons behind the move when he argued,

> I am of the opinion that European planters being thus right alongside the reserve would soon get their labour and they should be encouraged to offer the Wanyika [Giriama] small plots on signing contracts of labour for a stated period of time during the year.[5]

The Giriama were to be forced to work by restricting their access to the resource which enabled them to remain independent. Giriama only offered to work on plantations or on public works in times of crises such as famines. The British administration was prepared to manufacture a crisis in order to produce the required labour supply.

Resistance

In November 1913 Hobley received permission from the Governor to evacuate what he estimated to be 5,000 Giriama from the northern side of the

Sabaki River, to fine them for their 'past attitude toward government',[6] to declare the river as the northern boundary of the native reserve, and as a result of a complete misunderstanding of Giriama culture, to have them swear a traditional oath of loyalty to the government. The area was to be evacuated by 1 August 1914.

There were some misgivings over these tactics. The District Commissioner at Malindi wrote to Hobley in June 1914,

> In these circumstances it appears hard that they should lose their five thou-sand acres of good land out of what has always been considered their reserve. ... I trust you will pardon me again referring to the Wanyika [Giriama] rights to this particular piece of land, but I feel as the govern-ment allowed the Wanyika to stay so long north of the Sabaki, that they imagined they had a right to be there.[7]

By July 1914 it was obvious, despite repeated promises by headmen, that the Giriama had no intention of evacuating the land north of the Sabaki. The onset of the war with Germany on 4 August 1914 created an immediate de-mand for African labour to form a Carrier Corps and provided further reason to subdue the Giriama. Champion received a request to provide '1000 men urgently' and believed he had but ten days to comply with the instruction. Men from one of his patrols, sent into the hinterland south of the Sabaki to or-ganize this labour, allegedly raped a Giriama woman and were attacked with poisoned arrows which the Giriama used in hunting. The Giriama, already deeply suspicious of British motives towards them, were angered by the rape and the sudden demand for labour. Hobley seriously over-reacted to this at-tack and requested assistance from the King's African Rifles (KAR) to put down what was characterized as an 'uprising'.

The KAR spent six days sweeping on both side of the Sabaki River 'burning villages and attacking every Giriama they saw', a move which was met with 'more or less continuous opposition'.[8] An estimated forty-two Giriama were killed. They then withdrew. The Giriama, believing their resistance had forced the withdrawal, increased their attacks on Jilore and villages loyal to the Brit-ish. On 10 September the KAR began a second sweep in which 'they fired on all Giriama they met, whether or not they were hostile, and systematically con-fiscated goats and burned dwellings' (Brantley 1981: 117). The Giriama were forced to flee and to carry on their resistance by firing arrows from ambush positions in thick bush. An unknown number were killed in this second attack and most of their property and cultivations were destroyed.

The British at first refused two Giriama offers of peace, but the KAR were needed elsewhere in East Africa. In October 1914 they accepted a Giriama surrender on the conditions that all persons wanted on capital charges be handed over, the headmen and leaders of the rebellion formally submit to the government, 1,000 men be supplied to serve in the Carrier Corps, a fine of 100,000 rupees be paid in cash and the land north of the Sabaki River be evacuated (Brantley 1981: 121). After the troops were withdrawn the 'terms of peace and ... fines [were] imposed, [and] the work of driving the people from the north bank was carried on by Police patrols' (Leys 1925: 129).

However, in 1916 a commission of inquiry held into the legitimacy of the government actions in 1914 concluded,

> the area north of the Sabaki which in no small way contributed to the large export of grain from the Malindi District, is now spoken of as the "dispossessed Territory". ... The various removals of natives referred to in this report have undoubtedly interfered largely ... with general cultivation in the District, ... the present position has been rendered precarious by the failure of two successive crops, and ... there is danger of a serious famine in the immediate future.
>
> (Leys 1925: 129)

Ngonyo wa Mwavuo and other leaders appeared before the commission. Ngonyo argued that the land at Marafa had been given to him by Sir Arthur Hardinge in 1895 and he was deeply aggrieved at its loss and wanted to return there. Evidence was produced that there had been around 20,000 people living north of the Sabaki and not the 5,000 which Hobley had estimated.[9] The commission also found evidence against the British claim that the Giriama had no right to cross the Sabaki and occupy the land at Marafa. When they had crossed the river in 1895 there had been no legal reserve boundary in existence, they had observed customary payments to the Galla and they had been encouraged to settle the Marafa land by IBEAC and British government officials. The commission left the decision on the ownership of the Marafa lands to the Governor, but between 1916 and 1918, when Acting Governor Charles Bowring made a decision in favour of the Giriama, Ngonyo encouraged many people to return to the 'dispossessed Territory' and the provincial administration could do nothing to stop them. In 1919 the Giriama gained a legal communal title to the Marafa lands when they were added to the Nyika Reserve. Increased numbers of Giriama moved into the new reserve.

We have said little about the economy of the Giriama in the Sabaki valley and the Marafa area because we examine this question in some detail in the following chapter. However, the Giriama from these areas were recognized as the major contributors to the export trade in maize from Malindi from around 1900 until the mid-1920s. One major reason for the commission of inquiry in 1916 was the sudden decline in maize production in the area after the Giriama were forcibly removed from the Marafa land. By 1920 they had rebuilt this economy, but from 1920 to the beginning of World War II in 1939, their relative wealth was eroded by a combination of colonial taxes, regulations on maize trading and repeated droughts. Many Giriama continued to move back and forth between the hinterland and coastal land owned by Arabs, where they were viewed as a problem, because their insecurity of tenure was a disincentive to plant permanent crops and their exploitation of coconuts to make palm wine prevented the production of copra, an important commodity in the colonial economy.

Gede Settlement Scheme

Magarini was not the first settlement scheme in the vicinity of Malindi. In 1931 in a further attempt to control the 'Giriama squatter problem' on the coastal belt outside the reserves, the colonial administration began a project to resettle about 850 families rent free on 4,000 ha between Gede and Tezo. The Gede Settlement Scheme, extended in 1951 to an area of 10,450 ha with a capacity for over 2,000 settlers, had the object of stabilizing the Giriama by substituting permanent farming for the 'wasteful practice of shifting cultivation' (Ministry of Agriculture 1957: 188–9). What happened at Gede, in a far less marginal environment than Magarini, has many parallels to what was later to occur at Magarini.

The scheme did not achieve the objective of replacing shifting cultivation. Although the land was fertile enough to support the production of cash and subsistence crops in the initial phases of the project, in the absence of an improved rotation, settlers continued shifting cultivation on their 9-ha plots. At first the decline in productivity went unnoticed because, for development purposes, the scheme was given priority over all other areas in the district, and the effects of recurrent food shortages were cushioned by government assistance with food. Eventually, however, the long-term effects of soil exhaustion forced settlers on poorer land off their plots in search of more productive land and hence to become squatters again. Settlers on better land who were able to remain did secure ownership.

Nationalism and independence

Although from 1954 the Swynnerton Plan of land consolidation and registration, with its emphasis on 'areas of high potential', successfully encouraged the development of an African landowning class in the highlands, it initially had little impact on the coast. Slowly, however, enclaves of progress were established, mainly in the Gede Settlement Scheme and in the more prosperous areas in the southern coconut palm belt. Socio-economic differentiation became entrenched in the new possibilities for development engendered by individual land ownership. The greater wealth and development of the southern Giriama encouraged people there to become involved in the first stirrings of nationalist politics. A number of young men from the south, including Ronald Ngala, a Giriama school teacher, formed the Mijikenda Union. The Union launched Ngala on a political career which led to him almost being declared the first president of an independent Kenya.

Ngala represented the Mijikenda on the national political scene, but outside his political base of urban Mombasa, the Giriama whom he was supposed to represent became politically marginalized and overshadowed by the factional competition focused in the south. Political factions on the coast formed essentially on ethnic group alliances. With independence approaching, the coastal Arabs demanded autonomous self-government of the 10-mile coastal strip, which was technically still on lease from the Sultan of Zanzibar. This issue was vigorously opposed by the leading African politicians of the time, including all local Mijikenda politicians, who urged the colonial government 'to annex the area and then open it to settlement by squatters including landless Mijikenda families' (Herlehy 1985: 270). In early 1963, some months before independence, the Coastal Strip was formally released from the nominal imperialism of the Sultan and handed over to be administered as part of Kenya. As part of this agreement, to the dismay of the Mijikenda, all Arab and Swahili land claims were respected and transferred intact into the British system of individual titles.

Ngala's energy for local land reform had been diverted by his leadership, initially of the Coast African People's Union, and then to the presidency of the Kenya African Democratic Union (KADU). Ngala's party advocated safeguards for minority groups such as those making up its leadership and membership, in a popular regional campaign. The Kenyan African National Union, KANU, secure in its representation of the Kikuyu, the largest and most powerful ethnic group in the country, was concerned more with portraying an image of national mobilization. Ronald Ngala and Jomo Kenyatta were joint leaders of the interim government formed to prepare the way for the election of the independent government in 1963. Under Kenyatta's leadership, however, it was a foregone conclusion that KANU would lead Kenya into independence. Ngala dissolved KADU and joined KANU, but his popularity on the coast remained high, even among the non-Mijikenda, who feared domination by up-country Africans. He was offered a senior ministerial position in the government when he joined KANU, and right up until his death, retained a key position in national politics, a role which continued to draw him away from his people's interests at the coast.

After independence the scramble for land in the former White Highlands among the Kenyan élite distracted relevant administrative and material resources away from the coast, and policies for the further settlement of squatters there were shelved. Very little attention was given for the first decade after independence to assisting the Giriama and their Mijikenda neighbours with either agricultural development loans or land registration, the necessary prerequisite for titled ownership. This was, however, more of an issue in the southern areas of the Giriama region than the north.

'White with the bones of European experiments'

In the north, after independence, there was no effective effort by the government to settle the landless Giriama in Kilifi District. It was therefore ironic

that the location of the Magarini Settlement Project, begun in the name of 'landless' Giriama, was on the very land first occupied by Ngonyo wa Mwavuo north of the Sabaki River in 1895 and granted to him by the British colonial administration. Little imagination is required to understand that the people living in the proposed project area faced the prospect of more interference in their lives with deep trepidation. Since 1914, when they were forcibly removed from the land, but were allowed to return to it within two years, they have had to suffer numerous extemporary and almost completely unsuccessful efforts to 'develop' it. The Malindi Annual Report of 1924 could well have been written in 1975.

> [For] the past twelve years [the Giriama] have seen seven government and two mission stations started and abandoned, new crops introduced ... rubber, rice and potatoes which have turned out a failure. The district is white with the bones of European experiments of the past. It is hardly to be wondered at that suggested innovations are regarded with distrust.

THE MOST IMPORTANT POLITICAL ISSUE IN KENYA

The land at Magarini is marginal land, climatically difficult, with relatively infertile and erodible soils. Until the 1970s agriculturally marginal lands in Kenya had been of only marginal political interest. Recently they have become of central importance. To understand why this has occurred is to understand the links between land, agriculture and politics in Kenya. Chris Leo argues that 'without any qualification', the 'allocation and acquisition of land constitutes the single most important political issue in modern Kenya' (1984: 6). In a society where 85–90 per cent of people depend on increasingly smaller, scarcer and inequitably distributed pieces of land for all or part of their income, the distribution of land rights is a fundamental determinant of the distribution of wealth. Yet Kenya is said by many people to be one of the richest countries in Africa.

Kenya – 'the glittering economic jewel of Africa'

Kenya *is* rich. It is, as journalist Anver Versi describes it, 'the glittering jewel of Africa'. It is home of the WaBenzi, who, with their Nigerian cousins, are perhaps the richest tribe in Africa. Long lines of their Mercedes Benz cars weave through Nairobi's traffic-choked streets. But Nairobi, like the rest of Kenya, is full of contradictions. From the high-rise landscape of international tourist hotels and glass-fronted office blocks, it is a short step to Mathare, the largest slum in Africa. Here is found some of the most distressing poverty and disaffection on the African continent. But poverty in Kenya is not restricted to Nairobi.

To the extent that models are ever completely applied in practice, Kenya

Faces of Magarini Project: *Plate 6* On the development bandwagon (bottom left) *Plate 7* Magarini water supply (top left) *Plate 8* Tea shop (middle left) *Plate 9* Land rights: an inheritor? (bottom right) *Plate 10* Aged settlers (top right)

followed most of the popular modernization and 'open economy' propositions of development economics in the 1960s and 1970s (Cassen 1986: 340). Investment was concentrated in the modern sector, capital-intensive methods were favoured, manufacturing production rose and many opportunities existed for import substitution and supply to an expanding East African market. Between 1964 and 1972 these policies appeared to be working. GDP grew at an average of 6.5 per cent per year. Manufacturing grew at an estimated 12 per cent and agricultural output overall expanded at around 5 per cent (Hunt 1984: 19). Peasant agriculture, relieved of colonial constraints, expanded fast enough to support the foreign exchange needs of the modern sector, whereas population pressure in some areas served to keep agricultural wages low. But during the second decade of independence things began to go awry. The 'trickle down' effect of modern sector growth did not materialize. Employment growth remained lower than economic growth, which also declined rapidly, and fell below the rate of population growth. Diana Hunt demonstrates a probable lowering of average per capita income for the poorest and an increasing number of people in the poorest income groups. She estimates 45 per cent of the population live in absolute poverty (1984: 30).[10]

The vast majority, 85–90 per cent, of Kenya's population are rural and most live on smallholdings of less than 10 ha. Hunt explains, 'The highest single category of rural poor are small holder households whose farms are either too small or on land of too poor quality to enable them to achieve the basic needs level of income' (1984: 35). Landownership and income distribution are heavily skewed in Kenya. Around 30 per cent of smallholdings are under half a hectare and 54 per cent are under a hectare. Efforts to count the numbers of rural people with no access to land, 'is one of Kenya's longest running exercises in futility' (Leo 1984: 188). Wildly differing estimates are made. For instance, for Coast Province, a 1972 ILO report quoted a figure of 15,000, a 1977 Parliamentary Committee estimated 130,000 and a 1980 World Bank report estimated about 124,000 (Collier and Lal 1980; Hunt 1984; Livingstone 1986: 184). Hunt believes around 5.5 million people lived in poverty in Kenya's rural areas in the mid-1970s. The fact that most landless people are in Central and Rift Valley Provinces, a region from which the present government draws much of its legitimacy and stability, is not lost on Kenya's leaders and is directly related to repeated attempts throughout the history of the Magarini Project, to settle up-country people there.

Numerous factors have contributed to the steadily rising poverty in Kenya. One of the most acute problems Kenya faces is a burgeoning population. Over the past fifteen years population has been growing at world record annual rates of between 3.9 and 4.4 per cent. If population grows at around 3.5 per cent till the year 2000, the numbers of people of working age will almost double from 7.2 million in 1980 to 14.1 million. Until the mid-1970s it was argued that households forced off the land would find employment in small rural business enterprises, non-farm activities or agricultural labouring. By

1979 it was clear that many of the factors which made this so-called 'sponge effect' possible had ceased to exist. The once-off growth-inducing forces of hybrid maize and under-utilized high potential land had been largely spent and from 1972 to 1977 agricultural growth fell to about 2 per cent per annum, below the rate of population growth (Tidrick 1979: 25; Livingstone 1986: 187). The number of landless poor expanded rapidly, increasing the number of people in marginal informal sector occupations and accelerating the movement of people onto marginal land (Livingstone 1986: 187). Overwhelmingly, Kenyans live on the land and they will continue to do so for the foreseeable future, because 'the process of industrialisation or development of tertiary services has not and will not proceed at a pace fast enough, given population increases, to begin to meet the problem of unemployment' (Bienen 1974: 157).

Historical land alienation

The origins of Kenya's land problems have been traced by John Overton to the 'complex mesh of haphazard appropriation, bureaucratic chaos, fitful economic growth (by settlers and Africans), economic cooperation and conflict, and frontier readjustment' (1988: 109) which occurred during the massive alienation of land from its native owners during the early 1900s by the colonial government. The British declaration of a Protectorate over Kenya in 1895 opened the way for European settlement and appropriation of the more highly productive land. Much of the most fertile, high rainfall areas, and some of the drier land for ranching, was excised from the centre of Kenya to form the White Highlands. Africans who previously occupied this land were confined to native reserves and by various legislative and financial measures, including hut and poll taxes and restrictions on the production and marketing of cash crops, were forced onto the labour market.

A policy which created 'broad acres reserved for a few individuals alongside an African reserve where hunger existed' (EARC 1953–55: 60) maintained the bitterness and sense of loss. The 1935 Kenya Land Commission found 'abundant evidence' of a white settler sense of 'primordial superiority' (Rothchild 1973: 160) and immutable landownership, clashing with increasingly vigorous African claims for enlarged opportunities and the principle of corrective equity. Population growth within the reserves and African squatting on alienated land around the reserves increased the political tensions which surrounded land. During the 1920s and 1930s a small but growing élite group of progressive African farmers pressed their claims against the white settlers' monopoly of state patronage, to the point where Harold Macmillan, then British Under Secretary for the Colonies, warned in 1942 that population pressure and land scarcity would 'provoke serious peasant revolt within ten years' (Throup 1987: 4).

Concessions were made during the 1950s in a belated attempt to defuse political tension over the land issue. Traditional land claims were replaced with individual freehold titles. African cash cropping was actively encouraged, but the pressure for independence could not be contained. By 1960 the British Macmillan government, beset by the adverse publicity and costs of defeating the Mau Mau nationalists, decided to seek the means of transferring power in Kenya to the African majority while safeguarding the interests of the white settlers.

Settlement schemes – 'letting the steam out of the kettle'

The transfer of the land in the possession of white settlers to African ownership through the vehicles of individual title, farming companies, and settlement schemes was therefore a prominent feature of post-independence policy. The first 'low-density' resettlement of Africans in the former European highlands took place in 1961 before independence, but was seen as mere 'tokenism' (Rothchild 1973: 242). European good-will was maintained, a few relatively prosperous and loyal Africans benefited, while many thousands of rural dispossessed were neglected. Consequently, 'to lance the boil of land seizures and growing lawlessness' (Bienen 1974: 164), plans to settle more than 35,000 families on what came to be called the Million Acre Scheme were announced by the colonial government. Rural disaffection was to be nipped early through the establishment of a high-density scheme aimed at less experienced and less wealthy farmers. This scheme committed the government to purchase about 80,000 ha of land from white settlers each year for five years (Roberts 1967: 128; Leo 1984: 97). By 1966 almost all the land under the 467,000-ha high- and low-density settlement schemes had been settled (Rothchild 1973: 217).

Many African nationalists were critical of these schemes. The Luo leader Oginga Odinga maintained only élites would benefit, the old colonial norms of property would be reaffirmed, and British funding would create a situation in which Kenya would remain dependent on its former colonial masters (Harbeson 1973). Kenyatta persisted, however. He believed there was more to be gained by stepping into, or 'Africanizing', the existing systems of land-ownership, trade and the civil service than by dismantling them. He also understood the urgency of the situation and he knew the British government had promised funding on the condition the land titles were to be transferred to individuals rather than the state.[11] The British, pressured by 'panicky' white settler farmers, viewed the settlement schemes as a means of 'letting the steam out of the kettle' (Carey-Jones 1966; Segal 1968: 288).

Post-independence – a shifting series of coalitions

When Jomo Kenyatta led KANU to power at the first post-independence polls in Kenya in 1963, his party had no broad political base among the mass

of Kenyan people. Unable to build an all-embracing centralized party structure (Bennett and Rosberg 1961), KANU became vulnerable to the pressures
of different tribal groupings and factions (Bienen 1974: 72). Kenyatta skilfully
used land, already a dominating entity in the Kenyan political consciousness,
as a reward for patronage, together with government favours and civil service
jobs. Political stability since independence has been built on the re-allocation
of many of the large estates of the former White Highlands. Kenyatta also
feared that violence similar to that which characterized the Mau Mau movement might recur in Kenya following independence and the new government
would not be able to control its own supporters. Rapid and large-scale resettlement of Africans was therefore a precondition of political stability.
Although Kenyatta had few illusions about the economic impact of replacing
European farmers with undercapitalized Africans, visible tokens of independence were needed to give the new state a chance of achieving political
stability.

From independence to 1970, therefore, the major share of Kenyan public
investment went into land settlement programmes and over 30,000 African
families were resettled on individually titled plots. But although the settlement programmes were begun to deal with landlessness in a controlled way
and to restore social stability, they have become the preferred means of ad-
dressing four interrelated political objectives. First, the redistribution of
population to relieve tensions in densely settled areas; second, to distribute a
politically acceptable minimum level of social services; third, to reduce food
shortages and increase cash incomes in rural areas through agriculture and
other forms of income generation; and fourth, to avoid the political repercussions of genuine land reform by being seen to be helping the landless.

Settlement schemes of the immediate post-independence years did reduce
the discontent somewhat by effecting an inter-racial re-allocation of land
while maintaining the confidence of white settlers in the land market, but as
a solution to the overall land problem the results were far from satisfactory.
From the outset, settlement schemes barely scratched the surface of landlessness. By 1967 it was evident,

> on individual schemes there are wide income differences, with a minority
> of farmers achieving more than target incomes, a minority of comparable
> size having virtually no monetary income and sometimes working land on
> less than a full-time basis, and a majority of settlers failing to meet targets
> but still generating some cash incomes.
>
> (Segal 1968: 289)

Integrated rural development

The mid-1960s brought a significant change in Kenyan rural policies. The revised National Development Plan (1966–70) announced that, rather than

continuing to try and find land on which to mount further settlement schemes, farmers on existing schemes were to be assisted to increase their productivity substantially. This focus on the needs of existing farmers demanded the timely purchase and supply of productive inputs according to 'a strict set of interdependencies'. Integrated rural development had come to Kenya. The integrated approach demanded that,

> The supply system must be able to deliver the required input before rain brings the start of the planting season; credit agencies must be able to extend loans to farmers in time to pay for the new inputs; an extension service must have taught farmers how to use the inputs, markets for the increased output must be available; and roads must connect the farms and markets.
>
> (UN 1971)

The first generation of integrated approaches produced the highly successful cash crop development authorities, the best known of which is the Kenya Tea Development Authority. Government action integrated the provision of all services for one export crop: inputs, credit extension, markets and roads (Lamb and Muller 1982). Following on from these successes came the second generation, the area or regional integrated development project designed to 'improve multiple elements of the system simultaneously' (Wiggins 1985: 91). In Kenya IRDPs were known as Special Rural Development Programmes (SRDP) and from 1971 to 1977 operated in six divisions with populations of between 20,000 and 75,000. Five were sponsored by Britain, the Netherlands, Norway, Sweden, the United States, and one by the FAO. Kenya's experience with the SRDPs was better than the outcome of IRDPs in many other African countries (Wiggins 1985: 92). In contrast to many IRDPs which existed in isolation from surrounding administrative institutions, the Kenyan SRDPs attempted to work through existing administrative arrangements, and focused on marginal improvements to local level management (Chambers 1974). In parallel with the SRDP was the Integrated Area Development Programme (IADP). A design phase began in 1972 and the first implementations occurred between 1977 and 1981.

Marginal land

Until the early 1970s public investment in agriculture had focused on high-potential land, the 20 per cent of the country where rainfall is sufficient and relatively reliable. At that time, as Wiggins wryly noted, 'the drier and more remote the District, the less attention it gets at the centre' (Wiggins 1985: 101). By the mid-1970s, however, attention had focused on drylands. It was apparent that the easy options were becoming few and far between. During the 1960s it had been relatively easy to acquire land from white settlers for resettlement by Africans. Now, if the critical political problem of subdividing the large estates in the former White Highlands in the hands of the Kenyan élite, who wa Thiongo calls 'settlers under the skin' (1982: 15), was to be avoided, new frontiers had to be considered within the extensive northern and coastal regions. Coincidentally, arid and semi-arid area development had become fashionable in international agencies and their proselytizing was greeted enthusiastically by the Kenyan government. Support was immediately forthcoming for the newly established International Centre for Agricultural Research in Dryland Agriculture and the International Crops Research Institute for the Semi-Arid Tropics.

This increasing interest in drylands also coincided with the common under-pinnings of the second generation of IRDPs which came out of Washington and were concerned mainly with the distributional aspects of development, with equity and the plight of the poor. McNamara's landmark 1972 Presidential address to the World Bank expressed concern for the 'poverty of the poorest 40 per cent of the citizenry' of the Third World (1972: 9). In Kenya the new 'poverty focus' was taken up in a 1972 ILO study carried out as part of the World Employment Programme. The Kenya Mission Report incorporated a sharp change in emphasis, which reflected and influenced a widespread international shift in development opinion. On grounds of both productive efficiency and of equity, the emphasis was now to be placed on the possibilities for increasing the incomes of the poor, mainly in the activities in which they found themselves, rather than by trying to move them into a more prosperous sector (Van Arkardie *et al.* 1979). The intention, in policy at least, was now to adopt direct methods of raising living standards of the bulk of the population (Livingstone 1986: 2). Thus just as in the 1960s Kenya's ruling élite had whole-heartedly embraced the 'image of the relatively prosperous, independent, landowning and individualist farmer, with a conservative stake in the status quo and a progressive investment in improved farming practices' (Segal 1968: 290), in the 1970s they adopted, as enthusiastically, the plight of the poor pas-toralist or dryland farmer struggling to make ends meet on marginal land. 'Poverty alleviation' and 'marginal land' and 'dryland farming' became the central tenets of the new Kenya Development Plan 1974–78. Kenyan develop-ment planners were thus more than familiar with the concepts of integrated development which were to come from Australia during 1976 and 1977.

WHITE AUSTRALIA AND BLACK AFRICA

Nine thousand kilometres away on the other side of the Indian Ocean from Kenya lies the continent of Australia. The apparent similarities between the physical environments of Australia and Kenya have been put forward many times since the Magarini Project began as one reason why Australia should be involved in agricultural development in Kenya. But in 1970 the physical envi-ronment was about all these two countries had in common. Australia had been originally settled by blacks as long as 40,000 years ago, but white settle-ment from Britain from the 1800s had swept these Aboriginal people from their land and, those who survived, into reserves where they existed largely on meagre government handouts, in all except those areas considered by whites not worthy of occupation. Further migration was encouraged from Europe from 1946, but immigration policies which severely restricted the entry of Asians were dubbed as the 'White Australia' policy, a policy which had bi-partisan support.

During the 1960s Australia came under increasing criticism at inter-national fora like the Commonwealth and the United Nations on the issues of relations with South Africa and decolonization from the leaders of black African countries, Nkrumah in the early 1960s and Nyerere and Obote in the latter part of that decade. When Gough Whitlam's Labor government came to power in 1973, a sharp change occurred. A central part of foreign policy now became the removal of the perceived image in the Third World of Aus-tralia as a white, racist society. In contrast to his conservative predecessors, who had become disenchanted with the Commonwealth, Whitlam 'recognised the enormous goodwill which was to be gained from supporting developing nations in the two major affronts to their dignity – racial discrimination and colonialism'. At the same time Australia's relations with South Africa changed from a 'very close relationship' to 'little more than a slanging match' (Higgott 1981: 246). It was this foreign policy climate that eventually led to Australian involvement at Magarini. In the early stages at least, Australia showed more enthusiasm for some involvement than did Kenya.

Australian foreign aid administration

In 1976, Australia's overseas aid programme was administered by a semi-autonomous Bureau of the Department of Foreign Affairs, the Australian Development Assistance Bureau (ADAB). Prior to 1976, the administration of Australia's aid programme had been handled by seven different depart-ments to 1973, an interim office made up of the staff of five departments from 1973 to 1974, and a statutory authority, the Australian Development Assist-ance Agency (ADAA) from 1974 to 1976. Each new organization was formed by re-organizing and restructuring the resources and functions of its predeces-sor, a process which one inquiry found 'imposed considerable costs on the Australian aid program and the staff involved in its administration' (Public Accounts Committee 1982: 7). When ADAA was formed in 1973, the staff were not recruited for the purpose of administering aid, but many were simply transferred from the Department of External Affairs, where they had been largely responsible for the administration of Papua New Guinea, which be-came self-governing in 1973. Between 1973 and 1976, ADAA had 708 staff spread across nine branches in three divisions. No independent training or recruiting of professional and experienced aid staff was possible during this period.

Catchment communities and Kenyan politics

Australia's special skills were perceived by the rest of the world to lie in dryland farming and as early as 1972 FAO passed a recommendation to the Australian High Commission (AHC) in Nairobi that Australia provide Kenya with an expert in dryland farming. In 1973, less than twelve months after the election of the Labor government, Senator Willesee, Minister Assisting the Foreign Minister, visited seven African countries including Kenya, the first Australian minister to have done so. During his tour he is said to have 'received a number of requests for aid' but we are not aware of the details.[12] At the 1973 CHOGM meeting in Ottawa, Australia made a firm offer of technical assistance to the Kenyan Vice-President, and in July that year the AHC proposed to the Kenyan Vice-President that Australia provide an irrigation engineer or an arid-zone agronomist, and several times suggested a larger Australian involvement to the Kenyan Department of Agriculture but received no reply.[13]

Australian overtures to Kenya continued in the second part of 1973. The First Assistant Secretary of the Australian Department of Environment and Conservation visited Kenya in September 1973 and suggested to the AHC and the FAO Country Representative that Australia send a two-man team to Kenya to study marginal land northeast of Nairobi. Early in 1974 Kenya agreed to the visit, on the understanding that there would be no further commitment and a draft application for technical assistance for a 'dryland research project' aimed at developing farming systems in Eastern and Central Provinces was received by the AHC. In May 1974, Kenya approved a visit by Fred Morley and Henry Nix of the Commonwealth Scientific and Industrial Research Organization (CSIRO) to report on the Kenyan request for a dryland farming system research project.

Morley and Nix immediately recognized that many of Kenya's land degradation problems had social and economic origins, the problems needed urgent attention, and large and costly resource surveys, like an on-going Dutch soil survey, would be too late and would not provide practical solutions. They recommended a small-scale project to trial the establishment of 'catchment communities', in which the people living and farming in a catchment would be given control over decisions on land use and land management in the catchment and would be assisted to build and maintain proper soil and water conserving structures (Morley and Nix 1975). Before Kenyan government comments on this report had been received in Canberra, the Nairobi AHC informed AIDAB that this approach would not be acceptable to the Kenyan government, because it would jeopardize the way in which many Kenyan public servants and politicians held pieces of land around the country, but did not farm them, or farm them properly. The local community, under these recommendations would be able to insist that this land was properly farmed and protected. The AHC predicted the report would be rejected on the grounds it was not legally possible in Kenya to establish organizations like catchment communities. These predictions proved correct. The Kenyan response stated that, under the Kenyan Constitution, it was not possible to influence how 'private land' was used. Although Morley and Nix replied to AIDAB in detail, proposed means of adapting their ideas to the political realities in Kenya and questioned the legalistic basis of the rejection, they were not consulted again by AIDAB (AIDAB 23 August 1974 and 30 May 1975).

Selecting a project site

The next approach to Kenya was part of a visit to Africa in June 1975 of an Australian programme planning mission. Three Australians, Dennis Blight, a career public servant from Foreign Affairs, Kevin Stephens, an engineer from SMEC, and Ed Batt, who was working at Singida, a SMEC water supply project in Tanzania, set out on a tour of parts of Africa to identify possible development projects to be funded by the Australian government. In Kenya, officials had selected six sites for their consideration. Four sites were quickly eliminated. One in the north 'had cases of yellow fever and malaria was rife ... and wasn't much of a place to be working in'.[14] Another was very remote with difficult logistics, and a third near the Somali border was 'right out on a limb'. The choice narrowed down to two sites in the southeast of Coast Province. Just west of Mombasa was an area of good soils and rainfall with severe erosion problems which the Kenyans thought the Australians may be able to 'fix up'. But the area which appealed most to the Australians was located in Kilifi District near the coastal town of Malindi, where they had spent three days. Back in Australia AIDAB held further discussions with SMEC.

The Snowy Mountains Engineering Corporation is the commercial consulting extension of the Snowy Mountains Authority (SMA), the organization responsible for the construction of the Snowy Mountains Hydro-electric Scheme which diverted the headwaters of the Murrumbidgee River west beneath the Snowy Mountains in New South Wales, for the generation of power and the irrigation of cropland (Murphy 1985). The SMA designed, supervised and built sixteen dams, seven power stations, 150 km of tunnels, 80 km of aqueducts, 2000 km of roads, an administration headquarters, depots, 880 houses, complete townships, shopping centres and airfields, on schedule, over thirty years, within the original cost estimates of $800 million. This awesome display of efficiency attracted the attention of the then Australian Department of External Affairs (now the Ministry of Foreign Affairs and Trade) and as early as the 1960s SMA was given engineering projects in Thailand, Sabah, Papua New Guinea and Cambodia. SMEC was established by Act of Parliament in 1970 to ensure the expertise in design and construction in SMA was not lost with the completion of the Snowy Mountains scheme in 1975. By 1985, 40 per cent of SMEC's projects in thirty-six countries had been funded by AIDAB.

On 1 September 1975 AIDAB asked SMEC if they would be interested in 'taking up and applying the community catchment idea' in Kenya. SMEC agreed in principle and in further discussions on 3 September 1975 it was agreed AIDAB would provide up to $10 million over 5–7 years. SMEC proposed a broad plan which included an 'Appraisal Mission, an Implementation of Phased Programme of Work, a Data Collection Phase, and an Agricultural Advisory Phase'. The bare bones of this proposal are recognizable through all stages of the subsequent Magarini Settlement Project, except the last stage when an NGO was introduced. Also apparent in this genesis of the Magarini Project is confusion over goals. The AIDAB Consultative Committee were 'not fully receptive to the proposal for SMEC managing the Kenyan project' given their relative lack of experience in agricultural and community development, but it was thought this may have been the result of confusion over project titles like 'Catchment Community Project and Dryland Farming without any explanation of what will be involved' (AIDAB 3 September 1975). What was involved in SMEC's corporate mind was a large-scale water supply and agriculture project, which was the antithesis of Morley and Nix's recommendations.

In November 1975, Kevin Stephens and Ed Batt again visited Kenya and left a proposal with the Kenyan government for projects at the two sites near Mombasa and at Magarini. Meanwhile AIDAB was moving away from the Morley and Nix approach because of 'a level of complexity in implementation and a degree of hesitancy from Kenyan authorities', towards a 'broad survey of water resource development and conservation'. SMEC was therefore asked to prepare a proposal on this basis and in December 1975 their 'Water Conservation and Development Project' proposal was presented. It was decided a 'small initial technical input' was needed and SMEC's Kevin Stephens would travel to Kenya and carry out this work. In January 1976 the Kenyan government expressed a preference for Magarini. At almost the last minute, and partly because surplus funds remained in an AIDAB vote, it was decided to send AIDAB agriculturalist Harry Matthews to Kenya with Stephens. The proposal was now to,

> carry out a physical resource study of an area approved by the Kenyans and work it up from there to infrastructure and agricultural development as a pilot project. ... In view of the current financial situation we should at least send Mr Matthews to Magarini to examine the potential for agricultural development. Mr Matthews' report could then be integrated with Mr Stephens' and presented to the Kenyans as a complete feasibility study of proposed development in the Magarini area.
>
> (AIDAB 21 January 1976)

Stephens and Matthews' report is discussed in more detail in the following chapter, but in brief it recommended a phased project at Magarini. Phase I would involve resource investigation, especially water, and project design, to be completed around June 1978. If the Phase I investigations showed a project was feasible Phase II would involve the provision of settler plots, the introduction of cash and tree crops to enable settlers to earn K.pounds 150 per year, the establishment of a demonstration farm, provision of groundwater and surface water storages, the provision of machinery for soil and water conservation works and road construction, and the provision of water drilling rigs and crews, credit and marketing, agricultural extension and settler selection management by the Kenyans.

The managing agent

Tenders were called for a managing agent and on 10 September 1976 AIDAB's Technical Advisory Panel unanimously agreed that G.P. McGowan & Associates Pty Ltd was 'the only firm capable of efficiently handling the management of the project'. McGowans were to act as AIDAB's managing agent in the preparation of a detailed resources study, feasibility study and economic assessment, and if it proved viable, to undertake project preparation and planning for the initial development.

G.P. McGowan & Associates Pty Ltd was founded in 1961 as an agricultural consulting company by director Paul McGowan, a Victorian sheep farmer with university degrees in agriculture, commerce and psychology. McGowans worked initially in Australia, but during the economic recession of the 1970s went overseas in search of work, first to Argentina and then to the Middle East and Iran. By 1976 the company had carried out consultancies for the World Bank, FAO, the Asian Development Bank, the Government of Iran, the Iran Development Bank and the Government of Tunisia, in livestock, animal husbandry and agriculture (Anterson 1979: 104–5). McGowans had incorporated SMEC in a supporting role in their bid for Magarini and proposed to subcontract Coffey and Partners Pty Ltd, a geo-technical consulting group, to carry out the groundwater resource investigations. G.P. McGowan & Associates Pty Ltd became McGowans International Pty Ltd in 1981 and Paul McGowan retired from the directorship and from involvement at Magarini in 1982.

In October 1976 the Permanent Secretary of the Kenyan Ministry of Finance and Planning gave approval for the Magarini Settlement Project to begin. The Kenyan executing authority was to be the Ministry of Lands and Settlement (MOLS). McGowans appointed Harry Matthews, who had resigned from AIDAB, to be their first project manager at Magarini and responsibility for the management of the project was vested in him and a Kenyan representative of MOLS.

The site

The proposed project area at Magarini comprised a strip of land about 5 km inland and 15 km wide and 40 km long (Figure 2.2). The east coast of Kenya emerged from the sea only relatively recently, geologically speaking. The

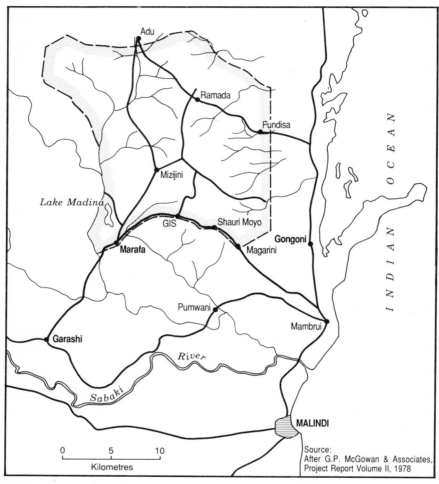

Figure 2.2 Location of Magarini Settlement Project in Malindi hinterland.

underlying rock is all of marine origin, limestones, marls, clays, pebbles and sands, the beds tilt gently towards the sea and the surface is covered with stabilized wind-blown sands. To the immediate south of the area is the Sabaki River valley 15 m above sea level. Land rises from the valley to a dissected plateau which is bordered on its southeastern and eastern side by a low ridge, the Magarini Ridge, which reaches 150 m above sea level at its highest point. Ephemeral streams drain the plateau to the west into the Gandi and Marafa rivers and to the east onto a coastal plain (Figure 2.3).

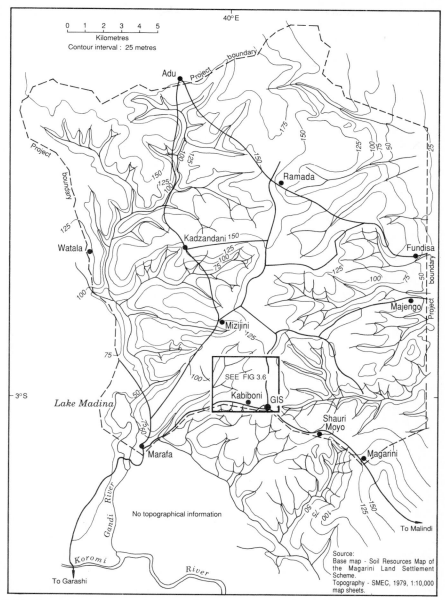

Figure 2.3 Magarini Settlement Project, topography and locations.

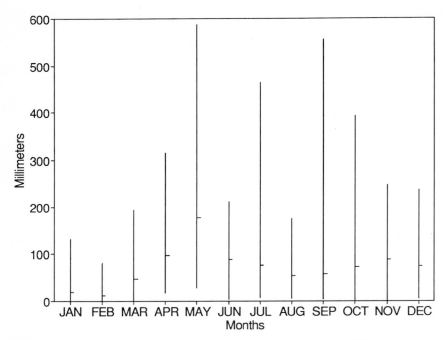

Figure 2.4 Marafa, 1937–86. Maximum, minimum and mean rainfall by month.

The pattern of soils is characterized by extreme complexity over short distances. Soils range from deep, well-draining red and yellow sands to fertile cracking clays, to poor-draining solonetz and solodized–solonetz soils. Both soil types contain high quantities of soluble salt in their lower horizons and are low in phosphorus, nitrogen and trace elements.

The problem with rainfall over this area is not that there is not enough of it on average, but that from year to year large and unpredictable deviations from the average are normal and that within the year, rainfall distribution is very lumpy. Average annual rainfall ranges from about 700 mm to 1,000 mm across Magarini. Most rain falls between April and June in a period known as the 'long' rains and most of the balance is received during the 'short' rains between October and December (Figures 2.4 and 2.5). The start of the long rains fluctuates considerably from year to year and the short rains are very unreliable. The Giriama coped by cultivating a range of soil types each year and by only planting a small area of land until enough rain had been received to assure a return on further planting. Because the short rains are so unreliable, very much larger areas were planted at the beginning of the long rains than at the beginning of the short rains.

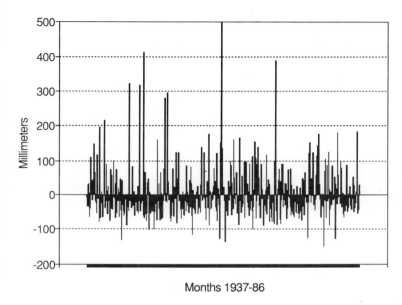

Figure 2.5 Marafa, 1937–86. Difference between mean monthly rainfall and actual monthly rainfall.

Every now and again, however, one or other rainy period fails and very little rain will be received for up to eight or nine months and sometimes longer. During these periodic droughts (Figure 2.6) virtually all Giriama crops fail and they face famine conditions. At other times extremely heavy rains or locusts have also caused severe food shortages. Famines recorded in Giriama oral history have occurred about once every four years between 1836 and 1980 (Appendix A), but the oral record deteriorates after the 1950s, when famine relief has reduced the severity of the events in human terms.

It was onto this environment that Australia's largest aid project in Africa was to be imposed.

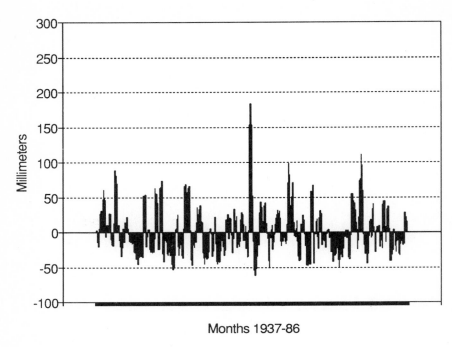

Figure 2.6 Marafa, 1937–86. Difference between actual and mean rainfall. Five month moving average.

Chapter 3

Agriculture: change and uncertainty

Kevin Stephens and Harry Matthews arrived at Malindi to begin their project appraisal in May 1976. As ambassadors to Malindi from across the Indian Ocean they were latecomers. Around 1417 a Chinese fleet is said to have visited Malindi to return a giraffe and a zebra, shipped from the port three years earlier as presents to the Chinese Emperor from the King of Bengal and which the Emperor believed should not be kept in China. The Portuguese navigator Vasco da Gama anchored off Malindi in April 1498 and found a thriving town peopled with Arabs, Indians and Africans (Martin 1973: 12–13, 19–20). Five hundred years later Malindi is a dusty little trading and fishing-port town of narrow pot-holed streets, rather run-down Arab and British-colonial residences and shops, rapidly becoming dominated by a handful of large multi-storey international tourist hotels with their inevitable following of souvenir sellers, drivers, guides, cleaners, barmen, maids, beggars and prostitutes of both sexes. Overweight and pale Germans, English and Italians sweat copiously on tennis courts and lie around swimming pools, endlessly eating and drinking, and turning a bright shade of pink in the equatorial sun. About 20 km north from Malindi across the muddy Sabaki River and inland about 10 km, was an area of rolling, thicket-covered land known locally as Magarini. The area appealed to the Australians because there was 'nothing there' and they would be able to 'do something Australia would be remembered for'.

SETTING THE PATTERN – PROJECT APPRAISAL, 1976

The course followed by the Magarini Project from 1978 to 1988 was cast in 1975. When the Morley and Nix report was rejected by the Kenyans, AIDAB had called on SMEC to follow a continuing interest in Kenya for a project. SMEC had come up with a proposal for a project in three phases: an appraisal, an implementation and an agricultural extension phase. AIDAB had in turn suggested a water resource survey, to which agriculture had been added. Stephens and Matthews' terms of reference were either, to formulate plans to demonstrate in the Magarini area the applicability of soil and water conservation measures to improving *agricultural productivity* in the semi-arid zone of Kenya

or,

to recommend some specific technical and/or staffing inputs which will contribute to the development of *agricultural activity* in the Magarini area (and possibly other similar areas) while ensuring that such contributions are complementary to overall development plans.

(ADAA 1976: 60–3, emphases added)

They were also required to recommend the most appropriate type of project and to investigate timing, funding, staffing, as well as to comment on the selection of settlers, the transfer of settlers onto the project, the resources base, the existing cropping pattern, rural living standards, land tenure systems, land suitability and water availability. Stephens and Matthews returned with a recommendation that Australia should participate in a *land settlement scheme* at Magarini. The project would develop between 2,000 and 8,000 ha of 'state land' and settle up to 1,600 'landless and destitute families' as a trial run, or a model for the later settlement of 8,000 families on 40,000 ha. They proposed Australians should train Kenyans in the engineering and agricultural inputs required for such land development.

To AIDAB in 1976 it is probable that only a very fine distinction existed between a project which had agricultural productivity as its primary objective and one which focused on land settlement. Nor was it unreasonable to assume that for 'landless and destitute' people, security of tenure was a prerequisite of increased agricultural productivity, and if that was what the Kenyans wanted, then there seemed to be no sound reasons why the project should not take this shape. From the Kenyan point of view, for reasons already made clear, land settlement was a primary objective, but if the Australians, who successfully farmed the driest continent in the world could apply their skills in dryland farming as part of a settlement project then national goals of increased food production and economic growth could also be satisfied.

A characteristic of the Magarini Project is that most of the serious environmental constraints were foreseen, but not taken seriously, or seriously enough, while many of the social and human constraints were not realized, by the Australians anyway, until the 1980s. The 1976 Appraisal Report noted erratic rainfall and variable crop yields inland, soil conservation problems and the way in which the ultimate success of the project would depend on being able to find enough water. On the occupation of the land, however, the report was confused and in places seriously wrong. It outlined the origins of the 'squatter problem' on the 10-mile strip and noted briefly the historical movement of the Giriama north from the Mombasa area and, more recently, east onto Arab land around Malindi. The insecurity of tenure there provided 'no incentive to improve the land and no opportunities to use the land as collateral for essential bank loans'. The situation was described as 'a major political problem' (ADAA 1976: 17). The squatter, it was said, 'exploits natural resources by cutting down trees and forests for charcoal burning, by poaching wild animals and by bush burning and by practising shifting cultivation with no fertiliser use or soil conservation measures'. The Appraisal Report described the Giriama as 'poor and illiterate people' and as 'a national environmental risk' (ADAA 1976: 18).

The object of the project was to move these so-called 'squatters' off the strip where population densities were 380 persons per km^2, west into the hinterland where densities were only 2 persons per km^2. Clearly the implication was that the great majority of Giriama were living in the coastal strip as 'squatters' and that they were to be moved inland onto land, the ownership of which was not specified in the report, but which, it was implied, was largely unoccupied, unalienated government land. This land was representative of the only land left in Kenya suitable for development, but because of its marginality, it would require 'substantial investment of capital' and this the project would provide. Many of these assumptions were incorrect, and the true situation of the land and the people at Magarini became apparent only after the project had succeeded in seriously disrupting their lives and their environment.

PEOPLE WITHOUT A PAST?

The Giriama people had believed since the 1890s that they owned the land on which the project intended to resettle them, and that many of the coastal strip 'squatters' also held land rights there. With the exception of the largely erroneous material presented in the 1976 Project Appraisal, most project documents until 1981 treat the Giriama of Magarini as a people without a past. No discussion of how they came to be in occupation of this land or of their past or present social, political or economic relationships with the people who now surround them can be found in any of the Phase I reports or annexes. It is almost as though they dropped out of the sky a few weeks before Harry Matthews and Kevin Stephens arrived.

Since the early 1800s, the steady northerly movement of the Giriama, which brought them into the Magarini area around 1890, was caused primarily by the slow but steady degradation of the environment by agriculture. Between 1920 and 1970 the pressures of British colonialism increased the vulnerability of the Giriama to drought and food shortages and caused further pressure on their land. Beginning in 1978 the project attempted to completely replace this farming system, but succeeded only in increasing the potential for rapid land degradation in the project area, and worsened the vulnerability of the settlers to food insecurity.

Traders and middlemen

By 1850, of all the Mijikenda, the Giriama had become the most consummate traders, skilled at forming and maintaining alliances in the then rapidly shifting political sands of the East African coast. Living between the coast and the interior they traded not only ivory, rhinoceros horn, gum copal and hides for cloth, beads and iron wire, but also maize, the American crop introduced to the East African coast by the Portuguese and adopted because of its ability to produce two crops in a year compared to one crop of millet. By 1850 maize had become a Giriama staple.

Giriama alliances served more than one purpose. During the frequent extended droughts and famines the Giriama could either use cash or draw on credit to obtain food from Swahili and Arab traders who could import grain by sea and who were willing, in difficult times, to help maintain the people who linked them to the interior. By keeping out of serious fights, making alliances with the strong, trading and producing surplus maize in good years and buying in food in bad ones, the Giriama became one of the most successful and prosperous peoples in the Malindi hinterland.

Maize producers

By the 1890s the Giriama had reached the Sabaki River valley and their agriculture reached new levels of productivity. Despite the serious famines from 1884 to 1885, Giriama maize made up most of the grain exported from Malindi during the 1890s. During the Mukufu famine of 1889–90 and the Magunia famine of 1899–1900 (see Appendix A) the Giriama on the Sabaki were able to provide food for less fortunate Mijikenda and nearby groups. Trade from inland, ivory in particular, to the coast remained an important part of the economy.

When Ngonyo and his followers were given explicit encouragement to move onto lands north of the Sabaki in 1895 they were able to establish themselves at Marafa in relative isolation from British colonial administrative influence and demands. Nearby was land held under lease by the Imperial British East Africa Company. One motive for encouraging the Giriama to cross the river was the hope that they would offer to work on the plantation. Instead they developed a thriving trade in maize to Malindi and Mambrui through Indian traders. But as Arab enterprises on the coast declined, increasing numbers of Giriama began to occupy Arab land in higher rainfall areas on the coastal strip, tapping coconuts for palm wine or *uchi*,[1] and growing maize and other crops using shifting cultivation, with the agreement of the Arab landowners. Once more they became the 'most dynamic element in the decaying coastal economy' (Brantley 1981: 54).

Whereas during the nineteenth century the Giriama had maintained themselves in their difficult environment by supplementing agriculture with trade, they now began to support themselves by gaining access to the best resources of the hinterland and the coast. In good years they could produce maize inland and palm wine and maize on the coastal strip, earning cash from the sale of surplus grain. In bad years they could subsist by using the cash to purchase supplementary food. Their production was such that in 1913 Malindi shop-keepers requested the colonial administration 'to build a trolley line by which Giriama grain and other produce can reach the port'.[2] But this prosperity was seriously jeopardized by the need of the colonial government to control its subjects, to extract surplus value from them and to press-gang them into wars not of their own making.

The first attempt to curb Giriama independence resulted in the military action of 1914. Even the British government admitted this was a blundering and illegal affair. The Giriama moved back onto their lands around Marafa and, with hardship and difficulty, re-established the maize trade. Local administrators were somewhat shaken to discover the degree to which the Malindi district depended on Giriama production. The years while they were barred from the north Sabaki land were years of low grain exports. Exports increased sharply after their return to the Marafa lands because of their need to sell much of the maize produced to pay off the fine and the interest on food borrowed from Arab and Swahili traders to see them through the serious famine of 1918. In 1920 it is reported,

> Many Giriama have returned to their old shambas on the north Sabaki and this area is becoming more and more closely cultivated ... there is no reason why it should not become one of the chief food producing areas on the coast ... the export figures of grain are rising.[3]

In 1911 grain exported from Malindi was worth £16,924, in 1924 £26,924 and in 1925 £56,552,[4] and this increase occurred in a period in which Arab farmers were said to be 'in trouble'.

Taxpayers

From 1920 to 1940, however, the colonial administration made a second, more gradual and ultimately more successful attempt to bring the Giriama into line, through compulsory public work and the imposition of hut and head taxes, which were increased throughout the period and took no account of good years or bad, nor ability to pay. The official view was that if people could not pay their taxes they should offer themselves for work, and if they chose not to then it served them right if they went hungry. The Giriama remained obdurate about contract labour and generally only worked for daily wages, leaving employment as soon as they had earned enough to pay the tax.[5] In years of good rains and hence good production the taxes could be met, but in poor years they could not. Some local officers were sympathetic. In 1934, the long rains failed partially, the short rains totally and locusts destroyed much of what was left. But,

Food shortages are being exacerbated by the tax rate which is too high. Even if the men work [on public works] the required amount of three months they earn only 5 shillings or 6 shillings which is insufficient to meet the tax requirement and they have to sell crops to make up the rest, hence food is always short. Prices are very poor at present. During the famine they bought food at 18 shillings a sack. Now they are selling for 3 shillings.[6]

Years of poor harvests (1929, 1932, 1934, 1936 and 1937) outnumbered exceptionally good years (1935 and 1938). Maize production by European farmers in the highlands increased during the 1930s and it was subsidized by cheap rail and shipping rates. The grain trade was regularized and export certificates were required to move maize out of a province. Only 'white' maize of the highest commercial grade was granted certificates. The Indian rupee was no longer legal tender in Kenya after 1931 and this curtailed grain exports from Malindi to Somalia (Waaijenberg 1985). Living standards steadily deteriorated and indebtedness increased north of the Sabaki. The destruction of the 2,000 year-old economic relationship between Arabs, Asians and Africans on the Kenyan coast between 1920 and 1940 by British colonialism proved much more damaging to the Giriama than the violent assault upon them in 1914.

In the ironic and contradictory ways of colonial administrations, the British made a number of attempts to persuade the Giriama to adopt cash crops to help them pay their taxes. In 1932 eight extension agents were assigned to teach the Giriama how to grow cotton as a replacement for maize (Martin 1973: 97). Fortunately the Giriama were sensible enough not to take the risk of basing their whole livelihood on an export crop. Production was 'good' in 1933 and 1935 but people quickly discovered the crop had a high labour requirement, which made it unpopular, and was as prone to suffer from lack of rain or too much rain at the wrong time, as other crops. When the world price collapsed in 1938 production virtually ceased, except on Arab land using paid labour. In 1939 a disease destroyed '90 per cent of the crop'.[7] Another government campaign in 1937, this time to encourage cashew nut production, was only applicable to people settled on the sandier soils where the trees grow best.[8]

World War II came to Malindi in 1940 when the Italian airforce dropped fifteen bombs on the town and the 'natives showed great steadiness' under fire. By 1944 47 per cent of all able-bodied males in Malindi district had been conscripted into labour gangs. It is not clear whether this contributed to food problems in 1943 and 1944. Although the north Sabaki was able to provide food relief for a famine in the Mombasa area in 1942,[9] in 1943 and 1944 there were 'severe food shortages' when the long and short rains failed twice in succession and the administration had to distribute relief food.[10]

Increases in population, land degradation and a capricious climate notwithstanding, between 1920 and 1940 British colonial policies which resulted in officers being involved in 'the almost continual collection of native hut and poll tax',[11] contributed to changing the Malindi District from a net exporter of maize to a net importer, and in reducing the Giriama from prosperity to indebtedness.

Colonial subjects

British policies after the War were based on the unofficial recognition that the land tenure situation on the coastal strip was virtually insoluble.[12] As early as 1943 an officer argued that policies which concentrated resources on the coastal strip, and Gede Settlement Scheme in particular, were shortsighted, because the land situation on the coast would prevent that area from being able to absorb the thus far neglected hinterland population and that 'the inland areas will always have to support a large part of the population and should therefore receive more attention'.[13] In 1947 District Commissioner J.D. Stringer instigated a programme of dam building and bore drilling and soil conservation known as the Coast Hinterland Scheme.

In 1948 the ephemeral Lake Madina, to the west of Marafa, was drained by headward erosion in the Koromi River, a forerunner of what was to happen in the Hinterland Scheme. In 1949, ten bores and forty-nine dams were constructed in the Malindi District and by 1952 another forty dams had been completed. Under the Scheme, dams were constructed at Waresa in 1951 and at Magarini and Fundisa in 1953 and bores put down at Adu and Marafa.[14] The Waresa dam failed within a year of being constructed and in 1952 labourers were being paid to repair dams constructed in the previous three years.[15] The Public Works Department found it was unable to maintain the bore holes and the pumps and motors and as early as 1949 the Local Native Council offered to pay for a hand pump to replace the diesel-powered pumps at two bores in the district.

A more serious problem associated with the Hinterland Scheme was the manner in which it was implemented. The District Commissioner at Kilifi in 1950 made his 'position quite clear'.

> I consider this work is by far the most important in the way of development that is going on in the district ... the chiefs have all had my personal instructions to build a dam and I wish to see that they carry this out ... if the people do not turn out for dam making they must be prosecuted immediately.[16]

And prosecuted they were, not only for refusing to work but also for failure to attend meetings at which the Scheme was to be explained to them. Demands for labour and arrests continued through periods of food shortages when relief food was being distributed. What the Giriama thought about being forced to work on dams which were quickly washed out and on bores which broke down frequently is not recorded, but it is unlikely they were encouraged to welcome further participation with authorities in the development of the hinterland. The legacy of this period of enforced participation was encountered thirty years later when an NGO associated with the Magarini Project attempted to use 'community participation' to develop surface water storages. The outcome is described in Chapter Five.

Peasant farmers

In 1976 the Giriama were viewed as a group of backward, poverty-stricken people, passive and malleable, waiting for somebody to come along and develop them. In 1985 a senior Kenyan official in the MOLS echoed the views of the Australians in 1976 when he observed, 'Before we came into this area there was nothing here. Nothing at all. We had to bring development for these people'. For AIDAB, and perhaps for McGowans, the first inklings of the real situation at Magarini were contained in Annex 6 (Sociology) of the 1977 Project Report, the culmination of Phase I of the project. Simon Chilungu, a Kenyan sociologist at the University of Nairobi conducted a survey in the project area in 1977 and found that 88 per cent of residents believed they owned the land on which they lived and farmed. On the basis of this and other findings[17] he concluded that the project was likely to 'alienate' the people whom it was supposed to benefit. Chilungu makes a plea for the project to avoid methods of 'subjugation' and 'power-coercive approaches to effecting change' and to ensure the people of Magarini 'participate' in the planning and implementation of the project.

Chilungu also questioned the economic viability of smallholder cropping at Magarini, and compared the policies underpinning Magarini to the *ujamaa* policy of Tanzania where small farmers were required to produce a grain surplus under conditions of inadequate rainfall in which they could barely feed themselves. His survey found that insecurity of food supply, lack of water, an unpredictable climate, poverty and indebtedness were said by the Giriama to be their greatest problems. Poor roads, poor health and education services also gave concern. But a full-blown social survey was not required to discover these matters and even a passing acquaintance with Giriama history would have revealed that people would not be willing to cooperate with any solution which separated them from their land. Although it is unlikely Chilungu thought his report would change Kenyan government policy, he may have believed he could communicate his concerns about Magarini to Australian consultants and aid administrators. However, his argument was lost on AIDAB until the 1980s.

'PRETTY PRIMITIVE' – GIRIAMA AGRICULTURE AND THE MAGARINI ENVIRONMENT

Although the Australians at Magarini made little effort to find out about Giriama history, they did attempt to investigate Giriama agriculture, although without a great deal of success. They had little or no experience with bush fallowing systems and determined very early in the project that the existing system had to be replaced, so understanding how it functioned was not of very great importance. Their Kenyan counterparts told them Giriama were not really farmers and would have to be taught how to farm by 'up-country' settlers. It is likely that as professional agriculturalists, many of the Australians arrived at Magarini with ideas about shifting cultivation very similar to those held by their Kenyan counterparts, who had inherited attitudes from the British that shifting cultivation is the most primitive form of agriculture.

Although a technical report on Giriama agriculture is notably missing from the numerous technical annexes of the Phase I Report, the adaptive advantages of Giriama bush fallowing, in particular the system's ability to recycle key nutrients, to protect the soil from surface erosion and the lack of weeding required in the first two cultivations, are recognized by some project workers in other annexes. Tim Reeves, the first project agronomist at Magarini, supplied details of the Giriama maize cultivation system to Hans Ruthenberg, an agronomist with extensive experience in East Africa. In his widely recognized book on farming systems Ruthenberg (1980: 57) concludes it will be almost impossible to change the Giriama system of agriculture because of local economic and environmental conditions. No project document argues this case and, perhaps out of ignorance of Giriama history, nowhere is it recognized that this agricultural system once produced the bulk of the grain exported from Malindi.

Giriama bush fallowing

Giriama bush fallowing at Magarini was a typical shifting cultivation system. On any particular area of land long periods of fallow were alternated with shorter periods of cultivation. The switch from fallow to cultivation was marked by the cutting, but importantly not necessarily the killing, of trees which had grown on the plot during the fallow. The branches and leaves of the trees were burned, releasing nitrogen, phosphorus, potassium and magnesium in larger amounts than that normally found in the Magarini soils, for immediate use by plants. Most commentators suggest the cultivation periods at Magarini were between two and three years and fallow periods around ten years. Cultivated areas were relatively large, between 2.5 and 5 ha. The area cultivated by any particular family was influenced by access to water and labour availability, with some families hiring labour for clearing, planting and weeding. By the end of the third year of cultivation, soil nutrients had declined, soil conditions had deteriorated, weeds and plant pests and diseases increased and crop yields had fallen sharply from those achieved in the first cultivation. At this point the plot was returned to fallow. Those trees not deliberately killed by ring barking and burning had begun to regenerate, and within a year the plot would be covered in a low thicket of regrowth. Commonly an area was initially opened up from forest and then the clearing extended over a period of years, so that some new land was being planted each year.

By far the most important food crop grown was maize with *simsim*, or sesame, the most important cash crop. Green grams and cowpeas were also grown for food and cash. Other grain crops grown included sorghum, bullrush millet and finger millet and, at times, rice. Sweet potato, peanuts, beans, pigeon peas, tomatoes, cassava, pineapples, watermelons, pawpaw and tobacco were also cultivated. Around homesteads coconuts, cashews, mangos, and a range of fruit trees were grown. Palms and trees could be bought and sold or pledged against loans, regardless of the ownership of the land on which they were growing. Maize was intercropped with green grams and cowpeas and simsim. Planting occurred with minimum disturbance tò the soil and weeding was usually not required until the second cultivation. Maize yields were low, around 400–600 kg/ha and labour inputs were only around 400–600 hours per year. Low planting densities of around 15,000 plants in 5,000 planting stations per hectare, and the use of cassava as a reserve food in case of a failure in the maize crop were adaptations to a risky climatic environment (Reeves 1979).

Fields were not cleared randomly from forest. Particular areas of land were known as garden plots and the characteristics of their soils and their past record of productivity was known. This was important because of the extremely complex soil pattern. The Giriama land use system clearly reflected different soil qualities. The sandy soils were favoured places for homesteads, tree crops and cassava, but not for maize, which grows poorly on the sands. The best maize-growing soils were the black cracking clays, while the solonetz soils were reasonable cropping soils in drier years but in wet years or following intensive downpours, waterlogging on these soils could kill a maize crop in a few hours. By cultivating two or three plots at once on a range of soil types, Giriama bush fallowers attempted to insure against the very high variability which is characteristic of Magarini rainfall.

Giriama fields look chaotic to the uninitiated. Dead and pollarded trees stand like ships' masts in the garden, with firewood stacked around their bases or stuck into forks in lower branches. The few trees which have been cut down lie higgledy-piggledy wherever they happened to fall. Crops appear to be planted at random and up to two dozen species may be interplanted in the same garden, with some crops planted into the same hole. Only when a careful inspection is made of the horizontal and vertical distribution of the crops and the trees in the garden, does a pattern appear. Different species are not planted at random and nor is the distribution of one species within the garden unrelated to others. Some species are planted near dead trees to take advantage of decaying roots, others, such as maize, are intercropped with a legume, like beans, because it is known the maize grows better when this is done. Crops which grow low to the ground may be planted beneath taller crops which shelter them from the sun. Crops which mature earlier are harvested and removed to reveal later maturers planted beneath them.

Fields like this present particular difficulties to the agronomist who wants hard data on crop yields. The garden is irregular in shape, planting densities vary across the garden and the yield of a particular plant species is influenced by its association with other nearby plants. Planting times, and hence maturing and harvesting times, are almost always staggered, even within one species. Yield will vary across the field and from year to year. One reason why the agronomists who were employed on the project did not gain a better understanding of Giriama agriculture is that they were rendered incapable, by professional prejudice, of seeking order in the apparent chaos. Instead of appreciating the Giriama garden as a present-day expression of knowledge gained by generations of empirical trial and error in the Magarini environment, they saw mostly primitive tradition.

The Giriama located their homesteads with reference to sources of surface water, such as pools in which rainwater collected, which were commonly deepened and extended, and soils suitable for gardening. In the periods between the rains, however, women carried water for long distances. In a typical household water collection could take up to three hours of a woman's day, but in the dry period just before the optimum maize planting time, it could take up to half of all household labour. People built temporary shelters in their gardens and sometimes stayed there during periods of hard work. The main house was a substantial building, often two tiered, with a granary constructed at one end over the main hearth so that smoke from the cooking fires kept the maize dry and reduced the losses from rot and insects. Despite this, however, post-harvest losses of up to 20 per cent were possible. About half of all Giriama families owned goats, but very few had cattle. These animals functioned mainly as walking banks, to be sold in times of scarcity and were only slaughtered on special occasions. Chickens were common and with ducks, provided most of the protein consumed. Many plants and condiments were collected from the secondary forest which surrounded the homesteads.

Average family cash incomes from the sale of crops was between K.sh2,000 and K.sh2,500 (1977 prices) and much of this had to be spent on buying water and in poor years, food. It is not known how many Magarini families were self-sufficient in food production most of the time, but a survey of farms in the Kilifi District (but not in the Magarini area) in 1983 found as few as 30 per cent of families in some areas and no more than 50 per cent in all areas surveyed, were self-sufficient in maize and were forced to rely on cassava and purchased maize flour, with many farmers engaging in off-farm work for this reason (Waaijenberg and Salim 1983). Estimates based on experimental work by project agronomist Reeves suggest that at Magarini, the average family would have faced a shortfall in maize in one in every 2–3 years, although in some years they would have had a considerable surplus.

Reeves (1979) produced an estimate of maize yields as a function of rainfall based on trials conducted at Marafa from 1977 to 1979 (Figure 3.1). Probable farmer production can be estimated by placing actual rainfall at Marafa

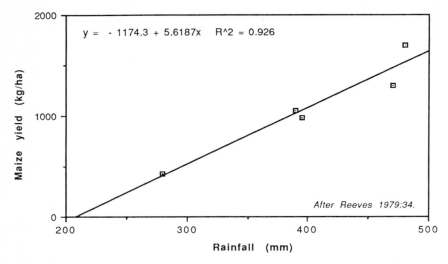

Figure 3.1 Maize yields as a function of rainfall during the growing season, Marafa.

between 1966 and 1986 into Reeves' function (Figure 3.2). The 1978 Phase I Project Report assumed farmer yields were 70 per cent of experimental yields. If, as Reeves estimated, the farmer was cultivating 3 ha of maize during the long rains and 0.75 ha during the short rains, and a family required 1,500 kg of maize per year to meet subsistence requirements but storage losses were 20 per cent so that total production had to be 1,900 kg to satisfy subsistence needs, then in the 21-year period the average family would produce less grain than that required for their subsistence in eight of the 21 years. If rainfall above 699 mm during the growing season is assumed to have destroyed much of the crop through waterlogging, the years of maize shortfall rise to eleven. Particularly striking are the 15 out of the 21 years in which the short rains are insufficient to produce a maize harvest. Not long after the project began, it was discovered that even 3 ha was beyond the capabilities of most Giriama families to cultivate unless they could afford to employ seasonal labour. Thus the actual annual shortfall of maize was probably greater than this estimate.

Sustainability

In the light of these regular annual shortfalls of maize at Magarini in the 1970s, how did the Giriama produce the large surpluses which made up the bulk of maize exported from Malindi in the late 1890s and early 1900s? When the Giriama crossed the Sabaki River and settled the area around Marafa in

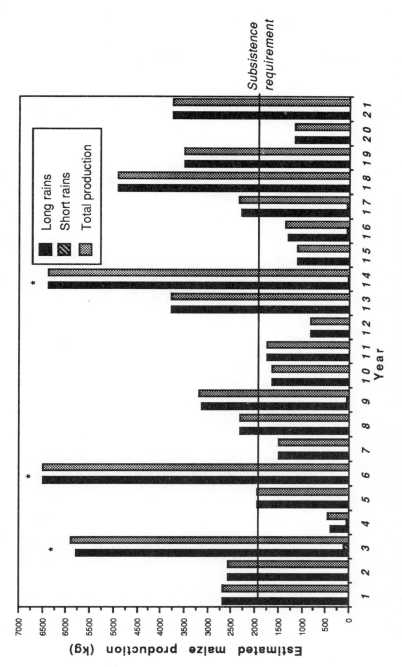

Figure 3.2 Estimated maize production based on rainfall at Marafa, 1966–86, and 1978 assumptions on area cultivated.

Note: Assumes 3-ha cultivated in long rains and 0.75 ha during short rains, and settler yields 70 per cent of experimental yields. An asterisk indicates years in which soil water-logging would probably have reduced yields substantially.

Plate 11 Mixed cropping – maize and cowpeas (top) *Plate 12* Giriama swidden farming (bottom)

the 1890s they were moving onto land which had been only lightly or never previously cultivated. In 1914 colonial officer Arthur Champion contrasted those north Sabaki areas which had been cultivated for some time with areas previously unoccupied, and although his prejudices against shifting cultivation caused him to see all forest cleared as forest destroyed, his observations are worth consideration.

> The soil is extraordinarily fertile, especially in its virgin condition. ... The soil under the bush is frequently loamy and full of decaying vegetable matter – so that no cultivation is necessary at all, the seeds, some two or three together, being pushed into holes made with a small hoe. The seeds spring up rapidly and a heavy crop is obtained, often without the necessity of even one weeding. Weeds do not grow under the bush as a rule so that the seeds of the weeds are not present. Thus a crop is not infrequently obtained with a minimum of labour. The Agiryama will never cultivate grass land if there is any bush at hand. He says that the soil is hard and would have to be turned up and weeds would be plentiful, both involving unnecessary labour. These methods have already turned the greater part of the southern and central Giryama into desert land. The protecting bush has been burnt off and the loam washed down into the rivers leaving exposed the bare hard subsoil. The forest trees which previously flourished when the bush protected their trunks and roots, though not cut down or rooted up by the cultivator, soon die from exposure if indeed they have not done so from the effects of fire. Thus the whole country is rapidly becoming denuded and presents a red gravelly waste, hard dry and scorchingly hot under the tropical sun. ... The tribe in their northern migration have carried the same destruction with them and much irretrievable damage has been done to the fine forest on the north side of the Sabaki (Galana) River.
>
> (Champion 1967: 8)

Champion's description, despite being overdrawn, matches what we would expect to find in an area where a shifting cultivation system has been pushed beyond the point where woody fallow plant successions can be maintained and stable grass communities begin to dominate. If fallow periods are too short to allow the same amount of living plant material, or biomass, that was growing on the plot prior to clearing for cultivation, to regrow before the next cultivation, more nutrients are being removed from the soil during the cultivation periods than are being replaced during the fallows. Ultimately this changes dominant fallow species, increases soil compaction, runoff and erosion, causes laterization, increases labour requirements, decreases yields, narrows the range of crop species and increases reliance on low-protein foods like cassava.[18] Champion observed many of these things at Marafa in 1914.

Since establishing themselves at Marafa in the 1890s the Giriama had been producing maize well beyond their own subsistence needs, for sale and to pay the British fines and taxes, and the interest on Arab loans. It is not surprising that they ran down the soil and forest resources there relatively quickly. The degradation they caused, however, was not the total devastation implied by Champion. They reduced medium-height forest to a lower thickety bush with patches of savannah-like grass and scattered trees. It was possible to continue cultivation of this land, and many people did that. Increasing numbers of Giriama began squatting on Arab land on the coastal strip. Others did what Giriama had done for at least the previous 100 years and moved north into taller forest. Adu, in the extreme north of the Magarini Project area, comprised only seventeen huts mostly belonging to Sanye people in 1917, but by 1932 the settlement was made up of 102 Giriama huts, and some Giriama had reached the Tana River. They were portrayed as 'notoriously a people who have a fondness for opening up new settlements for themselves beyond their fellows' (*Report of the Kenyan Land Commission 1933* 1934: 311).[19] Those who remained in the Marafa area, however, faced increasing problems of declining yields and labour shortages as larger areas had to be cultivated to meet subsistence requirements. From the 1950s food shortages were a regular feature of life here.

The Giriama bush fallowing system at Magarini in the 1970s was not sustainable in the long term.[20] If it took about 100 years or so to degrade the Marafa area to the condition it was in in 1977, then we may conclude that with no changes in the system, and with rising subsistence and cash earning demands from an increasing population being placed upon it, it would have taken only another 100 or so years to bring the rest of the area from Marafa to Adu and beyond, to the same condition. The obvious question appears to be, given that change was necessary, what sort of change was most appropriate? Because bush fallowing is a form of agro-forestry, some adaptation of the existing agricultural system would seem to have been the best route to follow, even though methods of intensifying bush fallowing systems and the establishment of agro-forestry systems were still experimental (see, for example, Rao and Westley 1989). Instead, after a year of intensive technical studies, the project proposed the complete replacement of the bush fallowing system. Important questions are raised by this decision, about how much longer marginal areas like Magarini can continue to be colonized through settlement projects, or spontaneous encroachment. It is worth observing, however, that the decision taken by the development workers on Magarini to replace the indigenous farming system was consistent with contemporary development practice worldwide. In 1976 John Hatch noted, 'the development profession suffers from an entrenched superiority complex with respect to the small farmer. We believe our modern technology is infinitely superior to his. We conduct our research and assistance efforts as if we know everything and our clients nothing' (1976: 75).

'IDENTIFY AND DEFINE A PROJECT': PHASE I, RESOURCE SURVEY, FEASIBILITY AND ECONOMIC ASSESSMENT

The gestation of the Magarini Project from the initial Matthews and Stephens' identification and report in June 1976 to the appointment of G.P. McGowan & Associates Pty Ltd as the managing agent in September 1976 and the approval of the government of Kenya in October 1976 has been described. In January 1977 Phase I of the project began. Termed a resource investigation in official documents, this phase was completed in May 1978 with the presentation of a report which comprised an Executive Summary, a Project Report and thirteen annexes of technical reports.

The Phase I investigations included technical studies of climate, land capability, soil conservation, surface water, geology and groundwater, livestock health and management, agronomy, forestry, infrastructure, surveying and mapping, engineering studies and a review of existing settlement schemes as well as the social and economic survey previously discussed. A more detailed soil survey was completed in 1980. In all, twelve Kenyans and twenty-one Australians were involved in these studies.

What happened during Phase I at Magarini is widespread in development practice. It occurs because, almost always, those who talk about development, those who work in the offices of the large funding agencies or the universities,

Plate 13 Giriama customary family homestead

are not the people who do development. The contrast between what is required of the talkers and the doers is the origin of what Paul McGowan calls
the development game. Every doer knows that rural development is difficult,
very difficult. 'After all', observes McGowan, 'if Magarini had been easy, it
would have been done long ago'. But if the bureaucrats in AIDAB, or elsewhere, were told the cold, hard facts about how difficult a project was going
to be, nothing would have happened, because 'they won't take risks, they're
too bloody frightened of making a mistake'. The game involves the doers
trying to persuade the talkers that everything will be all right, while the doers
get on with trying to solve some of the problems. McGowan was an archetypal
doer, but his colourful remarks contain an important truth. A former AIDAB
staffer agrees that a concern on the part of public servants to avoid mistakes,
'pervades government decision making in Canberra. Cautious bureaucrats
take the sting, the punch out of their work in a mindless pursuit of the safe
statement. There is no question of the Ministers being "*fearlessly* advised".
Facts are even casualties of the instinct of self-preservation'.

Robert Chambers provides a sympathetic yet critical description of doers,
whom he calls 'positive practitioners' (1983: 33–5). They are exposed to risk,
tied to deadlines of budgets and seasons, to targets and to political demands.
They look for what will go right in a project, not for what will go wrong.
Development depends on their energy, enthusiasm, entrepreneurship and
emotions. But there are dangers. Their very qualities get projects up and running but their drive and enthusiasm can cause them to misjudge the real
difficulties. They are often 'unable to accept or use discordant information'
and they are wont to see their critics as enemies not allies. Their use of 'selec-
tive perception and myth have their part to play in maintaining support, élan
and momentum; but in the long term the costs in benefits foregone and in
eventual disillusion may be high'. They tend to be technically oriented, professionals who have a strong need to do something and to be seen to have done
it. Finally they suffer from being overly optimistic,

> partly ... because over-estimates are needed to get proposals accepted in
> the first place; partly because of the ease with which social cost–benefits
> can be manipulated to produce whatever internal rate of return is thought
> necessary to get agreement and funding [see Chapter Four]. ... [But] Vision
> and hope are needed for action. Rural development is so difficult that some
> self-delusion may help to get things going at all.
>
> (Chambers 1983: 35)

In 1976 Paul McGowan saw Magarini as 'a beautiful project because you
had everything under your control, social, water, roads, survey settlement, agriculture. You had to do a package deal'. McGowan assumed that if the
components of the project which he believed to be critical (and the same components, plus some new add-ons, still appear in the burgeoning procedural
manuals of the major multilateral development agencies; see, for example,

Moris 1981: 35) were properly studied, he could design a project which could meet its objectives. He was a vastly more experienced practitioner than the AIDAB staff he was negotiating with and he used that knowledge to his advantage. 'We had a lot of experience in knowing what the international agencies required and perhaps AIDAB wasn't sure what they wanted ... I knew what was necessary and they didn't and I asked for this and got it.'

By the end of 1977, however, what he had was a high level of complexity, project goals which were almost certainly countervailing, information that the attitudes of the supposed beneficiaries were likely to seriously compromise the project's success and technical problems which appeared to have no solution. He was in the well-known 'muddled situation of reality' in which 'one may discover there are problems to be solved, but nobody knows enough to specify likely solutions' (Moris 1981: 42). Some of his 'experts' were also showing concern. Harry Matthews, the project manager in November 1977 was accused of showing a 'lack of faith' in the project when he questioned the scale of the proposed project and raised many of the problems which we are about to discuss.[21] He left Magarini shortly after the disagreement. What were these problems, how were they dealt with and why?

Land tenure and settlement

During 1977 Chilungu's survey revealed that most of the people who were to be involved in the project were not squatters, but residents who believed they held rights to the land on which they lived. The Kenyan government wanted the project to move these people from the land, which was legally government land held as a trust, subdivide it, resettle them and a similar number of up-country settlers back on it again, and issue them with Certificates of Occupation. Kenyan policy was that individual land titles promoted 'safe and easy land transactions', the 'removal of tribal and individual fears', the 'promotion of private incentive and industry' and security for credit, unavailable to holders of rights to land under community titles (McGowan 1978a: 69).

Settlers who took up their allocated plots would automatically incur a debt for the purchase price of the plot which was equivalent to about two years' earnings. They would also become eligible for a land development loan for building materials, fencing, tools and initial crop operating costs repayable over ten years with interest at 6.5 per cent per annum. 'At the end of the loan repayment period when all loans have been completely repaid and if satisfactory performance has been made, the title deeds should be handed over to the settlers' (McGowan 1978a: 78).

McGowan was aware of the project's potential to create landlessness among the Giriama, but if this possibility was raised directly with AIDAB the chances of the project going into Phase II were slim. AIDAB was involved because they believed this project would assist the Giriama, not turn them into a landless proletariat. The 1978 Project Report, therefore, devoted a whole chapter to land tenure, described the Kenyan land tenure system, the nature of the title at Magarini, and Kenyan policy on landownership. But it did not explain that, to many Giriama, the purchase price of a plot was equivalent to paying for land they already owned. Nor did it detail what would happen to the title if settlers could not repay the loans, or did not 'perform satisfactorily'. Instead the report contained one sentence which proclaimed that the 'rights of the existing occupiers should not be jeopardised' (McGowan 1978a: 72) and figures were produced showing that almost all the land within the proposed project area would be required for resettlement of existing occupiers.

McGowan justified this on two grounds: first, it was not the business of Australians to interfere in Kenyan government policy. The Kenyans had already made it clear they did not agree with the findings of the social survey. McGowan recounted, they had told him in meetings, 'Don't worry about it, it's nothing to do with you. They'll [the Giriama] do what they're told!'.[22] Second, he believed he could use the statement in the report to ensure all Giriama entitled to land at Magarini would get it and he believed it was 'a well-known fact that no one on Kenyan resettlement schemes repays their loans', so why should the Giriama?

Water

It had been obvious from the 1976 Appraisal that water was the critical factor at Magarini. If 4,000 families were to be spread evenly across the countryside on 13-ha plots and if the productivity of agriculture was to be increased, the hours of drudgery presently involved in carrying water had to be eliminated. McGowans had shrewdly included the engineering skills of SMEC in their bid for the project, in competition with SMEC's separate bid, and they subcontracted Coffey and Partners Ltd to oversee the groundwater investigations. The actual drilling at Magarini was to be carried out by Kenyans. The two bores drilled by the British suggested that sufficient water would soon be discovered. Unfortunately it was not and still has not been. Yet the project proceeded steadily into a flood of negative reports about water.

The search for groundwater during Phase I ran into two problems: first, the skills of the Kenyan drillers were limited, their equipment was unsuitable and it was six months into Phase I before they were sent to the project area;[23] and second, the strong possibility that water of sufficient quantity and quality did not exist beneath Magarini. The drilling programme was thus immediately behind schedule and in September 1977 a further $630,000, eight-month extension to the water exploration programme was approved by the Australian Foreign Minister. A technical annex on groundwater was produced in November 1977, and a report on the further exploration in July 1978. It is worth examining the language used in some of these reports in detail, because they provide an excellent illustration of professional over-optimism in action.

The 1977 Annex was extremely guarded about the likelihood of finding a suitable groundwater source; it included phrases like 'Ultimately the groundwater investigation will assess the amount of water which can be withdrawn safely from the aquifers in the long term without causing any harmful effects', 'borehole yields are not likely to be very high' and 'Until a better picture of the hydrogeology of the area is built up the ultimate yield of the aquifers cannot even be guessed at' (McGowan 1977c). Once again Volume II did not set out the details of the problem, although of course the Annex was available for anyone to read if they chose to.

Volume II read,

> Exploration has indicated the presence of groundwater under much of the project area. Further testing is required to establish safe yields and appropriate development techniques for production bores, but it seems likely that production rates of 5000 litres/bore/hour or better will be achieved. A 16 hour pumping day would produce 80,000 litres/day/bore. To meet domestic requirements 22 bores would be needed.
>
> The quality of groundwater tapped during the exploration program has generally been acceptable for human consumption. This source will provide a reliable supply of domestic water.

> (McGowan 1978a: 38)

And the Executive Summary read,

> All practical alternatives for water supply have been investigated and this study is continuing.
>
> The recommended plan is initially to provide a decentralised system from local bores, tapping the major aquifer. Each bore will have attached to it a diesel powered pump and a distribution system with hydrants at two kilometer spacings. Future domestic supplies could come either from more similar bores or if feasible and cheaper, from a pumped supply out of shallow aquifers along the Sabaki River. Roof catchments and storage tanks will supplement domestic supplies.

> (McGowan 1978b: 14)

This was a very worrying time for the consultants. The SMEC project manager Kevin Stephens recalls the water supply was always a concern. 'We were planning on going ahead and developing areas and not at all sure we were going to have enough water to supply people.' When asked how he slept at night during this period, Paul McGowan drawled, 'You get used to it'. Drilling continued under the extension. Under pressure from McGowan and the Kenyans to proceed into Phase II in July 1978, AIDAB expressed concern about the groundwater situation, among other things. Within a week McGowan was able to reply with a report from Coffeys on the results of the latest drillings. Coffey's report read,

[A]n aquifer apparently containing good quality water has been encountered over virtually all of the project area.

The Kenyan Water Ministry will commence construction of 10 production bores. These will be located strategically over the project area and, depending on yields obtained should be adequate for the first two years of operation of the project. In Year Three another 10 production bores are planned and these used in conjunction with proposed surface storages, should satisfy the water requirements of the settlement scheme.

No production bores have as yet been completed in the tertiary aquifers due to limitations of the cable tool drilling method. Rotary drilling techniques should enable production bores to be constructed without any unusual problems. The holes will be relatively deep (around 150m) and will have to be drilled with mud ... [Kenya] Ministry of Water Development does not have a lot of experience in mud drilling and hence will require guidance in these techniques.

(AIDAB August 1978)

The project proceeded into Phase II on the basis of this report, even though at this point only nine bores had been drilled. Seven were drilled into sands and found reasonable quality water, but were not properly screened and collapsed before production testing was possible. One contained water at 37°C and three times the salinity of seawater, one was dry and one was still in the final drilling stages.

Agriculture

The basis of almost all the agricultural problems which emerged at Magarini during 1977 was described in Annex 10 of the Phase I Report:

Rainfall is the major limiting factor on crop yields in both the amount received ... and more important in reliability. ... All crops are badly stressed for three years in four. Water is deficient in every month. ... A more important aspect is the occurrence of peak deficiency at flowering for all crops when moisture stress has the greatest influence on yields. Yield assurance is therefore low three years in four.

(McGowan 1977g: 10)

The Giriama attempted to compensate for this problem by planting larger areas, but they were constrained by shortages of labour at critical times in the agricultural cycle. If the project was to improve living standards and contribute to an increase in national food production, agricultural productivity had to be improved at Magarini. In the marginal semi-arid areas of Africa, an off-the-shelf 'green revolution' package of better crop varieties, more water and fertilizer and the use of pesticides and insecticides was not available and even if it had been, the majority of smallholders would have been unable to afford it. But rather than try to improve aspects of the existing agricultural system, the project sought to replace the whole system. It did this partly because the project was based on settlement and was going to put people whose existing agriculture was a form of shifting cultivation, on a 13-ha plot, and partly because the 'transformation model' of agricultural development derived from the successful application of machinery, fertilizers and new crop varieties in the United States and Australia from the 1930s was still seen as a superior model which could be successfully transferred to Africa with little modification.[24]

The decision to replace rather than improve the agricultural system had a problem-creating knock-on effect across the whole project. The solution of a problem in one area created two or three problems in other areas, and the solutions of these created further problems. In some cases these chains of problem–solution–problem led up a blind alley to an irresolvable situation, others circled back to the original problem. It is not necessary to examine all of these conundrums to understand what happened at Magarini. One example will suffice.

During Phase I an estimate was made of how much food and cash an average family would need in a year to provide a nutritionally satisfactory diet and enough money to purchase clothing, bedding, utensils, tools, mosquito nets, supplementary foods (like tea, salt and sugar), send their children to school and repay their loans. Based on crop yields derived from on-project trials and using a package of crops already grown by the Giriama, it was decided that to achieve the production necessary to provide the food and cash needed would require 6 ha under cultivation in an 'average' year.[25] A problem was immediately created. The adoption of this package demanded approximately three times the amount of labour the settlers were then investing in agriculture. Rather than backing off and trying another approach, the Phase I team at Magarini argued their way single-mindedly to a mechanical solution, against all advice to the contrary.

Some of this labour shortfall would be made up by bringing water close to every plot. Some settlers could afford to employ labour as some Giriama were doing in 1977, but the amount of labour required would not be available at Magarini. Oxen could be used but Giriama were not familiar with their use and Magarini was a tsetse fly zone. The only alternative was to use tractor-drawn machinery and as most of the settlers could not afford a tractor of their own, a tractor-hire service would have to be established.

This solution was in fact a problem in disguise. Annex 10 (Agronomy) of the Phase I Report had already quoted the Head of the Farm Mechanization Department at Kabete on the lack of success in the use of large tractors in Kenya; tasks were not completed on time, management and maintenance were poor, spare parts were scarce and, perhaps worst of all, the 'peasants became lazy' (McGowan 1977g: 21). But after listing further problems associated with tractor-hire services in Africa,[26] the report recommended a tractor-hire service of forty-eight 60–70 horsepower tractors, working a double shift of 60 hours per week for a 10-week season, supported by mobile workshops which would service every tractor every day. The lack of any semblance of reality in this proposal, particularly in the light of experience of groundwater exploration at Magarini, is passed off by arguing that the tractor support service at Magarini will be better because the project will ensure it is.

An unresolved dimension of the tractor problem related to the inability of settlers to weed their crops twice, which had been shown by project trials to be the only way to achieve the yields necessary to earn the required income. Annex 10 found the least-cost method was hand cultivation but insufficient home labour would be available for the whole area. The proposed solution was either inter-row cultivation using tractors, or two applications of 2,4-D, which the same report notes the farmers cannot afford and which in addition is a problem chemical.[27]

Another problem thrown up by the decision to use machinery was that if tree stumps, left in the ground under existing Giriama practice, were not removed, tractor cultivation would be impossible. Given the original labour shortage, the new settlers could not be expected to clear 6 ha of scrub from their plots and remove the stumps by hand. Therefore it was recommended that heavy bulldozers and local labour gangs be employed to clear 6 ha of scrub from each plot, and carry out an initial heavy discing. Immediately further problems were created. Technical Annex 9 (McGowan 1977f) on soil conservation read,

> [T]he removal of this vegetative protection exposes the soils to the hazards of erosion....
> [E]rosion hazards can be increased where tractors are used and machines are misused to produce structural breakdown in the soil. This risk is not present with hand cultivation. With machine cultivation particular care must be taken when cultivating dry ... minimum tillage practices and mulching are required wherever possible....
> [T]yned and not disced implements should always be used.

Volume II of the Project Report acknowledged the erosion hazard consequent on the removal of natural vegetation over large areas but plot layout designs and the building of soil conservation structures, contour banks and grassed waterways, were proposed to solve this problem. The other problems of machine cultivation were ignored.

Because the settlers were poor, and because of the high risk of not getting any response from fertilizer applications because of unpredictable rainfall, some form of on-farm nutrient recycling had to be found to substitute for the nutrients supplied by the bush fallowing system to be replaced. A legume–pasture ley, a grass fallow, would in theory not only produce nitrogen, but also provide a ground cover to protect the soil against erosion, and fodder for increased numbers of animals (McGowan 1977g: 5).

The availability of legume species in Kenya was thought not to be a problem. However, the low phosphorus levels of Magarini soils would almost certainly be a limiting factor for legume growth. Soil acidity could also induce a molybdenum deficiency. Therefore a phosphorus fertilizer and a molybdenum supplement would be needed to grow a legume ley successfully. But the settlers could not afford to use fertilizer and the risks of not getting a return on money invested in it were high. The only escape from this circular argument was to lamely recommend in Volume II that the use of fertilizers be re-examined after the project had been running for a time. The implications for the project of this apparent impasse were smoothed over in the Executive Summary by arguing that the problem 'may change with better technology and/ or improved marketing and will be reassessed continually during the project' (McGowan 1978a: 5).

Proceeding to Phase II

On the basis of these reports, the Magarini Settlement Project proceeded into Phase II. McGowans' position was that they had discovered greater difficulties than initially foreseen, but with people on two-year contracts it was pointless to postpone going into Phase II while some of the problems were solved on paper. Better to press on and solve problems on the run, which was what development was all about anyway. AIDAB staff were concerned about water in particular, but Coffey's July report was reassuring. With three years of time and money invested in the project, postponement would be administratively difficult, particularly trying to explain to the Minister why further short-term funding was required. To withdraw completely would seriously embarrass Australian interests in Kenya, where the government had already committed funds to the project. Kenyan comments on the Phase I reports were generally favourable; on agriculture, water and labour the reports were thought to be too optimistic, but the 'integrated' approach was liked and although the Kenyan government wanted to slow down the rate of general project development because of increasing problems with the national economy, MOLS proposed to speed up settlement to 15,000 ha in four years and to bring in 'Kikuyu farmers to give the Giriama a lead'. Following a withdrawal, AIDAB would be in the position of having to start over again in Kenya, assuming the Kenyans would countenance a continuing involvement.

Between July and September 1978, McGowan lobbied AIDAB in person and in writing. With his professional background he easily met technical queries raised by AIDAB staff, and he exuded confidence. He parried criticism in August by the Department of Finance, that the internal rate of return was too low, with a letter arguing that the yields presented in the reports were conservative, and that there were compelling political and social reasons for the project to proceed which were of equal weight to the internal rate of return. In September he presented AIDAB with three options for funding Phase II and AIDAB accepted the most conservative. In February 1979 the Minister approved funding and in July the Memorandum of Understanding was signed.

PHASE II: 'DISRUPTING A RELATIVELY SOUND FARMING SYSTEM'

The problems which beset the Magarini Settlement Project between January 1979 and September 1983, when Australian Foreign Minister Hayden refused to approve funding for Phase III, took three forms. First were those difficulties which came about because physical targets set in Phase I were not met. Second were the many problems clearly foreseen in Phase I, but which were not solved during Phase II. Third were problems which first appeared during Phase II.

Many of the chains of knock-on problem-solving and problem-causing which occurred in Phase II had been discussed but not resolved in the Phase I documents. All parts of the project were so integrated that an inability to meet a target, or an unsolved problem, in one area threw out of kilter plans to meet targets and solve problems in others. With a short-term, crisis management form of problem-solving forced onto project staff, they were unable to clearly relate day-to-day work to long-term objectives. Once again we examine these difficulties only in relation to settlement, water and agriculture.

Settlement

Settlement continued to place pressure on all other aspects of the project. Australian project staff complained of a 'settle at all costs' attitude on the part of their Kenyan counterparts. McGowans, having persuaded AIDAB to proceed to Phase II by down-playing the technical problems, were now concerned to slow down the rate of settlement until water supply and other technical matters could be addressed and argued that settlement should not go ahead 'without proper scientific and economic investigations'.[28] Unfortunately this was not what their Phase I reports had said, and the Kenyans were now determined to press ahead with settlement, always their prime objective.

By September 1979 a register of landholders eligible for compensation had been completed and a settler list started. Fortunately for McGowans, Kenyan teams who were surveying the plot boundaries quickly fell behind their targets and the settlement process was slowed more by this matter than by protestations from the Australians. Only 76 families had been settled by 1980 and by September 1983 only 1,075 families out of a target of 4,000 had been allocated plots. No further allocation of plots occurred until 1989 when a new settlement list of 400 families was approved by the District Development Committee, and forwarded to Nairobi.

A proportion of Giriama allocated plots either did not move onto their plot, or having moved on for a period, moved off again. The Kenyan project staff responsible for settlement, in cooperation with the district administration, threatened settlers that unless they occupied their blocks and built a residence there the plot would be re-allocated to another family. This led to houses being constructed which were never occupied, families splitting and living partly on a plot and partly elsewhere, and women occupying plots while their husbands worked elsewhere to earn the cash required to make up short-falls in food and to pay their children's school fees or to repay loans.[29] The reason why settlers were pressured to stay on their plots is complicated; first, the primary objective of the project in Kilifi District was to resettle Giriama squatters and if they did not move, the problem was not solved. But second, the political pressure on the settlement list from non-Giriama up-country applicants for land at Magarini was considerable and it was feared that if Giriama did not take up their plots and remain on them, they would lose access to the land for ever.

Water

Put simply, the Magarini Project failed to produce sufficient groundwater to meet the needs of the settlers. Of thirty bores drilled by 1983, nineteen had been abandoned, eight were producing, one was capped and four were being used for observation. A report commissioned by McGowans at AIDAB's request in 1987 found the groundwater resource was unproven at Magarini (Bell 1987). Despite the work in Phase I and Phase II virtually nothing was known of the detailed geology of the aquifers, the areal distribution of salinity, bore hole hydraulic characteristics or the long-term effects of pumping. The total water requirement of the project was estimated between 1,500 and 2,000 m^3 per day and estimates of total underflow in 1978 were 1,600 m^3 per day. But a re-examination of these data in 1987 suggested the most optimistic underflow was between 200 and 1,200 m^3 per day. This situation arose because the hydrogeology of the area was more complex than initially assumed. During the extended Phase I exploratory survey, although water was found in eight of nine bores drilled, only one could be tested. Before a further round of exploratory drilling and testing could be undertaken, the pressure of finding enough water for settlers coming onto plots caused the primary aim of the drilling programme to become the provision of water for the project. The collection of hydrogeological data became a secondary aim.

The reticulation system design assumed that water quantity and quality were absolutely secure. That was not the case. High levels of corrosion made it necessary for pump parts to be replaced at about three times the estimated rate and spare parts were difficult to obtain. By the end of 1980 only 9.5 km of a target 40 km of pipe had been laid, standpipes were on average 2 km from settled plots and considerably further from many. Low water pressure and the high rate of pump breakdowns made this supply unreliable. In February 1981 the sustainability of the reticulated supply was seriously questioned.[30]

Early in Phase II the project began construction of surface water storages, earth dams and excavated tanks, in an effort to offset the lack of progress in the groundwater programme. Because they were additional to the programme the layout of plots did not allow public access to them and they occupied land on allocated plots, reducing the area available for agriculture on those plots and increasing the likelihood of rapid siltation. AIDAB disapproved and stopped this work because of the perceived health risk of open water, in particular bilharzia and malaria. But the 1987 joint review of the project, which officially recognized the failure of the reticulated water scheme, recommended a renewed surface water programme, in association with 'catchment management groups' formed from the settlers occupying plots in the catchment of each dam, with assistance from an NGO (see also Chapter Five). It is sadly ironic how closely this mirrors the Fred Morley and Henry Nix recommendation for greater local control over water resources through the formation of catchment communities, forgotten for twelve years after AIDAB handed over the project preparation to SMEC.

Agriculture – the farm package

It should be no surprise that a tractor-hire service was never established at Magarini, and although some settlers could afford to hire tractors, most continued to cultivate by hand. They were unable to cultivate anywhere near the recommended 6 ha. Agronomist Reeves, who arrived on the project in 1978, devised a more appropriate package of food and cash crops, based on trials at the General Investigation Station, which involved the cultivation of only 2.75 ha. He argued that 'even when the land is initially prepared by tractor, and the task of water carrying is reduced by the closer proximity of water points, the typical family will still not be able to weed and harvest a larger crop area without additional labour' (Reeves 1979: 11).

This basic package was later adjusted to take account of the amount of labour available to settler families, but if families were only to repay their loans and have no other cash incomes, they needed to cultivate 3.75 ha, which required four adult-equivalent units of labour. To earn more than K.sh1,000 per year, 4.5 ha had to be cultivated, which demanded five labour units. In 1980, as a result of the policy of breaking up extended family hamlets and settling nuclear families on individual plots, 62 per cent of the seventy-six families then allocated plots had only two labour units available, 25 per cent had three and only 4 per cent had five (Staples et al. 1980: 90–2). Even without taking into account differences in land quality from plot to plot and rainfall from year to year, 87 per cent of families settled could not earn enough from their allocated plots to repay loans for the purchase costs of land they had believed was theirs.

Land quality was not unimportant, however. The Phase I Annexes on land capability argued that plot sizes and boundaries should reflect land quality and take into account the local topography. In practice neither recommendation was followed. Giriama farmers who previously took advantage of different soil qualities by living in one place and cultivating in two or three other places, now found themselves restricted to 13-ha plots, most of them on unfamiliar land, because fewer than 15 per cent were resettled on or near land they had formerly occupied. Because of the highly variable soils, plot demarcation could not take account of land quality because soil mapping could not be completed in time.

Agriculture – extension

The successful adoption of recommended farm packages required considerable control by extension staff over the settlers' labour and prevented settlers from seeking off-farm employment. Many settlers were not willing to take what appeared to be excessive risks in adopting the entire package being imposed on them. Settlers who did not adopt it were harangued and began to avoid contact with project extension staff, a marked contrast to the large numbers of Giriama farmers who attended field days at demonstration plots during Phase I. Tim Reeves ruefully observed, 'We could have done so much good, if it hadn't been for the project'. Relationships between settlers and project staff, already soured by the compulsory acquisition of land and forced removals of families, worsened. But this sort of relationship between extension services and their 'clients' in Kenya was not unusual and according to David Leonard (1977) the problems are due to the hierarchical organization of the extension services, the low morale of field staff, and the inability of recommended practices to solve the small farmers' problems. Leonard describes a Kenyan extension service field day on a model farm as pure 'theatre'; anyone who has visited the model farmers at Magarini will understand exactly what he means.

Giriama alienation from the project had serious repercussions on the ability of newly arrived Australian staff to learn and adapt their recommendations to local conditions. When Reeves completed his contract he found no way to pass on his accumulated wisdom to his successor. He likened the passing on of hard learned lessons about Magarini to the old story of the whispered message that changes 'Going to advance, send reinforcements', to 'Going to a dance, send three and fourpence'. By 1981 Reeves' successor was almost completely isolated from the Giriama. When Bob McCown visited in 1981 as part of the project review team, he went out with the Australian project agronomist.

> We went to Sosoni, the sandy soils, to the north, where the project had a substation. They had tried to grow a wide range of crops there, but except for cassava it was the most miserable situation you have ever seen. It was terrible. They didn't use fertilizer and it was a sandy, impoverished soil. They had a Giriama caretaker they employed who lived not far away. I asked him what he thought of this effort and he went into fits of laughter. Jim [a fictitious name – the Australian agronomist] was shattered by this, that this Giriama farmer thought the whole thing was a joke. I asked the

Giriama caretaker if he had a *shamba* nearby and he took us to his father's. It was literally a stone's throw away. It was very impressive. He had a good sesame crop just harvested, various other crops doing well. Jim had to admit he had never been in this *shamba*, although it was so close and he was employing the son of the owner. On the way back in the Land Rover, Jim's counterpart told me he was ashamed that they never talked to the farmers and that they should start, because the farmers obviously knew more than they did![31]

We have earlier noted the inability of many project staff to come to terms with Giriama agriculture because of what may be called professional biases. Although there has been recent widespread recognition of the variety, complexity and relevance of farmers' knowledge,[32] especially in research and development, the institutional character of project practice is such that local knowledge is often still judged not relevant to the new situation which a project is trying to achieve, and so is systematically devalued by the orientation toward the project's imperatives. In other cases, practitioners can 'see' that the farming systems or other indigenous practices make sense. But the way in which indigenous knowledge is organised is frequently inaccessible to the agriculturalist who seeks testable propositions of a cause-and-effect variety. Consequently, the farmer's knowledge is more likely treated as a 'confounding variable', or an externality which must be taken into account rather than used to provide lessons as to how to proceed. Indeed, where such considerations clash with other imperatives, of the strength seen at Magarini, they are unceremoniously dropped (cf. Redclift 1987: 200).

Agriculture – scrub clearing

Unforeseen difficulties also affected the timing of the scrub clearing, soil conservation and discing programme. It was originally planned to pull down the scrub with a large chain between two bulldozers, a technique well known in Australia and one used in Kenyan land development schemes during the 1950s. Suitable timber was to be removed for charcoal manufacture and the remaining debris burned in a chequer-board pattern to reduce erosion risk. Heavy discing was then to bring remaining roots to the surface from where gangs of labourers would remove and burn them. A local contracting company was hired to do the job. The chain to be used did not arrive from Australia until early 1980. The contractor began pushing the scrub into windrows with ordinary bulldozer blades, where it was burned. Charcoal manufacture was not organized. Blade pushing frequently resulted in topsoil being scraped or 'scalped' from plots and piled into the windrows. It was slow and the contractor's machinery broke down frequently; average machine down-time in 1979 and 1980 was 60 per cent. More local labour was hired and large areas of scrub were cleared by hand.

When the chain arrived it was discovered that the scrub species at Magarini tended to bend over rather than uproot. The chain was pulled in one direction and then in the other which doubled the cost of clearing and succeeded mainly in snapping off the scrub and larger trees, which were supposed to be left standing, about a metre above the ground. Leaving the damaged scrub to dry in the hope that a hot fire would kill it proved unsuccessful; after one rainy season vigorous regrowth occurred which would not burn. Areas which were unsuccessfully chained eventually had to be cleared by hand and blade pushing. The use of a root rake on the blades reduced the problem of scalping, but the scrub clearing programme rapidly fell behind schedule and by 1981 only 40 per cent of the target area had been cleared.

Because the heavy discing could not be done and the soil conservation works could not be constructed until the scrub was cleared, these programmes also fell behind target. Project machinery allocated to discing and building soil conservation banks had to be diverted to speed up the clearing, so that some land which had been successfully cleared and disced was left unprotected by soil conservation works through the long rains. The formula for contour bank spacing recommended in the Phase I Annex on soil conservation was found wanting by further work on soils during 1980 and it was recommended that slopes as low as 2 per cent be protected. Surface erosion on cultivated land on settler plots, rilling and widespread soil wash was observed and illustrated with photographs in this report (McGarrity 1980).

The scrub species at Magarini proved the better of the project in more ways than one. About a year after the scrub had been successfully removed and the land disced, the scrub began to regrow. The roots which had remained in the ground, chopped up by the discs and so increased in number, had retained the ability to regenerate. Bob McCown again,

> We were on the GIS, the experimental station inspecting a crop trial. What was interesting was there was all these suckers, shoots coming up. I asked Jim [a fictitious name] what they were going to be like next year, because they were obviously woody regrowth and they could have big impact on the crop next year. 'Nah, no problem', he said. There were some workers nearby, Giriama employed on the project, good practical people, so I said let's ask one of them. We had to use an interpreter. I asked one them, what will this stuff be like next year? He pointed up the slope to a neighbouring field where there was a thicket over your head! I was just stunned. Either Jim was trying to con me or he hadn't understood the problem. But the Giriama workers knew. That was the thing that struck me in 1981. The Australians doing the agricultural research did not know as much as the farmers.

The Australians were either unaware of, or discounted, very similar experiences in early post-War attempts to clear mallee and brigalow scrub in South Australia and Queensland.[33] The extent to which scrub cleared at Magarini regrew is not known, but some areas were recleared by repeated heavy discing

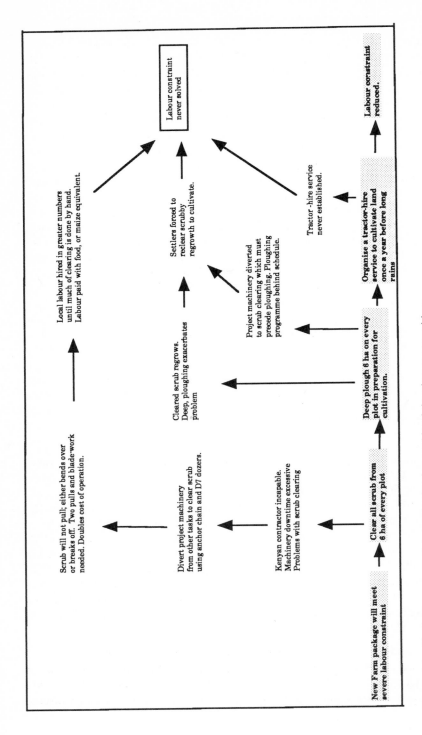

Figure 3.3 The labour constraint, scrub clearing and land development problem.

and large areas in the south of the project area are today completely bereft of any scrub or tree cover.

The practical conditions under which agricultural development is commonly practised can stretch the capabilities of the most knowledgeable person, however. As implementation proceeds and problems arise, personal perspectives narrow sharply and the need to solve immediate difficulties begin to override and even contradict broader objectives. Under circumstances of uncertainty people commonly are slow to realize the cumulative effects of a number of restricted decisions and they tend to hold even more firmly to arguments, although the circumstances are proving them to be inadequate (Slovic *et al.* 1982: 463–89). Attempts to maintain the rate of scrub clearing, solutions which clearly damaged the productive capabilities of the land and exacerbated the labour shortage, continued. The need to clear the bottle-neck in the discing and soil conservation programmes, and so get settlers on the plots, dominated and distracted project staff from the main issue (Figure 3.3).

Agriculture – a legume pasture rotation

The optimism of Phase I reached a peak in a proposal to replace the bush fallow rotation with a legume pasture rotation. The unresolved problem of fertilizer requirements has been discussed, but other, larger difficulties existed. John McGarrity, the project soils consultant in 1980 acknowledged the proposal had merit in theory but questioned whether, under the conditions at Magarini, tropical legumes would fix sufficient nitrogen and a grass fallow could provide the same protection against soil erosion as a bush fallow (1980: 25). The 1981 Project Review came straight to the point.

> There is no precedent for this system in the seasonally dry tropics, although analogous systems are proven in temperate and Mediterranean climates. Such a system is still being developed experimentally in tropical Australia, but, although results are promising the program is only in its early stages.
> (Staples *et al.* 1981: 54)

Experimentation with a tropical legume-ley was continuing in Australia in 1983 and its transfer to East Africa was still problematical. Significantly, the Australian system, if successful, will be based upon mechanization, and the annual use of herbicides and fertilizers (Jones and McCown 1984: 108–21), none of which will be affordable to the majority of Kenyan small farmers.

The process of transforming agriculture at Magarini had been begun in the absence of any proven superior replacement. Land had been cleared of forest and scrub, and continued to be cleared until 1987 when a joint review team tried to have further clearing stopped, with only partial success, but a rotation which could maintain soil fertility did not exist. The extension service which would have been critical in teaching former shifting cultivators how to become sedentary farmers had lost the confidence of the majority of the settlers. When

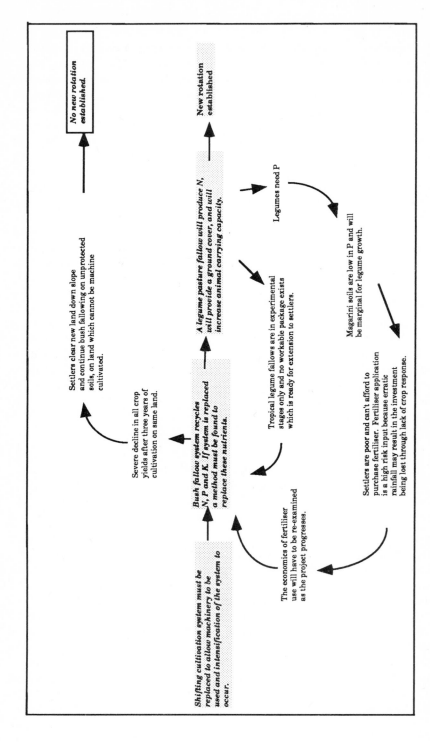

Figure 3.4 The bush fallowing system replacement problem.

Australian agronomists attempted to take their adjusted crop packages onto settlers' plots they discovered that the results from the GIS could not be replicated and labour requirements from the GIS trials appeared to be incorrect when applied on farmers' plots.[34] The complex variation in soils at Magarini was beginning to make itself felt, even though trials were established at a number of locations within the project. The 1981 Review recommended 'the wisdom of good local farmers should be tapped for guide-lines ... this is an important resource that has been overlooked by project staff, both Australian and Kenyan alike' (Staples *et al.* 1981: 57). But the Giriama, whose lives had been dislocated by government actions since the 1900s, were not about to lower their guard at the first sign of softness. Other things aside, their physical well-being was endangered.

The settlers, 1,075 families by 1983, faced severe falls in yields after the third crop on the same land. They faced the choice of clearing scrub regrowth on previously cleared areas or forest on uncleared land. We have no quantifiable measures of how settlers responded to this situation. Some walked away from it, others cleared and cultivated the regrowth and others, having discovered that the machine-cleared areas had lost much of their topsoil in the clearing process, set about practising shifting cultivation on the balance of their blocks. They cleared land downslope from and contiguous with the land cleared by the project. This land was not protected by contour banks, and the length of slope exposed to direct rainfall was increased and the slope itself became steeper. Some settlers cut into catchment protection reserves and firewood and building materials were taken from these areas (Figure 3.4).

Drought

The unwritten opinion of the 1981 review team was that the project was 'doomed', but Australia was 'committed politically and institutionally' and the Review Report was circumscribed by AIDAB's position.[35] Thus the drought which hit the project from 1980 until 1983 did no more than force acknowledgement of realities steadfastly denied until then. Drought is not widely discussed in the Phase I reports but the historical record shows it was inevitable during the life of the project. The short rains failed at the end of 1979 and when the long rains failed in 1980, severe food shortages were experienced by settlers. All maize in the north of the project area failed and yields in the south were half of those expected. After the 1980 short rains failed again all of the settler families already on the project and new families being allocated plots were placed on a food-for-work programme organized by the FAO World Food Program. The 1981 long rains were satisfactory but the short rains were twice the average and washed out culverts and roads, and caused widespread surface erosion and crop failures. The 1983 long and short rains failed and the food-for-work programme continued until August 1984.

Plate 14 Scrub clearing with bulldozers (top) *Plate 15* 'Developed' blocks and settler housing (bottom)

Agriculture – summary

This was a complex project and we have attempted to trace only the single issue of the labour constraint from its discovery during Phase I through to Phase II to illustrate how it influenced and was influenced by most other project components such as settlement, water, land clearing, agronomy and soil conservation. Solutions to problems which were created or appeared in each of these areas frequently only exacerbated the labour constraint problem; the failure to bring water to within half a kilometre of every plot, to clear scrub by machine, the employment of local labour to hand clear scrub, the unforeseen regrowth of the scrub, the steady decline in crop yields, the need to clear more land because no improved rotation was available and the food-for-work programme, all led to a worsening of labour problems, and coincidentally probably caused moderate land degradation and may ultimately be the cause of severe land degradation. When the settlers attempted to solve these difficulties rationally by working off their plots or abandoning them, they were harassed by the administration because they were invalidating a primary objective of the project (Figure 3.5; the changes planned and actual, wrought by the project, are illustrated in Figures 3.6a, b, c).

'THE ORDER OF THINGS'

A character in Milan Kundera's novel *The Joke* is shocked when he looks back on his life, only to realize that 'things conceived by error were every bit as real as things conceived by reason and necessity. So frequent, so common, were those errors that they cannot be considered mere exceptions, "aberrations" in the order of things; they were the order of things.' Magarini's catalogue of errors is not unique, but can be shown to have occurred repeatedly, perhaps in a slightly different form, on rural development projects all over the Third World. It is almost the sole topic of conversation whenever development practitioners meet and is the subject of numerous articles on project implementation.[36] The Magarini case allows an exploration of some of the reasons why these errors have become the order of things.

A comparative advantage?

Most literature on technical assistance assumes the individual 'experts' are competent to perform the tasks required of them. A now dated assessment of Australian technical assistance in Asia suggests that Australians 'make particularly good experts', especially in areas which involve practical application and the transmission of ideas because of their practical bent, capacity to innovate, and indifference to status (Boxer 1969: 96–7). The Australians at Magarini believed they were superior to experts from European countries in their ability to get along with African small farmers because they were either farmers themselves, or had worked extensively with farmers as farm advisers. Yet at least one Australian research scientist with extensive experience in

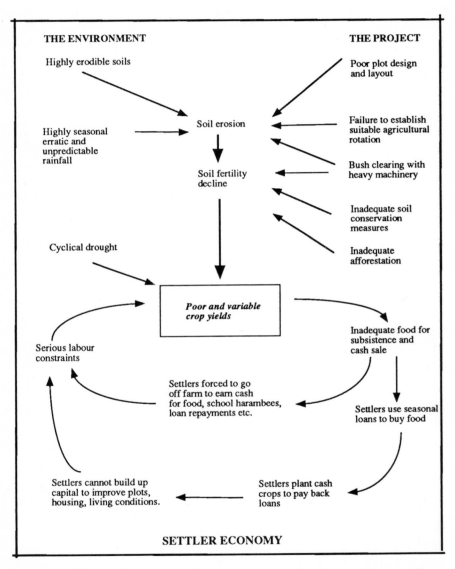

Figure 3.5 Relationships between the environment, project interventions and the settler economy.

A: Pre-project situation circa 1975.

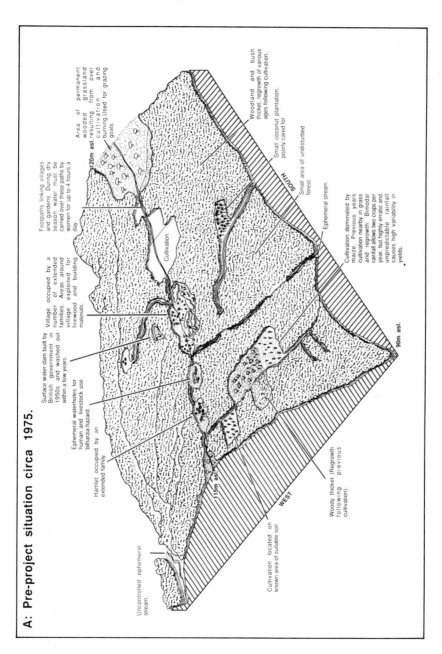

Surface water dam built by British government in 1950s and washed out within a few years.

Ephemeral waterholes for human and livestock use.

Hamlet occupied by an extended family.

Village occupied by a number of extended families. Areas around village exploited for firewood and building materials.

Footpaths linking villages and gardens. During dry season water must be carried over these paths by women for up to 4 hours a day.

Area of permanent wooded grassland resulting from over cultivation and burning. Used for grazing goats.

120m asl

Woodland and bush thicket, regrowth of various ages following cultivation.

Small coconut plantation, poorly cared for.

SOUTH

Small area of undisturbed forest.

Ephemeral stream.

Cultivation dominated by maize. Previous years cultivation nearby in grass and regrowth. Bimodal rainfall allows two crops per year, but highly erratic and unpredictable rainfall causes high variability in yields.

90m asl

Cultivation.

15m asl

WEST

Woody thicket (Regrowth following previous cultivation).

Cultivation located on known area of suitable soil.

Uncontrolled ephemeral stream.

Figure 3.6a Block diagram of Magarini Ridge – circa 1975 prior to the Magarini Settlement Project.

B: Planned outcomes.

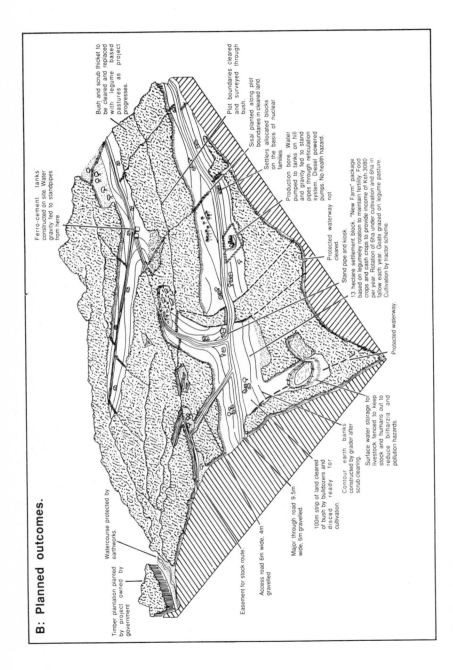

Ferro-cement tanks constructed on site. Water gravity fed to standpipes from here.

Bush and scrub thicket to be cleared and replaced with legume based pastures as project progresses.

Plot boundaries cleared and surveyed through bush.

Sisal planted along plot boundaries in cleared land.

Settlers allocated blocks on the basis of nuclear families.

Production bore. Water pumped to tanks on hill and gravity fed to stand pipes through reticulation system. Diesel powered pumps. No health hazard.

Protected waterway not cleared.

Stand pipe and kiosk.

13 hectare settlement block. "New Farm" package based on legume/ley rotation to maintain fertility. Food crops and cash crops to provide income of Ksh.3080 per year. Rotation of 6ha under cultivation and 6ha in fallow each year. Goats grazed on legume pasture. Cultivation by tractor scheme.

Protected waterway.

Timber plantation planned by project owned by government

Watercourse protected by earthworks.

Easement for stock route.

Access road 6m wide, 4m gravelled

Major through road 9.5m wide, 6m gravelled.

100m strip of land cleared of bush by bulldozers and disced ready for cultivation.

Contour earth banks constructed by grader after scrub clearing.

Surface water storage for livestock fenced to keep stock and humans out to reduce bilharzia and pollution hazards.

Figure 3.6b Block diagram of Magarini Ridge showing planned project outcomes.

C: Actual outcomes to circa 1988.

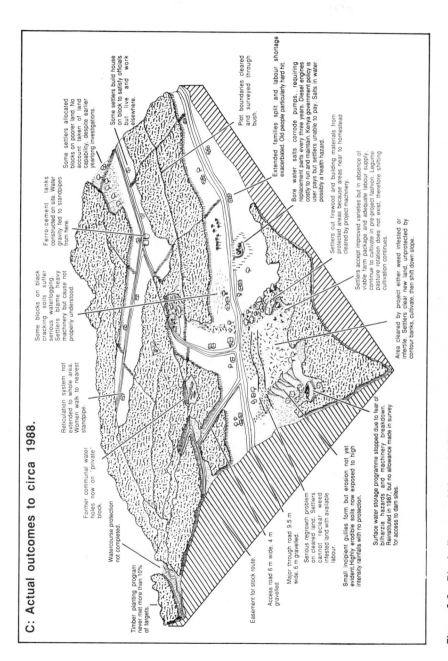

Former communal water holes now on 'private' block.

Reticulation system not extended to whole area. Women walk to nearest standpipe.

Some blocks on black cracking soils suffer serious waterlogging. Settlers blame heavy machinery but cause not properly understood.

Ferro-cement tanks constructed on site. Water gravity fed to standpipes from here.

Some settlers allocated blocks on poorer land. No account taken of land capability, despite earlier yearlong investigations.

Some settlers build house on block to satisfy officials but live and work elsewhere.

Plot boundaries cleared and surveyed through bush.

Extended families split and labour shortage exacerbated. Old people particularly hard hit.

Bore water salts corrode pumps, requiring replacement parts every three years. Diesel engines costly to run and maintain. Kenya government policy is user pays but settlers unable to pay. Salts in water possibly a health hazard.

Settlers cut firewood and building materials from protected areas because areas near to homestead cleared by project machinery.

Settlers accept improved varieties but in absence of viable farm package and adequate labour supply, continue to cultivate in pre-project fashion. Legume pasture rotation does not exist, therefore shifting cultivation continues.

Area cleared by project either weed infested or infertile. Settlers clear new land, unprotected by contour banks, cultivate, then shift down slope.

Timber planting program never met more than 10% of targets.

Watercourse protection not completed.

Easement for stock route.

Access road 6 m wide, 4 m gravelled

Major through road 9.5 m wide, 6 m gravelled

Serious regrowth problem on cleared land. Settlers cannot reclear weed infested land with available labour.

Small incipient gullies form but erosion not yet evident.Highly erodible soils now exposed to high intensity rainfalls with no protection.

Surface water storage programme stopped due to fear of bilharzia hazards and machinery breakdown. Reinstituted in 1987, but no allowance made in survey for access to dam sites.

Figure 3.6c Block diagram of Magarini Ridge showing actual project outcomes, circa 1988.

Africa believes 'it was simply ludicrous' to expect some of the people employed on the project to come to terms with Giriama agriculture and Giriama farmers. In Australia they had been competent, practical, sensible people, but in the Magarini environment they were technically and culturally out of their depth.

Leaving the question of individual competence to one side, what sort of corporate or national competence does Australia possess to be carrying out agricultural development in the semi-arid tropics of Kenya? The record of six large-scale public and private enterprise cropping development schemes in northern Australia is not one to instil confidence in the outcomes in Africa. A review of these schemes (Bauer 1977), all of which failed financially, includes phrases such as 'serious problems in management and planning', 'quite unrealistic in view of actual yields achieved', 'machinery was ill-suited to the environment', 'weeds were a major problem', 'targets set were impossible to meet' and 'created serious erosion problems'. Features common to all projects included a failure to use existing agronomic knowledge, decisions to proceed despite a known lack of knowledge and the lack of understanding of the severe constraints imposed by climate and soils in tropical Australia. All projects resulted in soil erosion, in one case severe. In 1982 another review of one of these six projects, the Ord River Project, noted,

> The decision to build the second stage of the project when it had been shown that farming was unprofitable suggests that the political advantages to be gained from proceeding with the project outweighed the economic advantages of not proceeding with it.
>
> (Davidson 1982: 20)

> The project moved from minor to major decisions, with the earlier low cost decisions creating precedents which made the later, high cost decision to proceed with Stage II, a seemingly inescapable commitment – despite failures and increasing problems.
>
> (Graham-Taylor 1982: 25)

Nor do Australians have a very good record of protecting a fragile marginal semi-arid environment on their own continent. In a recent review Judy Messer (1987) notes that land degradation is the single most significant threat to sustainable agriculture in many areas. The same paper recognizes political and economic causes to land degradation in Australia, similar to those we have identified in Kenya.

As late as 1983, AIDAB was arguing for a continuation of the Magarini Project into Phase III on the grounds that this was an agricultural project and 'Australia's dryland farming expertise is extensively used' (AIDAB 20 September 1983) and the 'availability in Australia of a comparative technical advantage' (AIDAB 14 December 1983). Do the northern Australia projects or the land degradation experience in Australia suggest Australia possesses no comparative advantage in dryland farming expertise? Not necessarily, but it does suggest that within Australia a great deal is yet to be learned about how to farm in the dry tropics. Australia's dryland farming expertise is mostly located in the temperate, Mediterranean climates of the southeast and, so far, attempts to transfer these legume-based systems into the tropics have not been very successful. But even if they were, there are significant differences between the Australian dry tropical environments and the African dry tropics, especially those areas like Magarini which have double maxima rainfall patterns (McCown *et al.* 1984).

Technology transfer – analogues or intellects?

Henry Nix, now Director of the Centre for Resource and Environmental Studies (CRES) at the Australian National University, believes the most common cause of problems in agricultural technology transfers is their reliance on the 'analogue approach' (1980: 107–10).[37] A long tradition in agricultural research is transfer by analogy, in which a system developed in one representative site is transferred to other sites which appear analogous in terms of vegetation, climate and soils. However, conditions at the representative site and the new location are rarely identical, and frequently social, economic or political differences can negate environmental similarities.

It is better, in Nix's view, to transfer the principles of how to solve an agricultural problem, than to attempt to transfer the actual solutions to an apparently analogous problem in a dissimilar physical, social, economic or political environment. Australia's comparative advantage is intellectual, not technical. Bob McCown agrees. Australia produces crops under water- and soil-limiting conditions and Australian agricultural researchers are famous for their contributions to an understanding of these conditions. What Australia can best offer Third World countries is not 'off-the-shelf' systems, but the principles and approaches required to develop systems which will meet localized conditions. Both McCown and Nix agree independently that what should have happened at Magarini was an experimental phase which had the objective of adapting local systems and building on local knowledge to increase productivity, not an attempt to replace one system with another. Nix favours a holistic approach using an interdisciplinary team.

Problems remain, however, with the use of a holistic approach under the conditions of certainty of outcomes and scheduling demanded by the existing procedures employed by most funding agencies. In systems theory, the manner in which the inputs to a system influence the outputs can be expressed mathematically. If the parameters of output behaviour are only constants or functions of time or of some factor external to the system, the relationships are linear, but if the output parameters depend on outputs from other components within the system, then the relationships are non-linear. Non-linear systems can have unforeseen and unexpected behaviour patterns (Beer and

Hills 1982). As James Gleick (1988: 44) explains,

> Traditionally, the dynamicist would believe that to write down a system's equations is to understand the system. How better to capture the essential features? ... But because of the little bits of nonlinearity in these equations, a dynamicist would find himself helpless to answer the easiest practical question about the future of the system.

So too a project planner. The more complex a project design, the greater the chance of an unpredictable outcome. The planner is faced with two types of uncertainty.

> One is caused by the lack of knowledge which must result when a society is being pushed towards an untested pattern of behaviour by social and economic change. The gaps in our knowledge will result in any model being poorly specified. The other form of uncertainty is mathematical ... we can anticipate unpredictable behaviour but we cannot forecast when and how a sudden change will occur.
>
> (Beer and Hills 1982: 21)

We have already raised a practical difficulty with the application of a systems approach to rural development projects. Practitioners, project managers, agronomists, land clearance supervisors, find it extremely difficult to hold on to systems concepts when confronted with the day-to-day problems of getting the job done, of meeting the targets. Under the practical conditions of achieving goals on the project, the system is unravelled and the components treated as though they exist in isolation one from another. To continue to see every action as having reactions everywhere else on the project creates conditions under which it becomes almost impossible to act, particularly after the original schedules go out of kilter as they are bound to do.

If a holistic systems approach is to be usefully employed in agricultural development projects, then the scheduling and targets set will have to be a great deal more flexible than they are under present procedures. The adoption of a genuine holistic approach implies less control, not more. It requires us to stop playing the 'development game', where we pretend to know before we start what the outcome will be, and to design projects which can change and adapt to the uncertain outcomes which systems theory and the Magarini Project and many other cases suggest is the only predictable thing about rural development.

ECOLOGY AND EQUITY

The Magarini Project proved to be economically unsustainable. But even if it had been successful in the short term, serious doubts exist about whether it would have been environmentally sustainable in the long term. Development theorists have been slow to recognize the relationship between environmental issues and development. In a recent review of literature on this matter Harold Brookfield (1988: 134) calls for theorists and practitioners to 'give up all notions of the environment as a "free good", cease to regard actual or probable future damage as "externalities" and be prepared to read, listen and learn'. Gordon Conway, a biologist, has vigorously argued for some time the relationships between environmental limits and development through the concept of the 'agro-ecosystem'. Conway's analysis (1984: 31–55) is based on four properties he imputes to agro-ecosystems: productivity, stability, sustainability and equitability. Bush fallowing systems like those at Magarini are generally low in productivity and stability, but high in sustainability and equity. Most recent attempts to 'improve' these system have resulted in increases in productivity but decreases in stability, sustainability and equity. Conway observes that these concepts are easy to define but difficult to measure. Work elsewhere in Kenya and in northern Australia by Australian scientists allows us to explore the long-term implications of agricultural intensification for these agro-ecosystem properties in marginal areas in Kenya similar to Magarini.

We have argued that the Giriama bush fallowing system practised at Magarini before the project began was not sustainable in the long term, and some change would have been required even in the absence of the project. But recent agronomic research in Kenya, when applied to the Magarini case, starkly illustrates the dilemmas created by interventions to enhance food security and equity in marginal environments throughout sub-Saharan Africa.

Since 1984, Kenyan agronomists and Australians associated with the CSIRO and the Australian Centre for International Agricultural Research (ACIAR)[38] have been developing and testing a version of the CERES-Maize Model, a computer model which will simulate maize production under known conditions of rainfall, soil–water conditions, soil fertility and inputs, such as mineral or organic fertilizers. The model was run to simulate a 125-year period of continuous cultivation under two conditions: one where fertilizer is applied at the rate of 40 kg of nitrogen per hectare each year and all crop residues are retained on the plot (a 'replacement' strategy); and second, with no fertilizer applications and only 10 per cent of crop residues retained (a 'mining' strategy). The simulation was undertaken on two Magarini soil types, the vertisols and the solonetz, and under Marafa rainfall conditions.[39] Figure 3.7 presents the outcome in graphical form.

Under the replacement strategy maize yields can be maintained indefinitely on both soils, but humic nitrogen declines steadily to one-third of the original level on the vertisol and to one-half on the solonetz. Under the mining strategy maize yields on the vertisol begin to decline after twenty-five years and eventually fall as low as those on the solonetz. On the solonetz yields fall significantly by thirty years and after about eighty years come to a low equilibrium. No allowance has been made for the consequences of cultivation on what are known to be highly erodible soils. The project soil consultant was

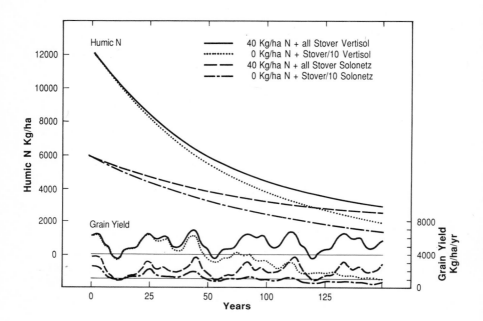

Figure 3.7 Simulated impact of 150 years of maize cultivation on yields and soil nitrogen levels, Marafa soils and rainfall.

Source: R. McCowan and B. Keating, ACIAR/CSIRO Dryland Project, Nairobi

uncertain about the efficacy of a grass fallow in providing protection against heavy rainstorms. Cultivation, even with a pasture fallow, could be expected to reduce the moisture-holding capability of the soil and even slow soil losses would reduce the depth available for roots to take hold.

The results of the simulation need to be placed in their social and political context. Development literature of the past five years, in particular, has been marked by exhortations to practitioners to consider the long-term implications for environmental sustainability of the interventions which occur within the shorter time frame of projects. The widely publicized report of the World Commission on Environment and Development, *Our Common Future*, puts the new ethos well. 'We have in the past, been concerned about the impacts of economic growth upon the environment. We are now forced to concern ourselves with the impacts of ecological stress: degradation of soils, water regimes, atmosphere, forests, upon our economic prospects' (WCED 1987: 5). The neglect of this relationship is commonly attributed to the short-term 'technocratic' orientation of development workers and is sometimes contrasted with what is called an 'ecocentric' view (see, for example, O'Riordan 1981). According to Michael Redclift (1987: 67), degradation is not simply the unpleasant consequence of food and energy shortages, but is 'the result of considering development assistance in terms of short-term production gains rather than long-term sustainability'. Yet despite the timeliness of this rebuke, we have found in the Magarini experience no instance where the development workers were unaware of the fact that even small numbers of people can have a dramatic impact on a marginal, fragile environment. The development literature is largely silent about the ethical dilemmas faced by development workers which are hugely distant from the tactical and everyday choices which they have to make in order to achieve short-term project ends.

Magarini is illustrative of these ethical challenges. It has been calculated that Kenya's labour force will double (from 1975 to 2000) with 8 million of these new entrants being forced to seek employment in agriculture (Hunt 1984; Livingstone 1986). With a relatively fixed land supply and high population pressures (currently increasing at more than 4 per cent a year), national policy focuses on the twin objectives of increasing yields per hectare and raising output per worker. Research has clearly favoured smallholder farming as the most likely strategy to achieve these ends.[40] Development workers, already aware of the likely costs of degradation through intensification, yet enjoined to consider the longer-term humanitarian and political imperatives reflected in government policy, must balance, too, the interests of the people in the locale of the project. Increasingly, these areas are ecologically marginal, and populated by resource-poor pastoralists, or swidden farmers. We are talking not of a marginal few, but about a global population estimated at 220 million subsistence farmers, pastoralists and landless by the year 2000 (WCED 1987: 13).

The historical experience of the Giriama is typical of a people whose food security has been steadily reduced by rapid population growth, alienation of grazing and farming lands (by demarcation of game areas, plantation and estate enclosures), and more recently, by movement first, onto lands with medium potential, and then onto marginal lands of which Magarini is typical. Their fundamental weakness in the face of historical and political pressures is indicated by Ian Livingstone's estimates that between 1969 and 1989 land in Kilifi District decreased from 0.53 ha to 0.28 ha per person (Livingstone 1986: 11).

As well as having to deal with this situation, the development practitioner must now face the predictions of the ACIAR model, the knowledge that resource-poor households will be disinclined to risk investment in an uncertain environment, government policy imperatives for intensification, and last-ly, the exhortations of the 'talkers' in the literature that the 'doers' should 'take more variables into account', 'not treat the environment as a free good', and place on the ground in a culturally appropriate and sustainable manner, the proposition that 'poverty and environmental degradation are closely intertwined'. Clearly this requires particular attention to the strategies adopted by development workers and, as we will see in the next chapter, to the techniques available for the appraisal of alternatives.

Chapter 4

Institutions for managing uncertainty

The Memorandum of Understanding (MOU) signed between the governments of Australia and Kenya for Phase II of the Magarini Settlement Project expired on 30 June 1981. In September 1983, AIDAB placed a submission before Foreign Minister Bill Hayden for approval to expend $7 million in Phase III. The Minister wrote two words on the bottom of the submission, 'Not approved'. For twenty-seven months the project had been in a state of 'crisis'.

The multitude of problems during Phase II had shaken AIDAB. The world economic recession during 1981 and 1982 meant the Kenyan government was unable to meet commitments under the Phase II MOU. Reluctant to participate at the same level in Phase III, they were still anxious to continue with the settlement aspects of the project. In Canberra, the Department of Finance, which had consistently opposed involvement in a major project at Magarini, again mounted strong criticisms of the Phase III proposals, this time with the added virtue of having been right twice before. In February 1983 Bob Hawke replaced Bill Hayden as Leader of the Opposition and then led the Labor Party to electoral victory in March. Hayden, Treasurer in the previous Whitlam Labor government became the new Foreign Minister, responsible for AIDAB. He insisted he would not approve Phase III at Magarini unless satisfied the project could meet the economic viability criteria being demanded by the Department of Finance.

Individuals within AIDAB, Foreign Affairs, the managing agent, and, indirectly, the government of Kenya, began trying to convince the Minister that the political benefits of keeping the project going and the costs of withdrawing from it, were greater than any measure of economic benefit. Meanwhile AIDAB also set about trying to satisfy the Minister and the Department of Finance that the project was 'economically viable'. A single measure of economic viability, the internal rate of return (IRR), began to dominate the debate. A number of times AIDAB complained that the Department of Finance would not specify what level of IRR would be acceptable and argued that normally acceptable levels were too high when applied to projects in marginal environments in Africa. The High Commission reported on IRR values used or not used by the major international aid agencies operating in Kenya.

The Minister decided to resolve this impasse by asking Professor Helen Hughes, 'an independent economist of standing', to provide an economic analysis of a redesigned Magarini Project. The 1984 Appraisal conducted by Hughes contained proposals to redesign the project, and to 'strengthen AIDAB control of the Australian input', an institutionalization plan for handing the project over to Kenyan government ministries and monitoring techniques to provide information on project progress. The 1984 Appraisal also contained a cost–benefit analysis which showed the redesigned project would achieve rates of return higher than the projected returns on comparable international aid projects in Kenya.

CONTROL-ORIENTATION

In the 1970s, the desire to control uncertainty gave rise to large pre-implementation surveys which collected information about all the components of a project which were considered to be important. The contradictions generated by this approach had to be overlooked, and the major difficulties of integrating all these components in time and space into a single system had to be denied, if projects which had strong political rationale to begin with, were to be implemented. Almost as soon as implementation began, these apparently tightly controlled components began to unravel rapidly, throwing programmes out of kilter and creating further knock-on effects across the whole project. The outcome, replicated in projects worldwide was unsustainability, or, as in the Magarini case, the so-called beneficiaries being left worse off than before the project began.

The application of better management techniques, logical frameworks, tight financial control and cost–benefit analyses, are responses found worldwide in major aid agencies to control the uncertainty created by rural development projects. We term this response a control-orientation. Control-orientation has taken place largely in the donor or financing agencies but is actively reproduced and often welcomed by recipient governments. Consequently control-orientation is being carried into every corner of development practice. We argue that control-orientation is the antithesis of good development practice.

This will prove to be an unpopular argument and, in an important sense, a hazardous one. It will be unpopular because these techniques are presently considered 'innovative' in development management and the staff of the donor agencies find the idea of greater control over their programmes attractive and reassuring from the point of view of being confident in achieving their stated goals in a climate of increasing scrutiny of the expenditure of public funds. They will not like being told that the very techniques which seem to offer them greater certainty of outcome for their programmes, will create greater long-term uncertainty and non-sustainability. It will be hazardous because any intervention in an economy or a society carries with it the concept of control. Control is part of the broader concept of development. Judgements of the sort, 'If I do this, can I reasonably hope to get that result', always imply that things are going to be controlled and manipulated to achieve a previously determined objective. The argument is also hazardous because within the major lending agencies are people who believe that rural development is a waste of resources and who argue that aid projects should be restricted to engineering construction tasks which can be strictly controlled. The baby may get thrown out with the bathwater. That is not our intention.

A history of control-oriented techniques

There can be little contention that a control-orientation has been present in development practice from the beginning. Control and order were the hallmarks of international development practice formalized by the Allies' Monetary and Financial Conference at Bretton Woods in 1944. World War II, the largest conflict in history, was not won on military strategy alone, but on the development of techniques of resource control and logistical planning at a level never previously experienced. Success in solving the logistical problems, such as the invasion of Europe, deeply influenced the approaches to economic development long after the War. UN Resolutions and United States Presidential Addresses, like Roosevelt's 'Four Freedoms' address and Truman's 'Point Four', emphasized the West's 'moral obligation' to help those living in 'primitive and stagnant' conditions by applying technical skills and economic know-how to resources.[1] But efforts to capture the world's imagination and loyalties did not reflect humanitarianism alone. More was at stake. The urgent problem according to one commentator of the time, was 'depriving the communists of their actual and potential "mass base" by an adequate programme of technical and economic reform' (Watnick 1952: 36).[2]

If the urgent problem was clear, so too were the strategies. These required a confident and accelerated transfusion of recent Western economic experience. From Bretton Woods emerged the United States' view that the post-War international economy would be run by expanding Western corporations according to the principles underlying the rapid technological and industrial advance of the West in the early twentieth century (Kolko 1968: 257; Preston 1982: 42).[3] The dramatic recovery of Western Europe under the Marshall Aid Plan led to a sense of optimism; development was almost an inevitable outcome of technology and money controlled on the basis of prescriptive economic theory. According to Brookfield, the prevailing view resembled 'a development vending machine: you put in the money, press the button and get growth' (Brookfield 1975: 39).[4]

Shorn of their moral and political dimensions, these early statements about development expressed a basic idea that persists to this day. Development practice is understood as the systematic application of a universal rationality at a societal level to achieve desired states of affairs through the control of human as well as natural resources. Development came to be seen as a 'problem' which could be broken down into a series of elements, like savings, growth rates, or literacy, according to known causal relations between them. Once identified, these elements could be re-assembled and manipulated in a controllable and predictable manner. Chapter Three illustrates the contemporary legacy of this outlook. These ideas are not new, but the intensity, purposiveness and assiduity with which this idea was expressed had no historical precedent (Preston 1982: 47; van Nieuwenhuijze 1982: 31–3). Development's designers did place certain caveats on their confidence. They foresaw impediments and obstacles but were assured that the technical and organizational imperatives of Western industrial development when brought to bear on 'the material economic environment' would weaken and destroy the obstacles.[5]

Institutions for creating certainty

Overcoming the impediments to planned and controlled manipulation of the future called for authoritative intervention on an international scale. Three levels of institutions have given effect to this idea of development. First, international agencies were needed to finance and manage intervention. By design these agencies possessed the degree of leverage necessary to ensure that the traditional, particularist or politically idiosyncratic features of a situation ('obstacles' and 'barriers') would not hold sway. Second, these institutions needed to be mirrored at the national level, to maintain political and economic control over the area in which development was to occur. This hegemony was in turn necessary at the local level. It was the role of a specific 'building-block' institution, the project, to provide the practical nexus of capital and technology.

The most prominent global institutions are the World Bank Group, namely the International Bank for Reconstruction and Development (IBRD), now the largest single source of development finance, and the International Monetary Fund (IMF), both established by the Bretton Woods conference. These agencies are said to give complete coverage in terms of varieties of development finance and in the universal procedures they establish for development. As Susan George points out, 'Our era is the first in history to place in direct contact the most powerful, hierarchical, elitist institutions in rich countries like the IMF and the poorest, most obscure, hungriest peasant or slum-dwellers in poor countries like Brazil or Zaire' (George 1988: 6). Accordingly, these agencies have been seen as 'landmarks on the road to a rationalisation of international decision-making' (White 1970: 5). These international, national and local institutions are said to protect development decisions from the idiosyncratic, the traditional or political influences on decision making. An Asian Development Bank historian illustrates this view.

[I]n helping to introduce the practice of fair, objective international competitive bidding in connection with the awarding of procurement contracts, [the ADB plays] a small but significant part in the erosion of certain unfortunate attitudes and practices which have long been a serious barrier to effective modern growth.

(Huang 1975: 147)

Largely controlled by Western powers,[6] development agencies were important sources of political stability and support for rapidly expanding Western corporations. They had a strong Promethean sense of purpose, but provided an 'objective and politically neutral' image, tending 'to neutralize the process somewhat, thus narrowing the field for political critics' (Huang 1975: 4, 3).[7] To match this role, development agencies were installed with sufficient authority to facilitate and direct rapidly growing national institutions and ensure that investment was carried out in an orderly and controlled political environment. Designers of national 'institution building' were susceptible to the conservative ethos of political order in the 1960s. Through such efforts, 'the State became ... the active instrument of a new policy aimed at the local reproduction of the characteristics of mature capitalist countries: industrialisation, agricultural modernization, infrastructure, increased provision of social services, and so forth' (Sunkel 1977: 7). The rapid concentration of power within nation states was seen as prerequisite for a more efficient penetration of investment by significantly reducing the irrationalities and uncertainties faced by foreign investors and aid agencies.

Projects: the 'privileged particles of development'

These attributes of development institutions are to be found in projects, the working face of practice. For many casual observers projects are synonymous with development itself. Nowadays an overwhelming proportion of development finance is destined for project-level activity. The World Bank, where over 90 per cent of loans since 1946 have been for specific projects, is indicative of the general pattern (Baum 1978: 10). Dennis Rondinelli (1979: 48) is correct in stating,

Projects are, and will remain, a dominant feature of organizing investment in developing countries ... projects have become one of the most important instruments of public and private management ... and a primary means of activating national and sectoral development plans.

The significance of projects is in accord with the basic idea of development. Projects reflect a hierarchy of logic that links specific local actions with the overall international effort. Each project contains a number of elements. At Magarini these were water, agriculture, roads, social infrastructure and so on. They are the minimum unit in a larger settlement and rural development programme which 'consists of an interrelated group of projects' (Goodman and Love 1979: 1). These are matched in a constellation of sectors which direct the overall pattern of intervention. An oft-quoted definition, from Albert Hirschman's (1967: 1) *Development Projects Observed*, reflects this rationality well.

> The development project is a special kind of investment. The term connotes purposefulness, some minimum size, a specific location, the introduction of something qualitatively new, and the expectation that a sequence of further development moves will be set in motion. ... Development projects ... are the privileged particles of the development process.

The project approach enables direct state (and through it international) control of investments that might otherwise be dispersed through multiple local agencies, and therefore 'invoke direct involvement by high, usually the highest, political authorities' (Hirschman 1967: 1; see also Arndt 1979: 40). This enables the application of project management procedures and techniques (appraisal, planning, implementation) and discourages traditional, personal or politically idiosyncratic practices; those 'unfortunate attitudes' and 'barriers' to the orderly and predictable manipulation of social change.

Defensive modernization

Faith in the 'vending-machine' model of development has been sorely tested by history. Although unprecedented investment supported considerable industrial expansion in some countries, the expected spin-offs were slow. By the early 1970s, as one World Bank economist observed, 'It became increasingly clear that a large proportion of the rural population lived, and would continue to live, on a near subsistence level unless development policies and lending for development were explicitly redirected' (Adler 1977: 34). This redirection was signalled by the 1973 Annual Address of World Bank President McNamara at Nairobi, where he expressed concern for 'the poor' and identified a special programme to deal with basic needs and the productivity of the rural poor (McNamara 1973). This social awareness has been seen as beginning in practice with Cochrane and Noronha's 1973 report on the use of anthropologists in the World Bank and shortly thereafter the appointment of a sociologist and an adviser on women's issues (Perrett and Lethem 1980: 2). Behind this shift in focus was a political rationale critics termed 'defensive modernization' (Ayres 1981: 11)[8] which signalled efforts to pre-empt the build-up of social and political pressures in rural areas by incorporating marginalized people more fully into development. It coincided in the early 1970s with a need for greater permissiveness. Severely repressive policies were becoming increasingly untenable for newly independent governments espousing egalitarianism. Politically, the poor became too great in number to ignore.

The popularity among development agencies of the new language of development, 'basic needs', 'growth with redistribution', 'social sector lending', was heralded as reflecting major changes in thinking. It is true, given the speed at which new catch-cries pass through development literature, that there have been changes in emphasis over the past decade. Juliet Hunt comments wryly, that 'one might be hard put to find many international trends in development strategies that AIDAB has not at some stage or other, incorporated into its policy rhetoric' (Hunt 1983; see also Robertson 1984: 24).

Incorporating more elements

Although these changes should not be trivialized, the extent to which the basic idea of development has changed remains open to question.[9] It is more appropriate to see the development policy in the 1970s as involving a more explicit adding-on of further variables to the existing equation. Ron Staples (pers. comm) characterized an AIDAB integrated rural development programme in the Philippines (Zamboanga del Sur) in the following terms,

[T]he rural development programme contained (in addition to the infrastructural element) the initial agricultural element. Incorporated into that was what we call an engineering extension element, a community health element was built into it, a rural water supply element was also built into it. There may be a number of small elements in there that have slipped my mind.

The core concept remains unchanged. The emergence of multi-sectoral, integrated projects represents the extension of an existing rationality into other areas (education, health, urban site and services) and their incorporation into a single format. Nevertheless, the broadening of scope, this adding-on of elements and multiple objectives, had important consequences in practice.

One consequence was confusion. A World Bank Department Director was reputed to have announced in the late 1970s, 'I don't know what the hell the goals are, but I'm moving ahead with projects' (quoted in Moss 1978: 94). In the Magarini Project much the same applied. Plans were made to move ahead but as we saw in Chapter Three, and as the 1981 Review Report recognized, there was an 'absence of definition' within and between elements which had led to an 'overemphasis [on] the technical production aspects of road construction, land clearing and plot survey, vehicle and plant maintenance at the expense of the technology transfer aspect of training people how to plan to do these tasks' (Staples, Price and Daw 1980: 105). Again, some members of the project team no doubt assimilated data in their own areas and developed an intuitive feeling for the optimal direction that the project should take, but little of this was coordinated with the strategy and so we see the ludicrous situations described in Chapter Three. The problems were not restricted to the project. Back in Canberra, AIDAB staff member Anthony Vale said to the Joint Parliamentary Committee for Public Accounts in 1983, 'The situation is very confused. Overall, there is no standard, clear line of approach to spell out what are the objectives. ... It is hit and miss. It is a bit here, it's a bit there. ... Over a period of time you simply lose policy coherence and that is precisely what has happened' (JCPA 1983: 453).

In response to this situation the 1981 Review and subsequent documents recommended adoption of more sophisticated techniques for project management. AIDAB was again following international trends. In the Magarini case, given that the project was now well and truly in the implementation phase, the review recommended the adoption of logical framework analysis and network planning (Cracknell and Rednall 1986; Cracknell 1988). Before we talk more about these techniques, it is important to recognize the wider context, in Africa, if not throughout the Third World, in which it made sense to make these recommendations.

A new orthodoxy

First, most projects, particularly integrated rural development projects, lacked internal coherence. Integration within the project and between respective government ministries was not occurring, and the broader economic circumstances of developing countries were deteriorating so rapidly that few ministries had the funds to meet their counterpart obligations.[10] The 1986 *Kenya Aid Effectiveness Study* undertaken by Robert Cassen and Associates (1986: 337–43) identified a litany of problems, from weak performance of public sector organizations ('a collapse of financial discipline' and 'crisis management'), overly complex design, termination of multi-sector projects, to severe sustainability problems in rural water and agricultural sectors. All this in a middle-income country by sub-Saharan standards.

But just as the collapse of commodity prices and the chronic debt situation in the Third World were forcing themselves on international attention, the new orthodoxy, a blend of monetarism and neo-classical economics, began to be asserted in development economics.[11] Although by as late as 1980 Robert McNamara, the World Bank, and reports like the Brandt Commission were still advocating basic needs and poverty policies, there was a clear shift of priorities from direct attacks on poverty to monetarist policy emphasizing economic efficiency. After a short lifespan, basic human needs policies were rapidly superseded and, as Mahbub ul Haq was reputed to have said on his resignation from the World Bank, 'the Goddess of Growth is returned to her pedestal'. The view, based on the perceived successes of some East and Southeast Asian Newly Industrializing Countries (NICs), was that fundamental development problems could be put right by economic growth and the freeing of world trade. The vehicle for these policies whereby developing countries would become 'outward looking' and 'put their macro-economic houses in order' was structural adjustment.

A structural adjustment programme has standardized elements. The most frequently imposed include drastic reduction of government expenditure, particularly welfare spending and elimination of food and other consumption subsidies; devaluation of the currency (to discourage imports and encourage exports); privatization of government parastatals and/or increases in prices charged by them (electricity, water, transportation, etc.) and the removal of price controls; 'demand management' (which means the curtailment of consumption) through wages ceilings, along with restriction of credit, and higher taxes and interest rates in an effort to reduce inflation (Payer 1985; George 1988: 52; Smith 1989: 23–4). There has been widespread debate about the IMF's approach to stabilization through adjustment policies and it is often argued, in the case of Africa, that this 'stabilisation approach per se is wholly inappropriate and unacceptable' (Smith 1989: 22). In Kenya's case the relationship between the IMF and the government has not been smooth and, as Tony Killick (1984: 208–9) observes, 'if successful stabilisation and good working relationships with the Fund are not feasible in Kenya, it is unclear where else in Africa they might be achieved'.

Getting it right in aid policy and practice

Structural adjustment policies have been extremely influential in bilateral aid policy. The attitude of structural adjustment fits well with donors' disenchantment and the view that most of the problems of aid practice are due to inadequacies on the recipient's part and 'current policies erroneously undertaken in the deluded belief that they would foster development' (Toye 1987: 25). Structural adjustment lending and conditionality at the higher levels has been matched with stricter efficiency and control measures at the level of sectoral assistance, programme support and project practices.[12] In Kenya, Robert Cassen (1986: 340) observes,

> there has been a marked increase in the proportion of aid funds taking the form of programme aid, among both bilateral and multilateral donors. The reasons for this change are perceived weaknesses in absorptive capacity for project funds, and the donors' views that institutional and policy reforms are crucial to sustained economic progress and to effective project implementation.[13]

Changes in intellectual climate have renewed emphasis on 'policy dialogues' and donor 'leverage' to ensure sufficient measure of 'political will' is present to put in place what are considered to be the right policies.

The new orthodoxy was fully translated into official Australian aid policy with the publication of the *Report of the Committee to Review the Australian Overseas Aid Program* (the Jackson Report) in March 1984. The Jackson Report mirrored World Bank/IMF orthodoxy in many places. Statements are made about the policy prerequisites of economic growth, its emphasis on political will, stability, the imperative to rein in public sector spending, and

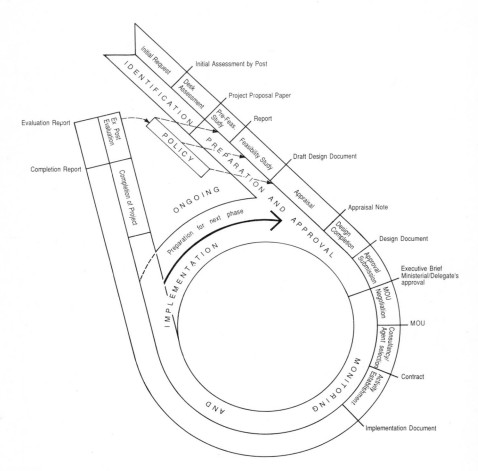

Figure 4.1 AIDAB's Project Cycle.

the litany of conditions commonly applied to structural adjustment recipes (Higgot 1986: 39–54).

Of greater significance was the manner in which prevailing economic thought was translated into development practice. The macro-economic commitments of the Jackson Report were to be matched by increased efficiency and professionalism in aid management. Indeed, the many administrative procedures and structural changes recommended by the Jackson Report (1984: 16) were designed to allow the necessary work to be done in a professional style. The tools of professional management were equally well spelled out. New procedures were introduced for country and sector programming, through to management, based on the World Bank 'Project Cycle' which takes the manager through each stage of a project from identification, appraisal, design and so on, to evaluation procedures designed to feed back results across projects, sectors and country programmes (Figure 4.1).

Amongst the array of techniques of appraisal and planning introduced to improve efficiency and effectiveness, the Jackson Report gave particular attention to cost–benefit analysis. For many, cost–benefit analysis came to epitomise AIDAB's commitment to improved control over aid management decisions in all aspects of the programme. Following the Report's publication, the Magarini Settlement Project was the first case where this commitment could be demonstrated in practice.

'SERIOUS CAUTIONINGS AND SUBSTANTIAL RESERVATIONS'

In October 1981 President Moi attended the Commonwealth Heads of Government Meeting (CHOGM) in Melbourne, together with a party of ministers and top level public servants. AIDAB arranged for Paul McGowan to brief the Minister of Agriculture K.N. Biwott and his Permanent Secretary J.S. Mathenge about how an important part of the project was making Australian rainfed agriculture useful to Kenya. Anthony Vale, AIDAB Africa Desk Officer, then met with Mr Biwott and President Moi's Private Secretary Andrew Ngeny and told them Magarini was 'making a gateway for introducing Australian agricultural techniques to Kenya', but that because the present Kenyan contributions to the project were insufficient, the gateway was only half open. Vale met the President himself at Melbourne airport the following day and again lobbied on behalf of the project. The purpose of these activities was to raise the political profile of the project in Kenya (AIDAB 8 October 1981).

From the time the Australian members of the 1980 Joint Review Team to Magarini reported their serious misgivings to AIDAB, strenuous efforts were made to try and reform the project rather than withdraw from it. AIDAB staff were handicapped by an 'extreme defensiveness' on the part of the Australian managing agent, and an increasing reluctance by the Kenyan government to make what was considered by AIDAB a sufficient commitment of staff and funds. During 1982, negotiations on the draft MOU for Phase III stuck on the level of the Kenyan commitment, the provision of credit for settlers, which Australia was not prepared to fund, and import duties on project vehicles used by the Australian staff (AIDAB 28 April 1982). But when AIDAB's submission to the Fraser government's Foreign Minister Tony Street, for $600,000 to extend Phase II for a further six months while negotiations continued, was viewed by the Department of Finance they replied,

in 1978 we expressed serious reservations concerning the economic viability of the scheme and we were unable to support the project. Our
principal concern now is that the latest evaluation report [the 1980 Review
Report] vindicates our earlier reservations and tends to confirm that the
project is, at best, only marginally viable. ... We consider the evaluation report effectively calls into question whether Australia should involve itself
with the substantial additional expenditure.

(AIDAB 25 March 1982)

The Department of Finance reluctantly agreed to the extension because nine
Australians were employed on the project and could not be abandoned there,
but they clearly flagged their future opposition to the project going into Phase
III. They also requested AIDAB to attach Finance's comments on the submission which was to be placed before the Minister.

With the project under pressure in Australia as well as in Kenya, AIDAB
detached Vale from normal duties to 'give absolute priority to redesign'. With
regional planner Graham Gaston, Vale formed a working group in Canberra
comprised of the members of the 1980 review team, ACIAR and McGowans.
This group rewrote the draft MOU amended by the Kenyans into two documents, a simplified MOU which became an enabling document, and a draft
design for Phase III. Vale and Gaston took these documents to Kenya in late
1982 and succeeded in having them accepted in principle by the Kenyan government (Vale and Gaston 1983). A notable feature of this period was the
deterioration in relations between AIDAB and Paul McGowan, who resented
the nature of the criticism and the extent to which AIDAB was attempting to
direct the project from Canberra.

During May 1983 McGowans presented to AIDAB the draft Phase III
Project Design. This is an unusual document for a project design and reflects
both the deep insights Paul McGowan had of many of the problems afflicting
the project, as well as his blind spots. The design contained three key components: human settlement, area development and production. Water was not
mentioned anywhere in the document. It described with feeling and accuracy
the difficulties the project had encountered in trying to reach the Giriama settlers, but it also held up the cooperative as a good example of how Australian
funds were helping the settlers when, as is now known, the cooperative was
viewed by the settlers as an imposition. The design introduced new concepts
which had not been raised in the previous discussions, such as sisal and cassava
processing, and described 'an enormous lift in agricultural productivity',
something which was being denied in every Quarterly Progress Report written
by McGowans staff on the project and received in AIDAB. The document also
contained, at AIDAB's request, a logical framework, a critical path analysis
and a cost–benefit analysis.

The cost–benefit analysis was examined by AIDAB and Department of
Finance staff. Both agreed it was unsatisfactory because it was based largely

on estimates of crop yields, farm incomes and family sizes, when data should have been available given that the project had been involved with settlement since 1979 (AIDAB 8 June 1983). Correspondence between Vale and Mc-Gowan became increasingly pointed. McGowans was either not prepared, or was unable, to swing the project away from its initial transformational approach to one which the Vale and Gaston report described as possessing 'more openness and humility'. But both AIDAB and McGowans, for their own reasons, wanted to keep the project going, and the major barrier to that course was the Department of Finance, although there were some 'adverse views of Magarini within the Bureau' (AIDAB 27 June 1983).

Their greatest ally in this struggle was the Australian High Commissioner in Nairobi who sent frequent lengthy reports back to Australia about the project, the 'flag carrier of our aid to Kenya'. In one he argued 'powerful Kenyans attach a great deal of importance' to the continuation of the project, that 'the Kenyan government turned to Australia because of our practical experience in dryland farming in marginal country' which the High Commission had 'gone to some pains to proclaim publicly', that a withdrawal would 'have a serious impact on our claims to expertise in dryland farming ... and would raise doubts of our sincerity regarding our wish to transfer appropriate and relevant technology to Africa'. This report also detailed internal rates of return on projects acceptable to the major international aid agencies operating in Kenya (AIDAB 30 September 1983). In May 1983 the mission reported a Kenyan Permanent Secretary had expressed his opinion to the High Commissioner that the key factor from the Kenyan point of view was to speed up settlement and that the introduction of up-country people would transform the project.

With the election of the Hawke government in March 1983 and the appointment of Hayden as Foreign Minister, AIDAB had to decide whether to explain the whole mess to the new Minister or to distance him from this project and other problem projects on their books. They chose the latter course, but Hayden was an experienced Minister, proud of his record as Treasurer in the Whitlam government and determined to see Australia's aid dollars spent as effectively as possible. Shortly after coming into office he instituted the Jackson Committee to examine Australia's aid programme. On 20 September AIDAB presented their submission, including Finance's comments, to fund Phase III at Magarini to Mr Hayden. He rejected it on the same day and requested AIDAB to ask the Department of Finance to provide an economic assessment of the project, 'emphasising the cost–benefit aspects'.

The Department of Finance provided AIDAB with their assessment on 14 November, 1983. It was damning. The data provided in the McGowans Phase III design proposal was so inadequate that a cost–benefit analysis could not be carried out. The project's 'long and troubled history' was referred to in terms of 'low economic returns, and its sensitivity to certain dubious assumptions'. Phase II had proceeded although the department had pointed out the inadequacy of water supplies 'which was crucial to the success of the project had still not been established', 'unsubstantiated assumptions on crop yields' and the 'possibility of labour shortages'. The 1981 Review had 'vindicated' the position of the department. Now it was proposed to proceed into Phase III 'on an extraordinary act of faith'. The department estimated the economic rate of return would still be around zero and 'major unresolved difficulties remained'. Australia had spent $11.8 million on Magarini to 30 June 1983 and a further $6.8 million was being proposed. No more should be spent until the detailed financial analysis, called for twice previously, had been done. The Minister wrote to AIDAB that he was 'absolutely staggered that the serious cautioning and substantial reservations ... could have been ignored in what was apparently a cavalier manner' (AIDAB 14 November 1983).

In one last attempt to defend its position on Magarini, AIDAB argued that it used more than just the economic rates of return to assess its projects: the priority to the recipient, conformity with Australian aid policy to that country, the availability in Australia of comparative technical advantage, the social and environmental impact of a project and its economic and financial viability were all taken into account. Magarini was likely to make a 'substantial contribution to settler living standards', and now had an 'assured groundwater supply'. The problem of agriculture was not addressed, but it was argued that in marginal areas like Magarini lower economic rates of return must be accepted. AIDAB's overall assessment was that Magarini was a 'valid developmental activity, which clearly focuses on major issues confronting Kenya' (AIDAB 14 December 1983). Within the Bureau, however, great frustration was experienced and opinions about the Department of Finance's report were less than generous with references to 'relentless economic determinists' and 'developmental Luddites'.

However, the Minister had decided that an independent economist should be asked to examine the project. Professor Helen Hughes was an Australian who had recently left the staff of the World Bank to head the National Centre for Development Studies at the Australian National University. Hughes knew something of Magarini and more of Kenya from her World Bank work and she believed Australia had allowed itself to become 'caught in an intensely political and almost certainly unwinnable situation' (AIDAB 4 January 1984). Hughes was a Deputy Chairperson of the Jackson Committee and was fully committed to other work, but she acceded to a personal request from Hayden to review the Magarini Project.

Meanwhile pressure for continuation of the project was mounting. In October journalist Michelle Gratten published an article in the *Melbourne Age* (4 October 1983: 3) which described the Magarini situation accurately, but concluded that Hayden's decision to end funding 'comes at a bad time for the perceptions black Africa is getting of Australian policy'.[14] A few days later the Nairobi mission informed Canberra that the new Kenyan Minister for Lands and Settlement had visited Magarini and reported favourably to President Moi. A precipitate decision to withdraw now could mean serious embarrassment for Australian Prime Minister Hawke at the forthcoming CHOGM conference in New Delhi where Moi would probably raise the question of an ongoing commitment to Magarini. Hayden informed Hawke, who was *en route* to New Delhi, of his decision to have Hughes review the project, but that the Prime Minister could reassure Moi that whatever the outcome of Hughes' investigation, Australia would find some way of rearranging the project or of finding a viable alternative to it, to fulfil Australia's commitment to provide aid to Kenya.

Hughes initially proposed a team of three economists, including the Deputy Director of ACIAR and a retired Director of Agriculture and Rural Development at the World Bank, should visit Magarini in August 1984. But AIDAB and the Minister required an earlier resolution of the problem so Hughes alone made a five-day trip to Africa the week before Easter 1984 and reported in May 1984. She concluded that 'essentially the project is for the right people and in the right place, but inappropriate design and naive implementation have resulted in heavy overcapitalisation, painfully slow progress and disturbingly low socio-economic returns' (AIDAB 1984: 5). She found it tempting to simply abandon the project, but this would have been at the cost of the Giriama people who would be left worse off than they were before the project began. Hughes, therefore, proposed a redesign strategy which included sending a team to Magarini to collect new data for appraisal of redesign options and to consult with Kenyan officials on the selection of a redesign option, economic analysis of the selected option, preparation of an appraisal document and the negotiation of the final form of Phase III.

THE 1984 APPRAISAL

The 1984 Appraisal, which followed Hughes' recommendations, reviewed four of six redesign options. Two of the six were rejected from the outset, namely a New Development Sequence, which implied large-scale land clearing and commercial agriculture preferred in a Kenyan review of March 1984, and the other the termination of Australian project inputs except for the provision of counterpart wheat aid funds, monetized by the Kenyan government to provide budgetary support for the MOLS who were responsible for project management. A withdrawal option (that is, from the Australian point of view) was retained for the purposes of comparison in the cost–benefit analysis,[15] and a 'continue as planned' option was rejected in favour of a redesign which increased settlement density either by an increase in the number of people on each plot, or a reduction 'within ecological limits' in plot size.

The Appraisal argued higher settler density would increase the potential number of beneficiaries, 'which is more in harmony with the Giriama traditional homestead unit of patrilocal, extended families' and, as a further advantage, would 'alleviate the problem of landlessness in the immediate district'. It was also argued that increased density would proportionally increase

agricultural production by overcoming reported shortages of labour for cultivation. The Appraisal noted warnings about the dangers of reducing plot size
'in this ecologically marginal area'. A person involved in the Appraisal has
since remarked, however, 'they needed to get a dramatic increase in the internal rate of return and that was one easy way to do it'. Without further
explanation in the Appraisal, this option, a reduction in plot size, was
favoured and it was to this option that a cost–benefit analysis was applied.

Cost–benefit analysis

The idea behind cost–benefit analysis is simple. It is a technique for objective-
ly determining whether the benefits derived from implementing a project are
greater than the costs, by an amount sufficient to make investment in the project worthwhile, for the economy as a whole. The analysis of an agricultural
project like Magarini commonly falls into two parts. The first part, known as
the financial analysis, concentrates on the farm and attempts to estimate the
extra income earned by the farmer after all costs of production, taxes and loan
repayments have been accounted for, that is, the net benefit gained by the
farmer as a result of participating in the project, over what would have been
earned in the absence of the project.

The net benefits from the farm and other benefits accruing in the local
economy determined by the financial analysis are carried into the second part
of the cost–benefit analysis, the economic analysis, which attempts to estimate
what effect this increased income has on the national economy. The lay person
can quickly grasp the logic of the financial analysis which is not unlike a profit-
and-loss account projected over twenty years, and here we restrict our
discussion to that level of analysis. We use as a basis of comparison between
what was done on Magarini and what might be considered a standard financial
analysis technique, Gittinger's text (1982), published by the World Bank,
which was the approach AIDAB requested McGowans to adopt when their
first Magarini Phase III cost–benefit analysis, presented in 1983, was unacceptable (AIDAB 8 June 1983).

The cost–benefit analysis applied in the 1984 Appraisal was supposed to be
of this standard form. The Appraisal Report noted 'The report is, in itself, a
demonstration of the commitment of AIDAB senior management to institute
effective financial and economic appraisal of projects as requested by the
Minister'. It was also to provide a model for application elsewhere in response
to the Jackson Report's recommendation that cost–benefit analysis should
become a more prominent feature of project appraisal. Hughes is strongly of
the opinion that if·a 'proper' cost–benefit analysis had been undertaken in
1978 the project would never have gone ahead in the form it did. On the basis
of the 1984 outcome we are less certain. That a full social cost–benefit analysis, where weightings are applied to the social distribution of benefits, was
not undertaken in 1984, or that a cost–benefit ratio was not presented, are of

little moment. The way in which cost–benefit analysis is commonly used in situations like this can be illustrated by focusing on the financial cost–benefit analysis at the level of the individual settler.

The internal rate of return

A central concept of cost–benefit analysis is the internal rate of return (IRR). The IRR is used by international agencies for practically all economic and financial analyses and it became critical during the impasse on Magarini during 1983 and 1984, although there are important debates about this (see also Irvin 1979: 14–19). The IRR may refer to a financial rate of return, that is, in the Magarini case the level of return to the farmer, or the economic rate of return, which refers to value of farmers' increased incomes to the national economy. We focus on the financial rate of return.

The IRR measures the worth of a project by finding the discount rate that makes the net present value (NPV) of the net benefits equal to zero. To discount is to recognize that the value of benefits will be worth less in the future than they are now. We know that $100 will be worth less than $100 in twenty years time. Even if there were no inflation it would still be more advantageous to take the $100 today and invest it at some rate of interest. If a discount rate of 10 per cent is assumed, $100 in twenty years time has a present value of $14. There is a discount rate which will result in a NPV of zero over the life of the project, that is, when all the benefits minus all of the costs, discounted over the life of the project, are equal to zero. By iteratively trying different discount rates until the NPV is near to zero, we can ascertain the IRR of the project.

The IRR is therefore equal to the maximum interest that a project or farmer can pay for the resources if the project is to recover the investment in it, meet the operating and maintenance costs and still break even (see Gittinger 1982: Ch.9 and Irvin 1979). This is the same as saying 'What is the return to the capital invested of the activities undertaken by the farmer or the project?' In strict economic terms a project which has an IRR of less than the opportunity cost of capital is rejected. Opportunity cost refers to the benefits foregone by using capital for one purpose instead of the next best alternative use. An acceptable IRR for a private enterprise is therefore normally the interest rate at which finance is available (Gittinger 1982: 331).

The farm survey

Fundamental to a farm financial analysis are reliable data on crop yields, areas planted, market prices of the main crops likely to be produced, and the costs of physical inputs, fertilizer, building materials, machinery hire, labour costs, loan repayments and debt servicing costs, as well as local food and water prices, school fees, the cost of local health services and transport. Gittinger (1982: 91) notes the farm analysis 'must be as realistic as possible to determine

108 Development in practice

what the farmer gains by participating in the project'. The draft Phase III design proposal submitted by McGowans was rejected because it was based on inadequate estimates of these data. Hughes recommended a team should travel to Magarini and conduct a farm survey to generate accurate data to be used in another cost–benefit analysis.

The team comprised two young Australians who had never previously conducted an agricultural survey in rural Kenya. With only two weeks available to them they used extension staff from the project to carry out the survey using Swahili or Giriama languages. We have already described the poor relations which developed between the settlers and project extension staff. One or other of the Australians had to be present for most of the farmer interviews because the Kenyan interviewers 'believed they elicited a better response with expatriates present'. Gittinger (1982: 92) believes the 'farmers are a crucial source of information' and 'great care should be taken to establish a good atmosphere in the interviews'. The Australians were aware their survey was less than satisfactory. On the subject of income and expenditure, they reported 'data obtained provided interesting insights but suffered from too many inconsistencies to be rigorously examined. ... An intensive, carefully planned and executed survey would be necessary to obtain credible data' (ADAB 1984: 51).

The standardized farm unit

Gittinger (1982: 89) states the financial projections must be based on 'at least one pattern of farm plan that is assumed for participating farmers – this is the model farm'. The 1984 Appraisal used the concept of the standardized farm unit or SFU. The SFU is an attempt to represent aggregate livestock, cropping patterns and crop yields across the project area. The SFU assumed a farm size of 12.5 ha, with 2.8 ha under crop, 1.2 ha for the homestead area, and the balance of 8.5 ha for livestock production. The Appraisal was at pains to point out that it 'should not be interpreted as a "typical" or "model" farm'. The SFU did not exist except in a theoretical sense. One of the Australians who carried out the farm survey explained to us, 'No one farmer could plant the crops in the patterns implied in the SFU because of variability of soil types, and so on'. The SFU was based on the random survey of forty-two farmers rather than a deliberate attempt to represent the whole range of soil types, possible cropping patterns and other farmer characteristics.

The SFU has a total annual area cropped of 2.8 ha and four crops cultivated: maize, pigeon peas, sesame and cassava (Table 4.1). Pigeon pea is used to represent all pulses, and cassava any other minor crops which the farmer might grow. It is assumed that initially maize will take up three-quarters of the total area cultivated, sesame 15 per cent and cassava 10 per cent, but pulses and cassava will gradually assume greater importance on the SFU and maize will be reduced to only half of the area cultivated after twenty years. Farmers

Table 4.1 Standard farm unit, 1984 Phase III Appraisal

Crop	Long rains			Short rains		
	Area (ha)	Proportion	Yield (kg/ha)	Area (ha)	Proportion	Yield (kg/ha)
Maize Pigeon pea	2.1	0.75	1000	0.4	0.8	1000
Sesame	0.42	0.15	400	0.1	0.2	400
Cassava	0.28	0.1	3000			
Total area	2.8	1.0		0.5	1.0	

Source: Magarini Settlement Project, Appraisal Phase III, October 1984.

will plant less during the short rains because of the increased unreliability of adequate rain for crop production.

THE FINANCIAL ANALYSIS

The financial analysis takes each crop in turn and, using estimated yields and the area cultivated, calculates the total production of that crop (see Table 4.1). Production is then multiplied by a price for that crop to produce a revenue figure for each crop. The costs of production are then deducted from the revenue to arrive at a gross margin for each crop. Table 4.2 illustrates this stage, using maize as an example. We merely observe that the 1984 Appraisal cost–benefit uses, without explanation, economic prices for maize and financial prices for other crops and it does not detail what items are included in input costs, nor what prices are used to calculate the costs. We address more

Table 4.2 Standard farm unit gross margin calculations, 1984 Phase III Appraisal

Crop	Year								
	1	2	3	4	5	6	...	20	21
Long rains Maize									
Area (ha)	2.1	2.07	2.03	2.0	1.96	1.93	...	1.44	1.40
Yield (kg/ha)	1000	1030	1061	1093	1126	1159	...	1753	1800
Total production	2100	2132	2154	2186	2207	2237	...	2524	2520
Price (K.sh)	2.00	2.05	2.05	2.05	2.28	2.28	...	2.28	2.28
Revenue	4200	4371	4416	4481	4524	5100	...	5755	5746
Input costs	2777	2737	2684	2644	2591	2552	...	1904	1851
Gross margin	1423	1634	1732	1837	1933	2548	...	3851	3895

Source: Magarini Settlement Project, Appraisal Phase III, October 1984.

serious problems below. The financial analysis in the 1984 Appraisal found the SFU would produce an IRR of 17.4 per cent over twenty-one years.

Errors

As it was presented in the Appraisal report the financial analysis contains a number of typographical and minor arithmetic errors. Columns and rows of figures do not add up, or are transposed. Most of the errors are typographical and are not carried through the whole analysis, however, and those that are originate in the calculations of the gross margins of a minor crop and so have little effect on the final outcome. Their correction reduces the financial rate of return from 17.4 per cent to 16.4 per cent. All subsequent discussion is based on the corrected figures.

Yield assumptions

A critical assumption which the 1984 Appraisal makes is that maize yields will increase by 3 per cent per year compounding, and pigeon peas and cassava yields will increase by 5 per cent per year. The Appraisal argues these aggregate growth rates for yields are considered sufficiently conservative to offset any likely climatic variations over the life of the project. The justification for these yield assumptions are further antecedent assumptions, notably that long-term adaptive research on dryland farming will occur, that a coherent and effective extension programme will be developed, that project staff will double effective working hours per day and all inadequacies in the supply of inputs and marketing will be overcome. Considering the history of Magarini to this point, it is beyond our comprehension how these assumptions could have been accepted as a plausible future reality.

Gittinger agrees that a project analysis must be based on a specific technological package, but that the 'effectiveness of the proposed technology must be realistically checked to ensure they reflect on farm conditions and *not those of an experimental station*' (emphasis added) (Gittinger 1982: 91). These yield assumptions did not even reflect conditions on the General Investigation Station at Magarini, where crop trials had been subject to the severe climatic variation since the beginning of the project. Chapter Three presents evidence of shortfalls in maize yields as a result of variation in rainfall, based on crop trials carried out at Magarini in 1978 and 1979. We also discussed the use of a computer simulation model of maize production. We have substituted in the SFU gross margin calculations, the Appraisal assumption of compounding increases in the yield of maize for twenty-one years, with yields based on actual rainfall at Marafa from 1966 to 1986, using first the crude 'Reeves' model' which was available from 1979, and second, with yields predicted by the more sophisticated ACIAR/CSIRO CERES-Maize Model for the same period. The outcomes are illustrated in Figures 4.2, 4.3 and 4.4. The major differences

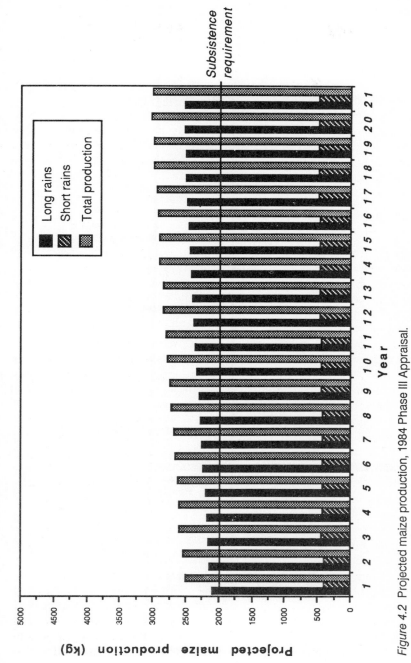

Figure 4.2 Projected maize production, 1984 Phase III Appraisal.

Note: Calculated on projected yields and areas cultivated from the Phase III Appraisal, pp. 91–2.

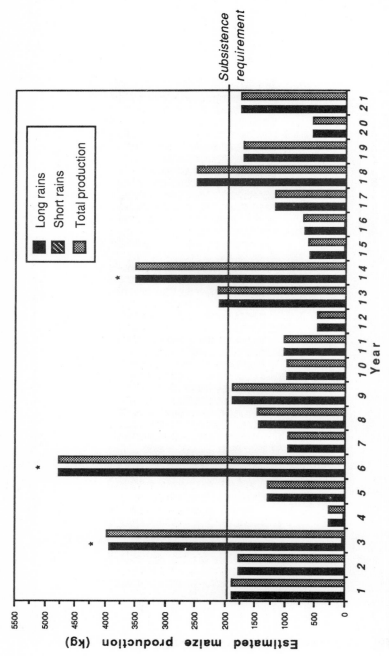

Figure 4.3 Estimated maize production, 1984 Phase III Appraisal assumptions and maize yields calculated as a function of actual rainfall at Marafa, 1966–86 (Reeves' model).

Note: Assumes same areas cultivated as 1984 Appraisal Standardized Farm Unit, and settler yields 70 per cent of experimental yields. An asterisk indicates years in which soil water-logging would probably have reduced yields substantially.

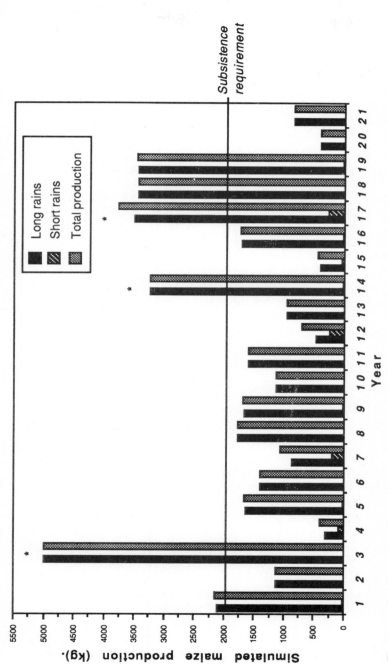

Figure 4.4 Simulated maize production, 1984 Phase III Appraisal assumptions and maize yields simulated by ACIAR/CSIRO CERES-Maize Model, Marafa soils and actual rainfall 1966–86.

Note: Assumes same areas cultivated as 1984 Appraisal Standardized Farm Unit, and settler yields 70 per cent of experimental yields. An asterisk indicates years in which soil water-logging would probably have reduced yields substantially.

between the two approaches are the regularly recurring shortfalls in the subsistence requirement predicted by the Reeves' model and the ACIAR/CSIRO model. Also notable are the large number of years in which the models predict that the short rains will fail to produce a crop. On the other hand, in some years, yields well above that assumed by the 1984 Appraisal are predicted and it could be argued that these good years could carry settlers through the bad years. But the manner in which two or even three bad years occur in a row, drives home the point that bad years at Magarini are normal years, and off-farm employment or some other options to earn an income were critical to the economic and physiological survival of the settlers.

The smallholder cash flow summary

The next stage in the financial analysis is to carry the gross margins for the crops grown on the farm into a cash flow summary. In the cash flow summary living costs, (which include the costs of labour foregone by working on the farm and not earning a wage elsewhere) and other outgoings like loan repayments, are deducted from the total gross margin to produce a net cash flow for each year. The net cash flows over the period being considered, twenty-one years in this case, are discounted to their net present value and the financial rate of return is derived. Table 4.3 reproduces the 1984 Appraisal cash flow summary, with years 7–19 excluded in the interests of space and clarity. A number of assumptions are made in the calculation of the net cash flow, some of which we believe are questionable.

The opportunity costs of farm labour

Farm work uses the settler family's time. The recommended approach to the problem of how to place a cost on that time is to use its opportunity cost, that is, the earnings the family will forego if they participate on the project rather than going out to work for wages (Gittinger 1982: 138–9). Under-estimation of the opportunity costs of farm labour is a significant reason for the wide discrepancy between IRR estimates before and after appraisals of projects.[16] The 1984 Appraisal cash flow summary is based on the opportunity costs of labour of one adult, but the farm survey undertaken specifically to provide data for the cost–benefit analysis finds that 'a typical farm has the following labour breakdown: fulltime = 3 people; part-time = 1–2 people; hired seasonally = 1' (ADAB 1984: 49). On these findings it would be justifiable to calculate the net cash flow on the basis of three adults, but instead we have recalculated it using two adults. The financial rate of return drops from 16.4 per cent to 6.3 per cent (Table 4.4).

It is also likely that the actual cost of the labour foregone has been under-valued. Peter Rohan (1984: 58), an economist who was involved in the 1984 farm survey, completed a Masters thesis on cost–benefit analysis using

Magarini as a case study. He considered the figure of K.sh1,890 used in the 1984 Appraisal was too low and used a value of K.sh2,250. The average disposable income of a rural household in Kilifi District in 1984 was K.sh3,500 and the K.sh1,890 used in the Appraisal is this figure multiplied by the World Bank shadow wage rate for unskilled labour in Kenya (0.54) (ADAB 1984: Annex III). This appears to be another example of how economic prices and financial prices have been conflated in the analysis. That problem aside, if the opportunity cost of labour is valued at K.sh2,250 the financial rate of return falls from 16.4 to 14.4, and if it is assumed two adults instead of one will forego earning this income, the IRR falls to 4.5.

Crop production

The 1984 farm survey does not describe how the areas under cultivation by the farmers surveyed were measured, but the areas cropped per year averaged 2.5 ha with a range from zero to 5.7 ha. In addition, 74 per cent of farmers interviewed reported labour to be insufficient. The Appraisal assumes an area of 2.8 ha will be cropped. If this figure is reduced by 10 per cent, the IRR falls from 16.4 to 12. If the increased cost of labour is included as well, the IRR falls to 10 per cent and if the number of adult labour units is increased to two, it falls to less than 1 per cent.

The major problem with the 1984 cost–benefit analysis is the unrealistic assumptions which it makes about crop yields. By 1984 clear warnings had been sounded about sustainable improvements in agricultural yields. Soils were highly variable, rainfall was erratic, and it was never convincingly demonstrated that the project's agricultural research could offer much to the settlers, let alone sustain an adequate extension service. If the gross margins from maize production based on the projected yields of maize predicted by the Reeves' model (Figure 4.3) and the CSIRO/ACIAR model (Figure 4.4) are substituted for the assumptions of the 1984 Appraisal, the IRR falls from 16.4 per cent to 7.8 and to 5.2 per cent respectively (Table 4.5). If any of the other assumptions we have questioned above are added in, the IRR becomes less than one.[17]

The financial analysis summarized

The various outcomes of the questioning of the assumptions of the 1984 Appraisal cost–benefit analysis are summarized in Table 4.6. The IRRs which result from changing the assumptions of the original Appraisal are at almost any stage well below two cut-off points at which the standard cost–benefit analysis would find that a project was not a wise use of resources. An IRR of around 12.3 per cent, according to standards that are implied in the 1984 Appraisal, is below the opportunity cost of capital for settlement projects in Kenya.[18] It is generally considered that the margin of error in the cost–benefit analysis method is such that any rate below 8 per cent should cause a project to be

Table 4.3 Standard farm unit and smallholder cash flow summary, 1984 Phase III
Appraisal (Kenyan shillings)

SPNV = 1.89   @ rate = 0.164

Gross margins					Year				
	1	2	3	4	5	6	...	20	21
Long rains									
Maize	1423	1634	1731	1837	1933	2548	...	3851	3895
Sesame	345	359	381	395	408	421	...	631	636
Cassava	380	417	473	516	580	630	...	2045	2189
Pigeon peas	0	1	5	13	25	41	...	896	1045
Short rains									
Maize	232	269	294	311	328	452	...	721	724
Sesame	55	60	66	64	69	75	...	95	99
Pigeon peas	0	12	2	5	9	11	...	293	336
Timber	555								
Charcoal	82								
Livestock	1400	1400	1400	1400	1400	1400	...	1400	1400
Total gross margin	4472	4153	4352	4540	4752	5578	...	9932	10324
Less living costs	1890	1890	1890	1890	1890	1890	...	1890	1890
Net income	2582	2263	2462	2650	2862	3688	...	8042	8434
Debt service									
Land purchase	−6780	0	530	530	530	530	...	530	530
Development loan	−8000	0	1300	1300	1300	1300			
Seasonal credit	0	400	400	400	400	400	...	400	400
Total repayments	−14,780	400	2230	2230	2230	2230	...	930	930
Net cash flow	−12,193	1863	232	420	632	1458	...	7110	7504

Notes: Typographical and arithmetic errors corrected. SPNV = social net present value.
Source: Magarini Settlement Project, Appraisal Phase III, October 1984.

CONSEQUENCES FOR THE SETTLERS

The re-examination of the 1984 Appraisal financial analysis took place with
the advantage of hindsight. We wanted to find out why what we knew had happened at Magarini since 1984 was so strikingly different from what the 1984
Appraisal assumed would happen. The differences are illustrated in Figure
4.5. The cumulative benefits, calculated by adding one year's benefits to the
next, predicted by the 1984 Appraisal, are compared to the cumulative benefits predicted when some of the 1984 assumptions are changed in the manner
described. If this is done, within the first six years, rather than receiving the
steadily increasing income predicted by the Appraisal, a settler on the SFU

Table 4.4 Standard farm unit and smallholder cash flow summary: living costs adjusted (Kenyan shillings)

Living costs: 2 adults opportunity costs = 3780
SPNV = −8.41 @ rate = 0.063

Gross margins	Year								
	1	2	3	4	5	6	...	20	21
Long rains									
Maize	1423	1634	1731	1837	1933	2548	...	3851	3895
Sesame	345	359	381	395	408	421	...	631	636
Cassava	380	417	473	516	580	630	...	2045	2189
Pigeon peas	0	1	5	13	25	41	...	896	1045
Short rains									
Maize	232	269	294	311	328	452	...	721	724
Sesame	55	60	66	64	69	75	...	95	99
Pigeon peas	0	12	2	5	9	11	...	293	336
Timber	555								
Charcoal	82								
Livestock	1400	1400	1400	1400	1400	1400	...	1400	1400
Total gross margin	4472	4153	4352	4540	4752	5578	...	9932	10324
Less living costs	3780	3780	3780	3780	3780	3780	...	3780	3780
Net income	692	373	572	760	972	1798	...	6152	6544
Debt service									
Land purchase	−6780	0	530	530	530	530	...	530	530
Development loan	−8000	0	1300	1300	1300	1300			
Seasonal credit	0								
Total repayments	−14,780	400	2230	2230	2230	2230	...	930	930
Net cash flow	−12,193	−27	−1658	−1470	−1258	−432	...	5582	5614

Source: Magarini Settlement Project, Appraisal Phase III, October 1984.

would have received no income for two years in succession (years 4 and 5) and, because of an inability to repay loans, would have gone steadily further into debt (Figure 4.5). The re-analysis predicts that in order to earn money to buy food (the 1984 farm survey found maize meal accounted for 60 per cent of household expenditure) the settlers would have been forced off their plots onto the local wage labour market. This is, in fact, what happened. As a consequence they faced threats of eviction by the project staff and were unable to carry out improvements to housing or land on their plots.

Four cases collected in 1988, of families who have been affected in different ways by the project, help give the numbers in the cost–benefit analysis a human dimension. None of these families, including that most advantaged, can derive the benefits assumed in the 1984 Appraisal.

Table 4.5 Standard farm unit and smallholder cash flow summary: maize yields adjusted to Reeves' (1979) model

SPNV = 6.46   @ rate = 0.0078

Gross margins	1	2	3	4	5	6	...	20	21
Long rains									
Maize	2402	2318	3650	–1242	1234	4145	...	197	3393
Sesame	345	359	381	395	408	421	...	631	636
Cassava	380	417	473	516	580	630	...	2045	2189
Pigeon peas	0	1	5	13	25	41	...	896	1045
Short rains									
Maize	–415	–437	–270	–350	–526	–526	...	–398	–326
Sesame	55	60	66	64	69	75	...	95	99
Pigeon peas	0	12	2	5	9	11	...	293	336
Timber	555								
Charcoal	82								
Livestock	1400	1400	1400	1400	1400	1400	...	1400	1400
Total gross margin	4803	4125	5706	800	3198	6198	...	5159	8773
Less living costs	2249	2249	2249	2249	2249	2249	...	2249	2249
Net income	2554	1876	3457	–1449	949	3949	...	2910	6524
Debt service									
Land purchase	–6780	0	530	530	530	530	...	530	530
Development loan	–8000	0	1300	1300	1300	1300			
Seasonal credit	0	400	400	400	400	400	...	400	400
Total repayments	–14,780	400	2230	2230	2230	2230	...	930	930
Net cash flow	–12,193	1476	1227	–3679	–1281	1719	...	1980	5594

Source: Magarini Settlement Project Appraisal Phase III, October 1984.

Johanna is one of the project's most progressive farmers. He took up his plot in 1982, but still runs his shop in a local trading centre. He inherited a plot of coconuts from his grandfather and received compensation from the project for a plot of cashews which are covered in long grass because the plots have not been allocated. Johanna and his brothers, who also have plots on Magarini were fortunate in that their soils do not suffer as badly from water-logging as others on the project and, depending on rain, they can get good maize harvests. In 1983 they had a reasonable harvest which lasted about eight months, and in 1984 they were able to sell a considerable amount. In 1986 they had enough maize only for subsistence, but in 1987 they were again able to sell some. Johanna is also making money from sesame and sorghum. An attempt at peanut production ended in a rotting crop, so he has given up on that crop.

Table 4.6 Adjusted assumptions and their impact on financial rates of return calculated in the 1984 Phase III Appraisal Report cost–benefit analysis

Unadjusted IRR = 17.44 *Assumptions Appraisal Phase III*	*Adjustment*	*Adjusted IRR*	*Comments*
1. Demonstration of effective financial and economic appraisal	**1.** *Correction of arithmetic errors*	**16.4**	Numerous typographical errors do not greatly affect IRR. Errors in minor crop gross margins have small effect
2. Opportunity costs of house-labour estimated at one adult	**2.** *At least 2 units of adult labour would be foregone by settlers in joining the project*	**6.3**	This is still a conservative estimate. Research on rival projects in Africa shows under-estimation of opportunity costs of labour as a primary reason why ex-poste IRR are low compared with ex-ante appraisals
3. Opportunity costs reflect living wage adjusted to 1984 prices	**3.** *Rohan (1985) argues that at 1978 prices likely potential income of settlers is <=K.sh2000. 1984 prices is K.sh2250*		Rohan collected field data for 1984 appraisal
	(a) Recalculation 1+2+3	**4.5**	
	(b) Recalculation 1+3	**14.4**	
4. Area of land cultivated or cultivable by a household is 2.8 ha	**4.** *Field assessment indicates 2.8ha achieved only where mechanical cultivation used. This is unlikely to be sustained. Reduce by 10%*		Approximates to cut-off for opportunity cost of capital of 12.3% FRR. It is unclear what FRR the Appraisal would have deemed acceptable, but the figure of 12.9 is noted as 'not relevant'. The maximum rate reported from comparable projects in Kenya in 1984 was 12.3%FRR
	(a) Recalculation 1+4	**12.0**	
	(b) Recalculation 1+3+4	**10.0**	
	(c) Recalculation 1+2+3+4	**<1.0**	
5. Maize yields. Assumed 3% compound increase per annum, ignored climatic effects	**5a.** *Maize yields recalculated as a function of actual rainfall using Reeves' (1979) trial results*		Recalculation of maize yields only. All other crops left the same as 1984 assumptions.
	(a) Recalculation 1+3+4+5a	**0.8**	In years above 699mm of rain during long rains maize yields are held at that level. In reality yields in years with that amount of rainfall would probably be substantially reduced, but because the reduction *in yields is not known, the more conservative approach has been used*
	(b) Recalculation 1+5a only	**7.8**	
	5b. *Maize yields recalculated by ACIAR-CSIRO CERES–Maize Model simulation based on rainfall and soil conditions*		
	(a) Recalculation 1+3+4+5b	**<1.0**	This figure ignores the effect of soil waterlogging. If soil waterlogging is taken into account the IRR falls to 1.0
	(b) Recalculation 1+5b only	**5.2**	

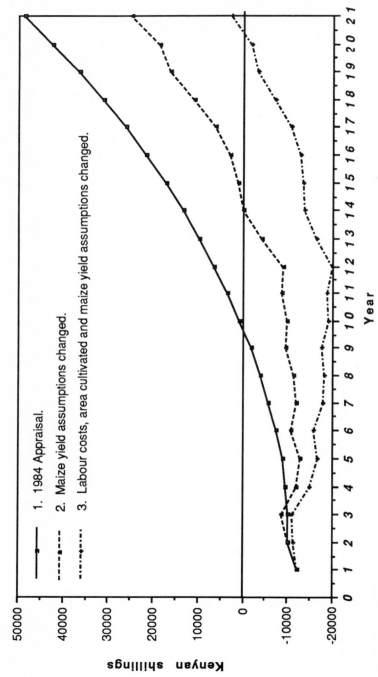

Figure 4.5 Cumulative net benefits, 1984 Phase III Appraisal, and adjusted maize yields, labour costs and area cultivated.

Notes:
1. Arithmetic and typographical errors corrected (IRR = 16.4).
2. Maize yields expressed as a function of rainfall (Reeves 1979) (IRR = 7.8).
3. Maize yields as above, opportunity cost of labour increased to 2 adults, cost of living increased from K.sh1890 to K.sh2250 and area cultivated reduced by 10 per cent (IRR = 0.8).

Johanna's financial position is good. Last year he spent K.sh2,150 on labour and bought his own oxen plough. He earns K.sh3,000 per year from his shop and now has six cattle, two oxen and thirty goats. He pays K.sh4,500 in school fees. Johanna is critical of the project, even though he has done well from it. He knows of families who are split up for much of the year while the men seek work or cultivate land off the project. Some men have gone as far north as the Tana River he says. He does not know how people can afford to send their children to school, when they cannot earn enough to eat. The schools demand the children are properly clothed and that is another expense.

Alfonse is the head teacher at a primary school in the Waresa area. As such he is an unusually well-educated and progressive settler. He has more than the normal amount of contact with project extension agents and has taken a K.sh10,000 farm development loan. This loan gave him two improved breed cattle and two water tanks. He and his family moved onto their plot in 1984, cleared land themselves and had such a good harvest that the maize lasted them for almost two years, until April 1986. In 1984, project bulldozers came in and cleared a large part of the plot of trees and ploughed the area. Extension agents insisted that Alfonse plant his crops there. The 1985 harvest was not as good and the 1986 and 1987 harvests were worse. Alfonse has also planted a smaller plot cleared in the forest further down on his plot which produced good yields last year. Alfonse earns K.sh600 per month from his teaching, but he cannot afford to pay the labour required to weed his project cultivations.

His household is made up of his wife and three children, his mother and his nephew. Alfonse's wife's family and her father's and mother's relatives also cultivate the land cleared by bulldozers on his plot and pool their labour during clearing, weeding and harvesting. His sister and her husband occupy a plot elsewhere on the project, but his sister is ill and can't work. The husband farms full time and breeds and sells ducks, but they are very poor and he is often forced to seek casual labour. Alfonse has also managed to get access to a small area of land off the project, half-a-day's walk away north near Adu. There the bush has not been cleared for years and large maize gardens are being planted. Yields are exceptional and weeding is not required for up to two years. Many people from the project seek work there and are paid in maize flour. Alfonse's brother has a plot nearby, but he has been walking to Adu to food-for-work, and brings back maize flour every week.

The failure of the 1987 harvest, after heavy rain flooded Alfonse's tractor-cleared field, has created serious problems for him. He owes K.sh575 to people who worked on his house and dug his latrine pit. The project has sent him a demand to pay 10 per cent or K.sh700 of his land development grant and he must pay off K.sh900 per month on his K.sh10,000 loan. He went to his family's home area in Jilore to sell a cow to get the K.sh700, but when he found she was in calf he decided not to sell her. Fortunately his uncle sold a piece of land in which Alfonse had a share, so he obtained the K.sh700 from that source. He is paying K.sh100 a month to his neighbour's children to have his goats herded. His family also make demands upon him. Just this week his brother did not come back from Adu so Alfonse has bought maize flour for his sister-in-law and last year he sold three cattle to pay school fees for children in his extended family. He must also spray his two cows against ticks and build a fence around their pasture.

Safari's family includes his two wives, their eight children, and his mother and father. He has lived in the Magarini area since 1975, when he, his father and his brothers cleared land and planted maize. Their first harvests were so good they always had surpluses to sell and were able to pay K.sh1,500 in wages for people to help clear the bush. In 1980 the extended family split up and occupied their plots. On Safari's plot the bulldozer cleared and ploughed some of the land before they took up occupation and the project staff told him to plant in the ploughed area. The first harvest was excellent and he built a large granary to accommodate it. They paid off their K.sh700 land development contribution. The extension staff kept telling them to plant within the cleared area, but production fell until they could not stay on the plot and have enough to eat. Safari and his wives and parents discuss together who will go out to earn money. His wives have independently made small gardens in the bush where they grow maize for roasting and selling. They spend the income from this enterprise on school books for their children. Safari works on pineapple farms, and cutting mangrove poles and at the salt works on the coast, travelling on a truck sent to the project area by the Indian salt works manager, or north in the Adu area to cultivate other people's fields. After off-farm work or labouring for others Safari claims he and his wives are too tired to work their own land properly.

Safari is angry about the project and its staff. He talks of wanting the British to come back to get rid of the people who steal everything. Some of his bitterness comes from the food-for-work scheme in which he alleges the workers were constantly given less food than they had earned and project staff sold the balance. He admits the new roads and the water supply are improvements, but he complains that since the project started, his family's diet has been reduced to maize flour and wild greens. He has tried to follow project advice, and has also independently planted palms, mangoes, citrus and cashews, but none of them will grow properly. He has been selling goats, so that of the 300 he moved onto his plot with he now has only 40. Safari now plans to move off the project to land north of Ramada. His project plot will never produce, he believes, because the maize rots after a period of reasonable rain. He has bought the rights to the northern land, about 2 ha for K.sh600, and is planting cassava and sweet potatoes there. Even then, he cannot see himself being able to pay his sons' secondary school fees unless he sells the rest of his goats.

Baya is an old man who, before the project, lived with his sons in the project area near Lake Madina. They owned 500 cashew trees there. They also had corporate clan rights to land from Magarini to Shauri Moyo and in the hillier north. Now he and his wife occupy a plot which neither of them is capable of farming, and their sons are scattered about the project and are often away working.

Baya's life has been deeply disturbed by the project. 'It makes me feel like I felt when my father has died. My head goes around and I can only sit and watch, and wonder what will happen.' He remembers the days when Magarini was a prime maize-producing area. 'Long ago there was rice, sorghum, cow-peas, greengrams, much food. I had two fields and many goats. If people were hungry they came here. Now we have to leave here to seek food elsewhere.' As an old man, Baya made a good living before the project producing honey from hives in the bush. But, 'the project destroyed all my 40 hives. They were in the trees. Now there are no trees left. They came with the bulldozers and knocked them all down. It is just grass here now. No trees, not even for shade. It is terrible.'

Baya and his wife, unable to cultivate more than a small part of their plot, make a small amount of money by stripping sisal which was planted along soil conservation banks and plot boundaries as a permanent marker, with which they buy maize flour from the store. They are poorly nourished and live in poverty.

COST–BENEFIT: SUSTAINABILITY AND CERTAINTY

The use of cost–benefit analysis in project management is a controversial yet routine practice. Cost–benefit does not address important aspects of project performance, such as the contribution of a project to the welfare of different groups, or institution building, economic self-reliance and environmental questions (Cassen 1986: 108). We do not criticize this aspect of the 1984 Appraisal. Instead we focus our discussion on the IRR because this Appraisal exemplifies a common occurrence, namely the elevation of a satisfactory IRR from a necessary condition of a 'good project' to a sufficient condition for the continuation of a bad one. It is not coincidental that Magarini also failed an extremely important criterion of success: sustainability.

The cost–benefit method has within it important features of control-orientation. It is designed to identify and predict which aspects of the project and its environment must be controlled for the desired outcomes to be achieved. But important contradictions exist between the single IRR figure and the factors which determine whether or not a project will be sustainable. A high IRR may suggest that a project will be an efficient converter of finan-cial resources into benefits, but this says nothing about whether it is an effective way of achieving other important ends, or, in the longer term, whether it will be sustainable.

Sustainability and the IRR

A recent study by Tiffen (1987: 361–77) of fifty irrigation projects which looked at the financial benefits estimated by the IRR before, during and after completion confirmed that IRR is consistently overestimated in pre-project cost–benefit analyses. Tiffen identified major drawbacks of a reliance on the IRR in project appraisal which included a bias against sustainability. Costs and benefits occurring in the more distant future are highly discounted. This assumes that initial capital costs are the scarce factor, whereas experience shows that the shortage of recurrent funds to operate and maintain capital investments such as the Magarini groundwater reticulation system is a major constraint on sustainability. As one review notes from the point of view of the IRR, there may be little difference between comparable investments in, say, the groundwater system and low technology hand-pumps or roof water catchments, yet one clearly has a greater likelihood of sustainability in terms of future operations and maintenance costs.[19] Moreover, the concept of discounting the future in cost–benefit analysis is a classic illustration of the short-term horizon of economic appraisal which diverts attention away from the long-term sustainability objectives of resource exploitation.

The IRR can also often cause excessive stress to be placed on rapid implementation to realize the benefits early in the life of a project. Correctly applied, the IRR should not bias against a slower build-up in project activities, but clearly, the sooner project benefits are realized, the greater their value in the calculation (Pearce 1971: 36). The impact on local institutional capacity ought to be obvious, whether we consider the farmers, or the government institutions expected to implement and maintain the facilities. For the farmer, the slower the build-up, the slower the pace at which new techniques of farming or marketing are introduced, the greater the likelihood of successful adaptation and 'institutionalization'. For counterpart government agencies, a rapid implementation rate frequently outstrips their capacity, calls for increased expatriate control and staffing, and adversely affects learning and accommodation to changes. Each point can be illustrated in the Magarini experience. An approach that is technically or economically inefficient in the short run may turn out to be efficient over time as a result of learning and skill effects (Fransman 1985).

The reliance on the single figure IRR often gives a false picture of the sensitivity of the outcomes to changed circumstances. Sensitivity analysis is a technique to test systematically what happens to the earning capacity of a project if events differ from those predicted in the financial analysis. In agricultural projects, sensitivity analysis commonly tests what happens to gross margins if prices, yields, costs of production or the timing of implementation vary from the values assumed in the farm analysis. What we have done above is an informal, non-systematic sensitivity analysis. Good sensitivity analysis examines what happens to the IRR if costs rise and prices or yields fall in a systematic manner. The 1984 Appraisal tested changes to the IRR only by separately examining increases or decreases in benefits and costs and concluded 'the project is stable with respect to changes in benefits and costs over its life' (AIDAB 1984: 23). It may be that more flexible designs have sub-optimal IRRs when compared with the highest IRR option. From the Magarini experience we can safely predict that projects will not run according to plan, yet the IRR gives no encouragement to consideration of more flexible options.

Politics and assumptions about certainties

Some points about the cost–benefit analysis we have analysed appear to be trivial. For instance, pointing out the mistakes made in the calculations serves no purpose other than to affirm that cost–benefit analysis is a procedure subject to human failings, a counterpoint to the technocratic mystique sometimes encouraged by proponents of the technique. But more important is the manner in which all attention focused on the 'bottom line' of the IRR. Even AIDAB's greatest critics, the Department of Finance, do not appear to have given the cost–benefit analysis more than a passing glance, which suggests the ritual of doing the analysis and producing an acceptable IRR was of more significance than its findings. There is an important sense in which the power of techniques like cost–benefit analyses lies not in their actual results, but in the promise that these results are available through their application. The essence of the promise of cost–benefit analysis lies in the legitimacy of the ritual applied economists go through. Van Houten and Goldman's conclusion about consultants is relevant to this point about cost–benefit analysis.

> Does it make sense ... for power brokers to employ experts in political struggles? Probably, whether the final report is unexpectedly too objective or downright poor may present only temporary problems. The legitimacy of the consulting process (the ritual) will only be marred in those cases when (and if) the product gets careful and wide scrutiny by the 'wrong' people. Otherwise the process can legitimate whatever was initially intended.[20]
>
> (Van Houten and Goldman 1981: 482)

In the same way, Ahmed remarks on his experience that 'the more technical and complex the presentation, the more the use of shadow prices, trade-offs, engineering coefficients, convincing evaluation or investment criteria, the better the chance of funding' (Ahmed 1975: 85; see also White 1976: 233).

When we consider the circumstances of crisis in which the cost–benefit analysis was undertaken during 1984, we move to a more significant level of concern. It is well known, and obvious from our cases above, that economic techniques can be used to justify decisions made on other grounds by achieving a satisfactory rate of return through an adjustment of the discount rate or the basic assumptions, like yields or labour costs. Whether or not the 1984 Magarini Appraisal cost–benefit analysis was deliberately manipulated to achieve a political or a humanitarian end is not of significance to our argument. A great deal of professional effort has gone into creating and refining techniques such as cost–benefit analysis in the principled belief that better judgements about resource allocations can occur. It is well appreciated by practitioners that cost–benefit studies incorporate an enormous amount of judgement and intuition on the part of the evaluator (see also Stewart 1978).

But inevitably, the introduction of sophisticated techniques and procedures for project appraisal tends to favour those with the resources and skills to manipulate those formats (Gasper 1987: 53). Room for interpretation and argument exists in many of the stages of the analysis; on Magarini this would include the choice of research design, the farmer survey methods, the seasonality and 'average' conditions during which the data were collected, assumptions about input costs, the adoption of agricultural packages, the quality of extension advice, likely prices/markets, the area to be planted and so on, through to the opportunity cost calculations – the 'opportunities' for manipulation of data are clear. Gasper (1987) systematically examines these opportunities for what he calls forging, fudging and framing during analysis. Without doubt these and other judgements require that political and ethical choices be made by the analyst at every turn. Proponents of cost–benefit typically refer to these as 'subjective judgements of fact' (Parrish 1978: 313; Porter 1986: 256–8), whereas for others the theory of cost–benefit analysis rests upon a philosophy of 'as if': values are derived as if a particular hypothetical configuration of the economy existed, lending an unreality to the study (see Dasgupta and Pearce 1978: 15). Cost–benefit analysis quite obviously provides no guidelines as to how the analyst is to resolve such matters. In the absence of guidelines it is distressing to see cost–benefit analysis subjected to the political manipulation it is designed to avert. Indeed, for some analysts we have talked to, this contravenes a sort of economist's Hippocratic Oath. If techniques like cost–benefit become devalued by blatant political usage, then there will be less inhibition in rejecting projects which claim high net returns, or retaining others which fare poorly. Already, the variable quality and consistency of assessments suggests, according to Gasper (1987: 34), 'a disturbingly ritualistic use of studies'.

COST–BENEFIT AND CONTROL

For the authors of the Phase III Appraisal, cost–benefit analysis clearly demonstrated a commitment to the control-orientation approach. We have suggested ways in which features of cost–benefit reproduce the problems of sustainability in projects. In this concluding section, we deal with this claim more systematically. To illustrate the generality of our claims we use as a guide a remarkable study of rural water development in nearby Tanzania by Ole

Therkildsen (1988) entitled *Watering White Elephants? Lessons from Donor Funded Planning and Implementation of Rural Water Supplies in Tanzania*. Therkildsen examines the planning and implementation work of five major donors and concludes they have all been control-oriented. By this he refers in general to five characteristics.

1   A focus in the medium- to long-term plans (3–5 years) on a set of future construction targets or physical goals;
2   a fairly detailed pre-implementation specification of the means to reach goals, indicating the various phases, priorities and financial needs, implementation rates, and so on;
3   substantial collection and analyses of information prior to implementation on the basis of which the plans are specified;
4   an implicit or explicit specification in the plans of the role of the intended beneficiaries either as recipients of services, or as participants in various predetermined activities, sometimes followed by attempts to mobilize beneficiaries to participate in these activities during implementation; and
5   a by-passing of recipient organizations at national, regional and district levels by the technical assistance teams, especially during the preparation of medium- and long-term plans, but also to a certain degree during implementation.

Therkildsen's study is intended to explain two features of experience in the Tanzanian water sector, namely that the plans are seldom used and that rural water sector activities are generally non-sustainable. Therkildsen is not alone in identifying the shortcomings of this approach, despite the fact that most major donors are still preoccupied with refinement of techniques for its application (see, for example, Waterson 1965; Lele 1975; Korten 1980; Johnston and Clark 1982).

The reason why non-sustainability is so prevalent and why plans and otherwise sensible documents are so often ignored in actual practice, is the outcome of many factors. Kenya had enjoyed a huge improvement in its terms of trade between 1976 and 1978 as tea and coffee prices boomed, but the expansion of the government sector continued well after the boom was over, supported largely by foreign borrowing. The national debt service ratio increased from 12.3 to 21.5 per cent between 1980 and 1982 and the second oil shock of 1979 created a major balance of payments problem which was at its worst at the time of the attempted coup in August 1982. By 1984 Kenya was in the grips of a budget rationalization which affected counterpart commitments to all aid programmes. There can be no doubt this had a detrimental impact on the government's capacity to honour Magarini funding, staffing and equipment commitments, despite Joint Reviews pointing up the obligations under the Memorandum of Understanding signed in 1979 during the boom years. Certainly, later Australian offers to hand over the project and responsibility for picking up the recurrent costs to Kenya were anxiously staved off

The human dimension: *Plate 16* A Giriama extended family (top) *Plate 17* A Giriama 'nuclear' family (bottom)

by Kenyan officials. How do the assumptions of the control-orientation in practice exacerbate these problems? The five characteristics identified by Ole Therkildsen can be dealt with in turn.

Common objectives?

The disappointing results in aid practice during the 1970s, whether judged in terms of unrealized equity/poverty aims or the pragmatist's difficulty in holding an increasing array of project components together, brought about a renewed emphasis on detailed statements of project objectives, priorities and attendant schedules of expenditure and implementation targets. In contrast, the Magarini Project shows that it cannot be assumed that the donor agency, their managing agents, the recipient agencies and the beneficiaries agree on common objectives.

For the Kenyan government Magarini necessarily had multiple and often conflicting objectives – to settle the landless, to alleviate up-country political pressure for land, to produce surplus food, to increase access of smallholders to government goods and services, to capture donor foreign exchange and budget support. An agreement on objectives implies that resources will be allocated, and this in turn means the satisfaction of some interests and the denial of others. Even within individual agencies there are different objectives ascendant at various times; in the AIDAB files over the years we find Magarini represented alternately as a land development project, a settlement project, and an integrated agricultural project, but also, as a chance to fly the Australian flag, to do something for the 'poor Giriama', as a testing ground for an unproven experiment in Australia's 'comparative advantage' in dryland farming, or an opportunity to demonstrate a commitment in policy to certain appraisal methods. All this is overlaid with the donor agency funding imperatives and bureaucratic incentives which reward the expenditure of funds according to a planned level of dispersement (see also Honadle and Klauss 1979). Most important are the unstated objectives (see also Morss and Gow 1985), not the sort that can be elicited by group reflection sessions or benevolent managers, but which are systematically blocked institutionally and are brought to the surface only by acts of sabotage or passive resistance, most often on the part of the intended beneficiaries.

Authoritative institutions

Second, as our review of the institutional history of development practice highlights, the implementation of a control-oriented strategy depends on the existence of one (or more in the case of integrated projects) 'authoritative and powerful' decision-making agency with the capacity to gain or enforce compliance. As has been said many times about developing countries, especially since the IMF–World Bank inspired curtailment of state fiscal capacity, the state's policy reach is nearly always beyond its operational grasp. That few powerful decision-making institutions exist in developing countries is a reflection of the general weakness of the state. Therkildsen (1988: 59; see also Hyden 1983) points out,

> Control is a central issue here. Correction of errors presupposes that the power to do so exists. Implicitly, many donors and recipients assume that blueprint plans[21] can be implemented because one or a few authoritative and powerful decision makers exist with the means and incentives to enforce compliance. This view may be based on wishful thinking or on faulty analyses of the nature of the state in developing countries.

Magarini and projects like it are littered with instances of overly optimistic and wishful thinking. On the part of both Australia and Kenya, commitments were entered into with full knowledge that the required actions had not occurred elsewhere, and that the Magarini situation was itself sufficiently unique as to make a repeat performance most unlikely.

There is also the tendency on the part of the managing agents and donor country bureaucrats to play down the fact, which is revealed sooner rather than later, that recipient country agencies cannot match the assumptions on which projects are based. They cannot mobilize the staff, equipment and resources to fulfil what is perceived by the donor to be their part of the bargain. It is as though all that is required for the defined purposes/inputs/outputs, and the development impact to be produced is for them to be written down and agreed upon in an MOU. At least one of the Australians involved lamented the trouble was due to 'AIDAB losing its nerve' and simply not insisting that the government of Kenya fulfil its part of the bargain. A primary objective of the 1987 Joint Review Mission was a determined but futile attempt to tie the Kenyan system down, through performance-based programme budgeting methods, to commitments which the AIDAB representative believed were 'entirely reasonable in the circumstances'. On the other side of the donor–recipient relationship, it is common knowledge that consultants and staff alike will have difficulty getting their project documents through the approval process if a realistic appraisal is made of the counterpart ministry's ability to meet their part of the bargain.

Future certainties

This brings us to the third feature of control-orientation. To get government approval at any stage, staff at all levels must express certainty of outcomes and of the conditions under which the actions and outcomes will occur. Detailed pre-implementation planning, or the mid-stream attempts represented by the Phase III Appraisal, pre-suppose that future economic, institutional and political conditions can be predicted, which in turn assumes the existence of operational information about key sector commitments of fiscally beleaguered governments. This is enshrined in the comprehensive operational guidelines donors like AIDAB now use to specify linkages between project inputs and outputs.[22] Yet unpredictability, environmental or institutional, lack of knowledge and operational information are typical of the project experience. How is it sensible for an Appraisal to reasonably predict how much farm labour will be available in three years time in an area where famine frequently drives people off the land to the towns in search of employment? As Therkildsen (1988: 166) notes, 'It not only mocks the uncertainty and complexity of conditions in developing countries, it also results in plans and project papers that frequently are not useful for implementers.'

Nowadays it is common for too much data about future conditions to be available and field staff are quite simply overwhelmed. Additionally, much of the information cannot be acted upon. Take, for example, the 1977 sociology report, written by a Kenyan, which contained clear warnings about how the Giriama would react to a settlement scheme, which had to be ignored because the primary objective of the Kenyan government in the project was to implement a settlement scheme. Much of the information is primary data from surveys which take little or no account of existing knowledge. Until the 1981 Review Report on Magarini, there is little evidence that planners, at any stage, consulted the large literature on settlement, rural planning and administration in Kenya. The 1984 Appraisal fell back into this approach. The specification of each stage of the project cycle is attended by separation between planners, implementers, and more so, between them and those on whose behalf the intervention is intended. It is apparently commonly assumed that project design knowledge can be generated separately from the organizations and individuals required for its utilization (Korten 1980: 499; see also Johnston and Clark 1982).

Bounded participation

It is somewhat ironic, therefore, that participation is so prominent in control-oriented planning. It is in essence, a covert recognition that somehow, the 'non-economic' variables (always the most troublesome knob on the development vending machine) need to be brought into the equation. The meanings attributed to 'participation' are manifold, but the common thread is that it is essential for the success and sustainability of the project interventions. However, under control-oriented planning, participation can play only a minor role. This may seem an odd claim given the statements constantly made in support of participation, in donors' project preparation guidelines today. However, with the degree of pre-definition given to the overall direction of the project, its objectives, inputs and outputs, participation can in practice occur only within the time and space and the intentions allocated to it (Mbithi and Rasmussen 1977: 30–1). The control-oriented approach is not administering support tailored to local circumstances, but spending money according to the terms of the 'performance contract' or the 'output-oriented programme budget'. Participation can be involved to the extent that it meets the enclosures set for it. Correction in mid-course through participation of people who say that 'the project is màking us worse off, not better off', is very difficult. In this situation, project 'beneficiaries' are left with only two forms of participation: violent opposition or resigned withdrawal. All other options involve only tinkering or embroidering the edges. People's choices remain bounded by the project, and so they often judge it better to stay away.

Participation, in the genuine sense required for it to realize its expected effects, tends to conflict with the desire by donors and the recipient government to control activities. By 1984 it was privately accepted by most parties to Magarini that settler participation was essential, and in the Phase III Appraisal we find exhortations to this effect. But this is unavoidably like tagging a sensitivity analysis onto the end of a cost–benefit. With the overall scheme intact and officially agreed to, it could only be hoped that already planned activities would fit beneficiary needs, and that their resource commitments and knowledge, if not their full compliance, could be mobilized at will if and when needed. But as Goran Hyden (1983) so amply demonstrates, planners and implementers can neither exert strong control over villagers, nor are villagers readily prepared to submit to 'capture', however benevolently intended. In Chapter Five we deal with this critical matter in some detail.

By-passing local institutions

Finally, to Therkildsen's point about by-passing local institutions. The World Bank (1983b), certainly not an opponent of control-oriented planning, in its *Toward Sustainable Development in Sub-Saharan Africa* concludes,

> [T]here are serious weaknesses in the institutions on which development depends. ... The capacity to formulate and implement economic policies and programmes has itself deteriorated. ... Donors must take some responsibility: the pressures they put on governments, the inappropriate design and selection of their projects, and the lack of co-ordination among themselves – have all contributed to the low rates of return on investment.
>
> (World Bank 1983b: 25)

The Magarini Settlement Project does not involve one of the most frequent examples of by-pass in the form of an entirely separate institution to implement the project. Not that this option was absent from the early investigations.[23] But as the Magarini Settlement Project, the venture did create a separate unit of project activity within the Department of Settlement of the Ministry of Lands and Settlement. As a result, executive authority for Magarini remained within the department and for bureaucratic reasons common the world over, there was considerable difficulty in involving other line ministries ultimately responsible for water, health and agriculture. Indeed, Australian officials found adequate grounds for 'withdrawal with honour' when it became evident in 1988 that the Department of Settlement had found a legislative loophole which guaranteed their continued control over funds from the sale of wheat aid which Australia had intended as a parting gift to respective line ministries.

There are, however, more insidious ways in which local institutions can be by-passed. The strict, and usually rapid implementation rates required by the donor, given their propensity to buy development in chunks of 3–5 years, tends to require imports of expatriate personnel, and installation of special project control and management procedures to achieve implementation rates. The donor's first concern is with efficiency and therefore with the perceived need to control implementation activities. But close behind is the desire to enforce financial accountability and to thwart attempts, which are seen by many expatriates as endemic in developing countries, to mis-use or embezzle project funds. Sometimes increased donor control through special executive authorities (such as top-level committees) also aim to favour the purchase of donor country consultant services, goods or equipment.

But as we noted with relation to the biases introduced by a reliance on IRRs, experience shows that there is little chance that recipient management capacity can be substituted for in the short run without serious long-term consequences. The project begins to march to the procedural tune, reimbursement schedule, and particular objectives of the respective donors (Honadle and Rosengard 1983).[24] In this situation there is little choice for donor-appointed managing agents but to take a more prominent role. The puzzling consequence is well put by Bernard Lecomte (1986: 62) in his analysis of the limitations of project aid:

> Paradoxically, agencies act as though they themselves were trying to reduce their own efficiency. They are constantly devising sets of rules, standards, and criteria that force their operations into a predetermined mould and then, to overcome that constraint, they call in outside aid administrators and consultants, who alone are privy to the rites and mysteries of aid procedure. That is bound to hamper the spread of management and monitoring capability in government in the recipient countries.[25]

The fundamental consequences for sustainability and development planning are illustrated by reports that after twenty-five years of development assistance by the European Community, 90 per cent of the contracts are still being performed by foreign firms (Lecomte 1986: 50). The reasons for this are well understood. Aid-dependent consultant companies are important and influential lobbies on donor governments anxious to assuage the trade interests at home.[26] Aid agencies, and in many cases recipient governments, distrust local brain power and doubt their competence. Larger foreign consultancies can respond quickly to donor/financier needs, they can field staff quickly, and important from the client's point of view, they can, in the words of a senior

AIDAB official, 'be leaned on', and made to perform to the donor's requirements. By placing people on the ground for the short assignment (and two
years is still short) they are in no position to pay regard to the peculiarities of
the local situation, nor to pass on to local institutions the knowledge generated during their stay.

The consequences are clear, although seldom examined by the donor countries who produce most of the development plans. Recipient governments and
local agencies rarely concern themselves with the content of feasibility studies
or design documents produced by foreign teams. Wiggins cites this in a list of
reasons why the Kenyan Special Rural Development Programme of the 1970s
failed (Wiggins 1985).[27] Skill transfer rarely occurs. As one of the Australian
staff at Magarini put it, 'With the pressure to perform to targets, you have to
make a choice between training and targets – the choice is clear'.[28] This, combined with common attitudes toward foreign control, means that little
prospect exists for the development of local skills. At Magarini the Kenyan
project staff questioned the expertise of the Australians. Improving efficiency
and effectiveness at Magarini often depended on factors quite removed from
foreign technical expertise. If many of the constraints on meeting the targets
are due to a lack of diesel fuel or spare parts, or an inadequate reward and
incentive system for government staff, or where the impediments to local mobilization are the legacy of still current practices whereby people are
immobilized by handouts at critical political moments, what can the foreign
'expert' offer here? Goran Hyden (1983: 92) leads us into the next chapter
with his observation that 'the more an organisation closes itself out from the
prevailing social forces in society, by insisting on the application of modern
management techniques, the more likely it is to socially alienate itself from
people'.

Chapter 5

Strengthening the people's hand?

In late 1984 approaches were made to a non-government organization (NGO) to become involved at Magarini. The lack of participation by the project's beneficiaries had been of concern to AIDAB staff for some time and the Phase III Appraisal recommended an NGO component be added to the project in order 'to strengthen the resources and organisation of the settler community'. The Appraisal stated the NGO should be involved in 'community development works', in particular 'community health, women's education and income-activities and the farmers' cooperative'.

This was not AIDAB's first attempt to involve an NGO in the Magarini Project. In 1982 discussions were held with Community Aid Abroad (CAA) with a view to CAA running a health programme at Magarini. CAA representatives resident in Africa visited the project and reported reasonably favourably. A further visit was made by an Australian staff member of CAA who was less impressed. In August 1983, without reference to AIDAB, CAA published a news sheet about Australian aid in Africa, using Magarini as a case study, which criticized the impact of the project on the Giriama and the Magarini environment. McGowans immediately drew AIDAB's attention to what they called 'a carefully manipulated lobby of criticism' (AIDAB 9 September 1982). AIDAB staff were 'acutely disappointed' at what they viewed as immaturity on the part of CAA. AIDAB staff who had fruitlessly attempted to impress upon McGowans the need for greater social awareness hoped the involvement of an Australian NGO would achieve this objective by stealth. Instead the NGO 'blew the whistle' on AIDAB's handling of the project. An internal minute suggested CAA had confused its role in the project. As a 'participant' CAA could not also be a 'commentator', particularly when they had been provided with confidential information to allow them to prepare a submission to AIDAB. The same minute noted that if NGOs were to be involved at Magarini, AIDAB's guidelines might have to be amended to ensure an acceptable measure of shared objectives (AIDAB 16 September 1982). CAA was said to be contrite. Both organizations had learned that NGO involvement in formal development projects was likely to be anything but straightforward.

In January 1985 Australian Freedom From Hunger Campaign (AFFHC), one of the larger Australian NGOs, was approached and terms of reference for a feasibility study at Magarini were negotiated. The terms required AFFHC to involve a Kenyan NGO to assess the institutional environment and recommend a plan which would identify the most appropriate activities for the NGO to become involved with and allow for the local community to take over after withdrawal of NGO support.

The Magarini case offers a rare opportunity to examine the control-oriented strategy of conventional development assistance alongside the undertakings of an NGO, and to examine the differences between the two approaches. In the space available we will consider only two issues in detail. First, the NGO's claim, implied in the use of words like 'participation', 'real needs', 'the poorest of the poor', and 'bottom up strategies', that the NGO approach to development is significantly different from conventional approaches. Second, we examine the charge that NGO efforts are merely fragmentary and isolated bits of projects, and that because they do not integrate with the broader programming context they are neither sustainable nor capable of responding to the enormous tasks asked of them.

The fashionable alternative

By 1984 many AIDAB staff saw Magarini in the same terms as their Minister Bill Hayden, as a 'dud' project.[1] It was economically unsustainable, would probably contribute to landlessness in the area, and would most likely accelerate land degradation through the restriction of a formerly extensive system of swidden farming onto small plots of highly erodible soils of varying fertility. The project could no longer be said to be in the interests of the Giriama beneficiaries. Within AIDAB there was a range of opinions on what to do about Magarini and the involvement of an NGO had a number of appealing advantages. For some, the NGO would provide a convenient means of 'withdrawing with honour' from Magarini. 'Support to the NGOs', one staffer quipped at the time, 'is being seen to make a commitment without having to make a real commitment.' Others took the 'pragmatic cost-effectiveness' view – the NGO could become a cheaper managing agent and hopefully assume many of the functions being performed by McGowans.

But it is difficult to sustain a completely cynical interpretation of why AIDAB wanted to involve an NGO at Magarini. There was a serious humanitarian concern over what had happened. Peter Vardos, then AIDAB representative in Nairobi, urged NGO involvement saying, 'The situation of the Giriama community is quite terrible. They are probably worse off now than before the project began. They are getting shafted by the government, you really must strengthen their hand.' Further, although the invitation extended to AFFHC was an innovation for AIDAB, it did not occur in a policy vacuum. Just as the application of cost–benefit analysis was encouraged by the

Jackson Report, so was the involvement of NGOs. Jackson was less than fully enthusiastic about NGO claims but followed international fashion in support of NGOs because they could help donors and recipient governments to go into certain areas where 'administrative bottlenecks' and long chains of decision making 'alienate recipient communities'. NGOs, Jackson reported, can sometimes 'bypass such obstructions and respond more flexibly to local needs and involve local communities' (Jackson Report 1984: 110).

A feature of Western democracies since World War II has been government absorption of many functions of community or voluntary organizations in the provision of social services. The phenomenal growth of NGOs (or PVOs, private voluntary organizations, as they are known in the US), has thus been all the more notable (cf. Kramer 1981). Public contributions to aid NGOs in Europe, Canada and the US more than tripled from US$331.9 million in 1973 to US$1.18 billion in 1983. The OECD Development Centre is now preparing an up-dated directory listing over 4,000 NGOs involved in development work. In Japan, a country where NGOs are still in the formative stages, 131 NGOs were listed in 1985 and by 1986 the number had increased to 257 agencies (OECD 1988: 16).

The international popularity of NGOs reflects the pragmatic considerations discussed in the previous chapter. The vendors of international aid blamed the recurring tendency for economic development plans to go awry, on inadequate attention to 'the human factor'. For the human factor we may read 'the need to overcome social and cultural obstructions to the successful implementation of projects'. The rise of NGOs is a direct outcome of the inability of most development projects to reach the poor, and to create local institutions which will serve the interests of the poorer majority. The Australian government invitation for NGO involvement in Magarini was part of a broad disaffection with the delivery of development aid, particularly in Africa, through centralized state institutions. A recent OECD publication observes that this form of development assistance:

> has not provided productivity and distributive benefits. It has led to activities focused for a long time on individual (pilot) farmers, to enforced co-operativism or service-intensive and often narrowly sectoral programs. It has diverted attention from farmers' and villagers' groups and their own needs, aspirations and potential contributions.
>
> (OECD 1988: 41)

The remarkable popularity of NGOs today is also the outcome of two otherwise contending forces, acting in concert: liberal calls for wider participation in governance, and for more equity in wealth distribution, and the disaffection of neo-classical economics with public sector meddling in the market. This is a very shaky alliance. A recent World Bank publication (1988) extols the virtues of NGOs in development in the same terms that many NGOs would argue their own comparative advantage. NGOs can reach poor communities in remote areas that have few basic resources or infrastructure, and where government services are limited or ineffective; they have the ability to promote local participation in the design and implementation of public programmes by building self-confidence and strengthening the organizational capability among low-income people; they use low-cost technologies, streamlined services and have low operating costs; and they are innovative and adaptable in the identification of local needs, can build upon existing resources and transfer technologies developed elsewhere.

But these virtues may also lead to vices. According to the World Bank (1988: 2) they include: limited replicability, poor integration within a sector or region, and politicization, because 'some NGOs combine development with political or religious objectives that may limit how much the Bank can work with them while safeguarding its primary relationship with the member government'. NGOs can do well, says the Bank, if they limit themselves and 'relieve suffering, promote the interests of the poor, protect the environment or undertake community development'. International institutional support is enthusiastic, but sharply limited.

AFFHC were nervous about AIDAB's invitation. A member of the executive cautioned in a letter, 'I find I still have strong misgivings as to whether AFFHC should be involved at all, taking account of the negative aspects inherent in the project because of MSP history. It seems we really do like to test ourselves to the utmost.' Acceptance of AIDAB support carried with it implications which went beyond Magarini. A senior AIDAB official had suggested, 'If you go down the drain on this one, it will affect all AIDAB–NGO funding in the future'. AFFHC moved carefully therefore. After first consultations with AIDAB and Kenyan NGOs it was apparent that:

> The NGO, all of us, are unclear on what we should do. That's one of the best features of the program so far. We know a) something needs to be done, something "affordable" locally, b) we have a role – we can, so it seems, control a lot of the agenda, and c) we know what not to do.

The question arises, why did AFFHC·respond positively at all, since in the beginning it had no way of judging the likelihood of success? Are NGOs afflicted with the same sort of optimism as 'positive practitioners'?

To answer this question we must move away from Magarini briefly and consider the manner in which NGOs, including AFFHC, present themselves as viable alternatives to formal government and commercial development agencies. Perhaps the most outstanding feature of NGO propaganda is its diversity and the often inchoate views it presents of NGOs and their objectives.[2] Despite this heterogeneity, two common threads can be traced through the NGO ethos. The first is a healthy scepticism toward the received wisdom on development. Their detractors claim NGOs are too critical, but NGOs are generally disapproving of the excessively aggregative and impersonal type of development practised by the major bilateral and multilateral agencies. But as often as this criticism is justified, so it is overdrawn to the point of being almost a dogma. NGO criticism is characterized by chants that official development is too top-down, too large-scale, too trickle-down oriented, and too supportive of élites and corrupt officials.

The second common thread is how NGOs claim to relate to people. Tim Brodhead found, after his review of Canadian NGOs,

> Voluntary development agencies routinely claim that one of the principal differences between their operations and those of others – official donors, local governments, or private sector firms – lies in the way in which they relate to the people with whom they work. Thus, for example, NGOs speak of their 'grass roots' style, of a 'participatory' approach to development, of development being 'from the bottom up', of 'fostering local capacities of self-reliance', or of 'empowering communities and facilitating' development.
>
> (Brodhead *et al.* 1988: 119)

The essential difference between NGO views of development and conventional attitudes is said by NGOs to be the ideal towards which NGOs aspire, of development workers as bearers of values rather than as pragmatists bent on gaining a larger slice of the aid funds cake. In the 1980s words like participation, community, equity and self-reliance pepper the rhetoric of all development organizations, but it is fair to conclude that most NGOs are committed to the view that development must embrace a strong humanitarian concern. If allowance is made for diversity of meaning, NGOs uphold three related principles: the right of people to the basic material necessities of life; the right of people to participate in affairs which govern their lives; and the right to the dignity and self-respect which is derived from increased material welfare and control over their own affairs.

The first principle stems from traditional concerns with poverty and relief. Most NGOs concede that economic growth is essential to ensure people have the means of overcoming the indignity and misery arising from lack of food, shelter, health and security. But material entitlement, they argue, must be seen as a means of development, and not as the ultimate objective (Porter and Clark 1985: 11). The second principle stems from the recognition that material entitlements can only be achieved if people have a measure of control over the means of production. From this point of view, appropriate technology is more about control over the means of production than with whether or not the techniques of production fit the beneficiaries' culture or circumstances. The third principle is centred on words like self-respect, identity and self-esteem found in NGO literature. Denis Goulet (1977: 90) has expressed this principle in a way consistent with NGO views,

> As long as esteem or respect was dispensed on grounds other than material achievement, it was possible to resign oneself to poverty without feeling

disdained. Conversely, once the prevailing image of the better life includes material welfare as one of the essential ingredients, it becomes difficult for the materially underdeveloped to feel respected or esteemed. ... Development is legitimized as a goal because it is an important, perhaps even an indispensable way of gaining esteem.

But does this alternative vision of development lead to alternative strategies of development? The cynics argue that the academic debates and the rhetoric are seldom related to what NGOs actually do. More importantly, however, the predominant NGO focus on small-scale activities like shallow wells, health care centres and vegetable growing projects does nothing to distinguish them from conventional views of their development role. Thus, far from challenging the hegemony of the conventional development strategy, NGOs are assisting in the advance of state prerogatives by the penetration and occupation of places (and people) which, by the government's own admission, it is having trouble occupying. Rather than challenging conventional development practice, the NGOs are frequently merely providing a component, an add-on, to the larger predetermined strategy.

Much has been written about the ways in which NGOs have been influenced by development theory during the 1970s,[3] but to append any particular theory or ideology to NGOs like AFFHC, to dub them revolutionary or transformational, reformist or palliative, is to misunderstand the reason why they have attracted support from across the political spectrum. In another context, Peter Brown (1973) in his timeless book, *Smallcreep's Day*, explains why.

> Similarly, there is a distinction not between revolution and reform, but on the one hand between the kind of revolution which installs a different gang of rulers or the kind of reform which makes oppression more palatable or more efficient, and on the other those social changes, whether revolutionary or reformist, through which people enlarge their autonomy and reduce their subjection to external authority.

That part of the NGO humanitarian concern which refers to 'political control', a phrase which worries conservative supporters of NGOs and multilateral funders alike, is not an ideological or party statement. It is simply an echo of the populist's concern over a single, state-centred perspective of development in which one group of people make the decisions, exercise the control and limit the choices, while the great majority must accept these decisions, submit to this control and act within the limits of externally imposed choices. The thread which makes it sensible to speak of 'an NGO perspective', is a view that development is about creating more options for more people. Development involves people and their organizations, the enhancement of people's ability to amass and manage resources in such a way that the greatest number of people have the greatest number of options.[4] Understandably, this perspective cannot be 'neutral about pluralism in culture, democratic freedom, active participation in politics, and preservation of the environment, which fit; or about authoritarianism, oppressive social or gender relations, or religious intolerance, which do not fit' (de Kadt 1985: 553).

In this belief, NGOs claim a special privilege in development. Tim Brodhead indicates the bedrock of this privilege when he says,

> Much of the credibility and legitimacy of Northern NGOs and their defence of their autonomy rests on their claim to have *unique access to, and knowledge of the real needs and aspirations of people* in the countries in which they work. It is this, they say, which qualifies them to act as advocates for the poor, to promote and/or oppose various government aid or foreign policies, and to insist on the relevance of their own work.
>
> (Brodhead *et al.* 1988: 47, emphasis added)

This belief lay at the heart of the positive response to AIDAB's invitation to AFFHC and three Kenyan NGOs they began to work with, to become part of the Magarini Project. They believed they could be responsive to the real needs and interests of the predominantly Giriama population, and that through a participatory approach, they could assist people to mobilize and manage their resources to produce sustainable benefits in an equitable manner.

THE 'NGO COMPONENT' AT MAGARINI

Kenyan government policy was supportive of NGO involvement. Much is made in Kenya of the view that NGOs are complementary to government initiatives in development. In 1984 the new District Focus for Rural Development policy had been announced which defined a legitimate role for NGOs in district-level development. The counterparts chosen in Kenya were Kenya Freedom From Hunger Council (KFFHC), who had been assisted by Australian FFHC in small-scale irrigation projects around Lake Victoria, and two other NGOs (the Undugu Society of Kenya and the recently formed Kenya Water for Health Organization), who had considerable experience working with government ministries.

Even so, the idea of NGO involvement in Magarini was greeted with almost total hostility by government officials in Nairobi. Despite the joint government endorsement of the 1984 Appraisal Report recommendations, the NGO component was clearly seen as AIDAB's idea. At this time the Memorandum of Understanding for Phase III had not been finalized and the arrival of Australian NGO people was seen as a further unwelcome sign of AIDAB's intention, declared in the Phase III Appraisal, to 'diligently monitor Kenyan performance'. On the first courtesy call by AFFHC to the Deputy Secretary of MOLS, permission to visit the project was refused. This decision was later reversed with the proviso that the Kenyan and Australian NGO team would be accompanied by MOLS officials and closely monitored by state security personnel.

The origins of this reaction to the intrusion of the Australian NGO are many. The political temperature was high at Magarini. The previous year had been marked by sometimes violent clashes, when project staff, backed on occasion by armed police, forced Giriama off plots which had been allocated to outsiders. Project files of 1984 record, for instance, that the land of Kambi Sakira had allegedly been taken over by the Project Manager, Kaganzu Joseph's land was claimed by the Forest Officer at Magarini, and so the list of grievances went on. Public questioning of the classification of 'reserved' to a growing number of surveyed plots had led to the disbanding of the Land Allocation Committee, as it was then called, in October 1983. Giriama people felt they were being systematically and rapidly excluded from the project's benefits. The Australian Team Leader employed by McGowans, Charles Adamson, wrote to the Australian High Commission in Nairobi during September 1984 and noted,

> At one time there was a significant training programme for local people who were employed in semi-skilled positions such as level operators, compass readers, mechanics, storemen, map tracers and draftsmen. Virtually all these people have been made redundant and replaced with up country people, predominantly Kikuyu. The latest action is for all Giriama drivers to be transferred out of the project.

In forwarding Adamson's report to Canberra, the High Commissioner appended his view, 'If Australia does not continue with the project, it would be like declaring "open season" for other tribes to move into the project and displace the already beleaguered Giriama'. A measure of the intensity of the conflict is underscored by the Kenyan project manager putting his concerns in writing to MOLS. The land problem, as he termed it, 'had far reaching effects on overall development in that it was feared to destabilise the whole project development strategy' (Confidential source).

The reluctance of government field staff about NGO entry into the area was also rooted in a normal bureaucratic reluctance to give up areas in which hitherto it had enjoyed full sway, and the fact that the intruders' tickets were paid for by the Australian government simply fuelled their unhappiness. It was possible that the NGO, Kenyan or Australian, would uncover sensitive issues concerning patronage and what the Australians had euphemistically termed 'mismanagement of funds'. There is evidence that these practices are widespread in relation to Magarini. It is probable that early Australian dominance in project management fostered an added degree of 'mismanagement' on the part of some Kenyans. In this vein, a senior Kenyan official remarked during 1985, 'In the early stages, MSP was very controlled by the Australians. Too much control when you look back because the Kenyan staff thought, since this is Australian controlled they weren't scared to do anything. They just ate as much as they could.' The basis of this reluctance is understandable. Magarini had involved the direction of considerable resources into a hitherto neglected area. Roads, water pipes, farm inputs, the cooperative, special agricultural extension services and the allocation of land had been the spoils enjoyed by groups who had been able to mobilize and control political processes in their favour. An NGO programme, if true to rhetoric, would result in the disruption of prevailing lines of patronage and divert resources away from those who had traditionally enjoyed the benefits of development.

Nor was the path to the people any easier. At first field workers reported that the Giriama considered 'the NGO are just another bunch of up-country people and there is no major distinction in their mind between government people and others like the NGO'. Then, when relations between the NGO and the Giriama improved, NGO field staff found themselves caught up in the conflict between the Giriama and the project staff. As one member of the field team remarked 'the conflict with outsiders is quite apparent. It's a cold war, full of subterfuge and propaganda.' The NGO was put on trial by both the Giriama community and the project staff, Australian and Kenyan. NGO activities required immediate legitimacy from the community. But the kinds of issues being raised by the Giriama, and more particularly Giriama who were indicating readiness to work with the NGO, placed the NGO in a difficult position. The NGO was unable to take up a neutral position between the project staff and the Giriama. One report from the field explained, 'our problem at the moment in selecting leaders is that there are no moderates, the lines are clearly drawn and the ones the community want to follow with the NGO would have us in the District Commissioner's office quickly.'

First lessons in tactics and strategy

The Feasibility Study Report prepared by AFFHC and KFFHC between February and April 1985, identified certain principles of approach which reflect how the NGOs came to understand both their role and the presumed 'needs' of the people. This report referred at length to a participatory approach which was to enhance people's control over their affairs. It emphasized a process whereby people are brought to a new understanding of their situation; are provided with the skills to consider strategies for change, and to mobilize resources and maintain control of them to secure their interests.

It quickly became apparent that there are many interpretations of 'participation'. The NGO approach received assent from government staff during an orientation workshop convened by the NGO. On the virtues of participation, a senior MOLS official enthused, 'It is important that junior staff [at the workshop] participate freely without fear of seniors, and if they don't participate freely, I will tell them to'. Moments later, a District Officer enjoined all his colleagues to participate in drawing up the plan for the NGO programme. 'Then', he said, 'once it is drawn up, we will help you [the NGO] go out and tell the people what they are expected to do.' Here is a practical example of what commentators on participation have often said; participation is applauded by all, but is extremely difficult to define operationally. It can be both an end in itself and a means to other ends. By and large, external intervention by hierarchical organizations through project aid is the single most important factor in defeating genuine participatory development.[5]

The most pressing issues faced by the Kenya FFHC, as the lead agency, were not, however, theoretical conundrums about participation. It was obvious that the people's needs had to be established from the ground up, and not through the District Officer's helpful offer to sort things out on the people's behalf. But programmes do not grow in isolation. From their earliest beginnings they create expectations in the minds of many people. At Magarini the most powerful expectations were motivated by the pecuniary interest of those who had previously benefited from project funds, by bureaucratic jealousy, and by a stated concern to 'do something for the Giriama', whether simply to keep the lid on things, or to relieve what was for them, an increasingly dismal future. It was no surprise that the NGO programme should create expectations. What is surprising is that few of the 'How to do it' manuals on NGO practice consider the implications for NGO activities of these expectations.

The NGO decided it had to undertake two kinds of fieldwork. The nature and weight of the expectations held by AIDAB and the Kenyan government officials had to be determined. On these expectations depended the NGO's initial legitimacy and its political survival. It was also necessary to rapidly establish some indication from the Giriama as to their needs and from this outline a strategy. The findings of the first fieldwork would largely determine the political space available in which to devise a strategy to meet what the second fieldwork would reveal. The former were quick to reveal themselves. A local NGO field organizer reported in March 1985,

> The power of the chiefs and government appointees and [Magarini] project staff is very much. We will have to be very careful in what we say. The government is already quite clear about what they expect the NGO to do, and if we try something different, even If it is what the groups want, we could get into hot water very quick.

Official expectations

It should be no surprise to the reader that the first overt requirement of the NGO from the project was, to 'put pressure on settlers to take up allocated plots'. The Kenyan project manager could see no other purpose to NGO involvement. He said, 'Unless the NGO can help us with the settler problem and make them stay, I really don't see why the NGO should be allowed in.' By 1985, however, a confidential report prepared for the Office of the President had acknowledged that Magarini should never have been a resettlement scheme. The problems should have been dealt with through the process of land adjudication in which existing use rights would have been confirmed. The author of this report conceded privately to NGO staff,

[T]he whole thing was ill-conceived, both by the Kenyan government who knew only other settlement schemes as their model, and by Australians who really spent no time looking at our experience and what land meant to Kenyans after colonialism. There's not enough land in the scheme to allo-cate to all those who were compensated [who had first priority], we know that now. But it's just not possible to do adjudication in the remaining areas.

In one of those strange twists of politics, the 'mismanagement' of the land allo-cation procedures at Magarini which had resulted in an unknown number of people being added to the allocation lists at the behest of powerful politicians, now meant it was not the 'government's wish' that the NGO should become involved in hastening a process of settlement which would bring this discrep-ancy more quickly to public awareness.

Nevertheless, the government saw plenty for the NGO to go on with. There was the ailing farmers' cooperative for one thing. Farmer participation in the cooperative was dismal, and there was the matter of a large unpaid loan from the project to the cooperative of which, it was hoped, the NGO could 'facili-tate' repayment. Water was also high on the agenda. The NGO was expected to assist water users to take over responsibility for operations and mainten-ance costs of water reticulation on the project, which exceeded the entire water operations budget of Kilifi District. Then there was the question of women's interests and the educational and income-generating activities which the Australian authors of the Appraisal Report had identified as being within the purview of an NGO component.

The NGO brought some of this growing list on itself by its own actions. In an analysis of the local situation, NGO staff had examined many aspects of Magarini, the water reticulation system, land settlement, agriculture and extension services, and had publicized their concern. NGO notes of a meeting late in 1985 with MOLS and Ministry of Water Development (MOWD) officials in Nairobi reported,

It seems as though we are to get it all now. MOWD are adamant that the NGO should take over all research on water options and extend to live-stock, operations and maintenance of the GWRS [ground water reticulation system], hand over of the reticulation to settlers and organise the settlers' revenue contributions. The Deputy Director of Water just decided this and copied his decision to the PS in OP! [Permanent Secretary in the Office of the President]. This is obviously us reaping the 'rewards' for pointing out, via [KFFHC water engineer and KWAHO engineer's] visit to MSP, that the whole thing was likely to be unsustainable. Now MOWD want to avoid responsibility. The problem for us is not so much taking on these responsibilities, there's simply no way we could or would want to, but rather the consequences of refusing. KFFHC have two other programmes which depend on MOWD counterpart support. The NGO can't at this stage simply say no. Then MOLS/DOS raved on about the NGO changing settlers' attitudes, assimilating the up-country people, getting the agricultural packages (whatever they are) adopted by the farmers – generally everything but the kitchen sink for the NGO.

The intention of the Kenyan government was to prompt KFFHC into quick and concrete actions. But at another level was the presumption, perhaps the hope, that the NGO knew how to save the situation. Not only were the tasks of the NGO circumscribed, but the channels the NGO would use and the scale of response were well established in the government mind. We do not have a record of statements from the Kenyan side, but Australian FFHC correspondence to AIDAB indicates what was expected of them. First, it was expected that the NGO would work through existing groups, but,

> Experience shows that members of 'representative' groups like existing women's groups or local leaders are frequently the more privileged members of the community and cannot be expected to act in the interests of the broader 'non-member' population. But in the eyes of local authorities, it is expected that the NGO will work initially at least, through existing institutions and groups. The task for the NGO is to begin in such a way that maintains their political legitimacy in terms of these expectations and yet also succeeds in establishing lasting relations with the people most in need of assistance. This is an extremely difficult task
>
> (AFFHC 4 December 1985)

Magarini Project staff expected a large-scale intervention from the NGO,

> Unless the NGO program is developed in a participatory manner it will not gain the confidence, and therefore the legitimacy of the target groups. In terms of legitimacy, we start with a big handicap. ... A big-bang-heaps-of-people-and-dollars approach will not work. An NGO program must be small and extremely modest to begin with. This way we can minimise the damage of mistakes (which are inevitable) and maximise the flexibility to change direction and grasp opportunities as they arise.
>
> (AFFHC 11 April 1985)

As evidenced by the project manager's remark about 'letting the NGO in', it was fully expected that the NGO would fall within the management structure of the project, that is, it would become a component in the established project strategy.

Assessing the people's needs

Although little was known on the project about the history and social anthropology of the Giriama people, even less was known about single-women headed households and unemployed or landless youth, two groups of particular interest to the NGO. This part of the community was largely silent, unorganized, without leaders and heavily patronized by others. Enough was known about these people to be sceptical about the official versions of community need. An NGO trainer/organizer pointed out, 'MSP is a building without foundations. And we're being asked to help the landlord to rent it out'. It was also apparent that women's interests had been disregarded by the project but, other than providing support to the semi-obligatory women's group craft clubs so often a part of NGO reponses to women's interests, it was difficult to know what to do. For, as Alan Robertson (1984: 173) observes, 'The notion of discrete "women's interests" is ideologically fashionable, but notoriously vague and unreal in the context of the local community.' Other messages coming back to the NGO from its field staff were less easy to understand. Everyone assumed the water 'problem' would be agreed by all parties, but one fieldworker commented, at the height of the dry season, 'of course we talked about water to the people. ... But it seems pretty clear from our first three months in the field that water is not the major issue for them.'

How then did the NGO first gain access to and then assess the needs of the Giriama people? The Feasibility Study considered five approaches to these matters, and decided to limit direct intervention in the area to three training and organizing specialists from the Undugu Society of Kenya. This society is a large indigenous NGO which grew out of work with urban slum dwellers in Nairobi, and which specializes in group formation, leadership training and support to economic enterprise development. Although AIDAB and the Kenyan government had agreed to the proposals of the Feasibility Report, this report made no concrete commitments to specific development activities beyond what was known as Pre-Phase I which was to run from May to December 1985. The intention of Pre-Phase I was to identify around twenty people who could at one level be conventional NGO extension agents, while at another would have primary responsibility to their local communities and not to the NGO. They were to be known as 'Animators', and in the original French sense of the word, would act as motivators of the community in which they lived. In the event nine Animators were selected following their participation in a number of workshops where they discussed the results of a listening survey they conducted in their home areas. The listening surveys were undertaken to give the Animators a more critical awareness of community needs, to assist them to understand the concept of 'participatory facilitation' and to provide the NGO with a means of identifying the most important local concerns. The Animators also identified what David Korten (1989: 3) calls 'member-accountable people's organisations', existing or potential local organizations which would ensure accountability of leaders to their members.

The NGO intended that the programme would be developed from issues, needs and interests expressed by the communities in a participatory manner. But it became clear that there were considerable constraints to proper participation. We have mentioned the alienation of the Giriama from the project, official surveillance and the dependency-forming consequences of ten years of experience with food-for-work and other Magarini activities. People's participation, even within their own organizations, is influenced by their 'life chances', which means that different people participate in their organizations with different levels of intensity. These life chances mean that the poor tend also to be the physically weak, the uneducated, those without experience in meetings, and those so taken up with survival that little time is available for other pursuits. Consequently, Magarini's model farmers tended to dominate existing men's associations; educated women dominated the executive functions and crowded-out 'speaking space' of women without schooling; young people tended to be silent when their elders were present, as were women when men were present. Considerable effort was needed to develop peoples' skills in the analysis of issues to enable them to consider how their objectives were being distorted by existing leadership and patterns of community control, and to allow them to speak about their needs confidentially, before it would be possible to move further than the shopping list of wants that is so often the outcome of the participatory needs identification NGOs pride themselves on.

Toward the end of 1985, KFFHC and Undugu Society staff were able to draw together a list of five priority concerns which they regarded as the real interests of the Giriama people in the Magarini area. In order of significance and in the words of the field records (Malindi NGO Programme 1986), these were:

Land security. Local people believe that pre-colonial and colonial activities displaced them from their birth-right of land ownership and use. MSP has added to this problem. The pattern of land settlement within the scheme is seen as going against the Giriama traditional ways of arranging their homesteads which ensure in-built social and economic security systems through inter-dependency of the wider family.

Traditional Giriama identity and institutions. Closely associated with a relationship to the land, but also includes several activities and groups – such as religious, traditional song and dance clubs, tribal and clan festivals and ceremonies and traditional leadership and decision making systems, all of which were seen as under threat from 'development'. Traditional ways of organizing life are commonly seen as being more democratic and participatory – perhaps with a tinge of romanticism – than contemporary life. Identity, like land was being sold off to foreigners.

Poverty. Due to unjustified trade systems and imposed foreign values, poverty has afflicted the community badly. Women, children and old people are seen as the hardest hit by this; and MSP has passed them by. But when looking at the usual activities trying to overcome poverty, like poultry, rabbit and goat rearing, bakery and other group-based income activities, the wrong target, inappropriate designs and the like were such that these were cited as a hindrance to achieving the objectives.

Diseases and ill-health. This reflects the chronic seasonal food deficits in the area, but the interest is based on a contrast between traditional and scientific health care systems. People have a strong appreciation of both systems, but scientific medicine was found to be inadequate and subject to abuse, whereas traditional medicine was very much directed towards the mysterious causes of diseases rather than visible and felt symptoms. Here also was the first mention of water as a contributing factor to ill-health.

Ignorance. Ignorance of basic rights and entitlements, of the way in which élite patronage systems were capturing government resources.

Three features of this list deserve comment. First is the obvious contrast between official versions of the people's needs and what the NGO believed the Giriama people themselves considered to be their greatest needs. Second is the preoccupation of project and official versions of the people's need with materialist considerations. Clearly material needs are not unrelated to people's aspirations, cultural needs or personal self-actualization. But the NGO list contains a clear warning for development practitioners schooled in the Western understanding of how needs are to be placed in a hierarchy. Abraham Maslow's famous (1970) 'hierarchy of needs' is pervasive in development assistance (Figure 5.1) and persuades us that the fulfilment of physiological needs such as food and water precedes the consideration of questions of identity and esteem, or the fundamentals of cultural values. The third feature of the NGO list of needs is that the official version not only failed to mention any of them, but systematically blocked their discussion.

THE POLITICS OF RESPONDING TO THE PEOPLE'S NEEDS: STRATEGIES VERSUS TACTICS

The Magarini Project had been from its beginnings, a settlement project designed to dismantle traditional extended families and replace an existing farming system. It was a designated project of national importance, intended to break down ethnic identity and to contribute to the struggle to form 'One Kenya'. In its desire to meet the expressed needs of the Giriama, the NGO also had to acknowledge these fundamental political realities. It attempted to do this by distinguishing between what it called its tactics and its strategy. But this distinction was not a simple matter and it remains today, within the NGO,

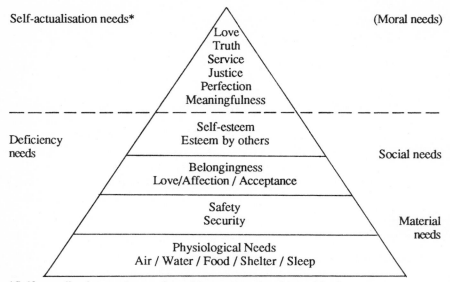

Self-actualisation needs*   (Moral needs)

Love
Truth
Service
Justice
Perfection
Meaningfulness

Deficiency   Self-esteem
needs   Esteem by others   Social needs

Belongingness
Love/Affection / Acceptance

Safety
Security   Material
needs

Physiological Needs
Air / Water / Food / Shelter / Sleep

*Self-actualization needs are of equal importance (not hierarchical)

Figure 5.1 Maslow's (1970) hierarchy of needs.

Source: Maslow, (1970)

the most intensely debated aspect of the programme at Magarini.

Tactically, the NGO had to be seen to be responding to the official versions of need which were far removed from, and at times antagonistic to, expressed community interests. The NGO's presence in the area was tenuous, and dependent on powerful national political support which could be withdrawn at any time. Kenyan NGOs, like most in east and southern Africa, are politically weak and are allowed to operate because they are judged to be complementary to government policy (see Hyden 1983: 111). The NGO therefore produced a statement of objectives as a tactical move designed to satisfy national and district political interests and to create a space for activities which would lead to the achievement of strategic objectives. The tactical objectives were:

1 to strengthen the contribution of programme participants in operating and maintaining water reticulation and surface water storage facilities;
2 to undertake community development activities related to the use and maintenance of water facilities in health and nutrition, food production and income generation;

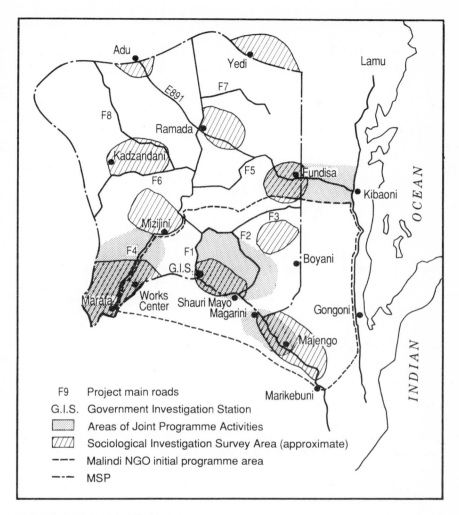

Figure 5.2 Malindi NGO programme.

3 to assist the target group to acquire the technical, financial and institutional resources to ensure programme activities are self-sustaining after the withdrawal of NGO support.

To further avoid incorporation in the overall management structure of the Magarini Project, the NGO programme argued their area of operations should not include all the the Magarini Project area, and in fact should incorporate other locations to the south and east of the project on the basis that this was where the project intended to extend in the future (Figure 5.2). The NGO operations could therefore prepare the ground for future settlement activities. With this accepted, it was agreed that the NGO should relate directly to the District Development Committee and not the project management.

Thus the NGO programme developed around three key activity areas – water, health and nutrition, and credit and income, which were clearly supportive of project objectives. But each of these activities was also viewed as an entry point for other activities which would attempt to enhance people's capacities to assess and act on other interests. Politically, it was impossible for the NGO, in particular the Animators working through existing community groups, to make a direct or open approach to the community on these latter issues. But improved water supply was of importance to local people and was also an officially approved activity. It could therefore be approached directly by the NGO, as the beginning, or entry point, to a longer and more circuitous course of action to the people's real interests. This approach has its dangers, political as well as practical. A practical danger, which we discuss further below, is the possibility that entry point activities like building a well, or providing management training to a women's group, become ends in themselves. Just as the project staff lost sight of the longer term aims of agricultural sustainability amidst the practical problems of clearing the scrub, so too can the NGO easily lose sight of its longer term strategies, in the flurries of a tactical battle. The sequence of the NGO project activities is listed in the chronology in Chapter One (Appendix 1).

EVALUATION: 'CALLING IN THE JURY'

If NGOs are frequently forced to conceal their real or strategic objectives behind a front of officially approved, or tactical objectives, how do their sponsors judge achievements of these tactical objectives? More importantly, how does an NGO judge for itself whether or not it has met its strategic objectives? There are some in the NGO community who believe it is not possible to assess the effectiveness of small-scale NGO development assistance because criteria for objectives such as enhancing the self-confidence of the poor or changing their awareness about the structural problems that deny them access to basic entitlements, are too difficult to determine (B. Smith 1987). Nevertheless, two aspects of the Malindi NGO programme are of particular relevance to an enquiry into the evaluation of NGO projects and of the NGO role in development in general. First, we can look closely at what NGOs take to be their primary comparative advantage, their responsiveness to real needs and participatory methods. Second, we can examine what is fast becoming the NGOs' Achilles' Heel. Following increased funding of NGOs in the 1980s, government and multilateral aid agencies are beginning to call in the jury and ask whether NGOs have any relevance beyond the highly localized, fragmentary project. NGOs are being faced with the vexed problem of how to ensure the sustainability of their operations with an increase in scale, whilst retaining the essential qualities of responsiveness, autonomy and community control possible at the small scale.[6]

It is doubtful whether the NGO programme at Magarini has met the expectations AIDAB heaped upon it at the beginning of 1985. AIDAB views have wavered according to the mood and disposition of the desk officer responsible at the time, around five or six over the four years, but one theme runs through all five AIDAB reviews of the NGO programme:

> The NGO component is well programmed, developmentally sound and of direct relevance to the community management approach, and will probably result in a significant transfer of information and technology in terms of the approach required to develop a successful community management approach to water development.
>
> (AIDAB November 1986)

These remarks need to be read in the knowledge that for some time AIDAB staff had been conscious of having a problem project on their hands. The 1987 Joint Review Mission (JRM) made a last, if futile, attempt to salvage critical issues concerning water and food security, and nothing the NGO has done since then has ameliorated the distressing water, food and environmental future projected for the area. But it is not easy to get out of a bad project, particularly when the project has left people worse off than before it began. In 1989, Bob Dun, Director General of AIDAB, acknowledged this difficulty and conceded that AIDAB support to the NGO for this reason was possibly open-ended. Thus AIDAB's formal opinion of the NGO programme, whatever its developmental merits, is coloured by the opportunity the programme has offered for AIDAB to 'withdraw with honour' from Magarini. Direct Australian financial contributions to Magarini have declined to about A$230,000 in the 1989/90 year, a fraction of Phase III annual expenditure until its termination in mid-1988, although funds are still flowing to the project through the sale of Australian wheat in Kenya. This matter aside, does the NGO performance at Magarini demonstrate that special talent attributed to NGOs, that they can uniquely facilitate the participation of the poor, and mobilize resources, skills and capacity for development that is sustainable and equitable?[7] We examine only the entry point activities of the health/nutrition, income-generating and water activities, which featured in the statement of programme objectives.

Health and nutrition

Studies elsewhere indicate that NGOs can make significant headway in the areas of health and nutrition.[8] The Health/Nutrition Activity began in July 1986 with a twelve-month programme of research by an anthropologist (Thompson) which aimed, to analyse the relationship between available scientific medical knowledge and indigenous Giriama diagnoses and treatment of illnesses; to formulate a health intervention programme reflecting this research; and to establish a low cost system of monitoring health and nutrition.

(KFFHC November 1988)

The prime purpose of this study was to determine how illnesses are socially interpreted and what explanations of causality are used in diagnoses and treatment, in the belief that NGO interventions would be more effective if they did not conflict with, and as far as possible drew on the legitimacy of traditional knowledge.

The research established that three water-related illnesses (malaria, bilharzia [urinary schistosomiasis] and diarrhoea) together accounted for a large proportion of an infant mortality rate reported as 180 per thousand in Kilifi District (the second highest in Kenya). In collaboration with the Division of Vector Borne Diseases of the Ministry of Health, the NGO embarked on a three-phased programme of testing and treatment for bilharzia and malaria (and, in 1988, added intestinal worms and protozoa) which was intended to provide a vehicle for health education and household follow-up activities in disease prevention. During 1989 these follow-up activities were expanded to environmental sanitation (latrines, rubbish pits, food storage and preparation facilities), water storage (roof catchments) and food production and income-generating activities, in each of the five study locales (Figure 5.2). A 1988 review of progress indicated bilharzia infection rates in school children tested had dropped (between March 1986 and July 1988) from 54 per cent to 6.6 per cent in the most improved locale and from 28 per cent to 3.4 per cent in the community with least impact. This compares with an infection rate of over 60 per cent in a community introduced to the programme during July 1988 (KFFHC November 1988: 5).

Small group commercial activities

In contrast to this broad-based activity, KFFHC began intensive work with between twenty and thirty existing, predominantly women's groups, concentrating on income-generating activities ranging from livestock raising and poultry production to collectively operated shops, bakeries and tea kiosks. This is politically the most difficult area of the NGO activity because of the attention that small projects receive from would-be political patrons. At the beginning of this programme a MOLS official warned NGO staff,

Politics in Kenya is the politics of small projects. In place of party politics we have project politics. So in politics to succeed, you must design yourself, or buy yourself a project. So you, as the NGO, if you have a good project, some politician will find it, and that applies to the individual women's group you help as much as to the big project.

In Kenya during the 1970s, what is known as the 'ten thousand shilling mentality' resulted in the formation of thousands of small rural groups like the Magarini women's groups. Many Kenyan NGOs view them as the single most important factor undermining local initiatives. George Omondi, Director of the NGO programme explained,

> Once a politician attaches himself to a project, you run the risk of being labelled as a supporter of that politician. In one sense this might be okay if the politician is a 'champion of the poor', or if he sees things our way. But what happens if he challenges a Minister of the Government?

To avoid these debilitating effects of throwing money at group enterprises, and in the knowledge that the main problems of existing groups did not include a shortage of capital, the NGO programme withheld financial assistance to participating groups for three years. Group activities such as the health and water activities were also used to extend organizing skills and analytical capacity to the community. KFFHC staff at Magarini were aware that group enterprises seldom succeed in rural Kenya, but they believed that wilful community actions had to be backed by productive capacity to be sustainable in the long run. Therefore a group-managed credit and finance scheme was developed in 1988 and 1989 with selected groups which provides small loans to individual member enterprises. The time taken for these activities to gain momentum was a notable feature of the programme and is a major point of contrast with the quick and decisive action expected by the official sponsors of the NGO programme.

Reaching the poorest of the poor?

Another claim of NGOs is that they can reach the poorest sections of the community. The Magarini experience, together with experience elsewhere, suggests that reaching the poorest members of a community directly is very difficult. It also suggests that if NGOs believe too strongly in their own rhetoric they may miss more important points. Some activities are very difficult to manage if the whole community has to be consulted before a decision can be made and it is not always the case that the activities being promoted by these projects are automatically 'better' if the whole community, including the poorest, participate fully. On the other hand, some things which will improve the life of the poor require the involvement and acquiescence of the rich. It was not possible at Magarini, for example, to deal with the bilharzia problem of the poor, without the cooperation of the whole community. If water was to be made available to the landless, access to isolated water sources had to be secured from landowners. Even in situations where clear-cut divisions exist between groups in a community, there is often little choice but to work with the community's existing leaders who are more than likely the élite. At Magarini, after a prolonged period of reflection in workshops about leadership styles and participation led by the NGO, when communities were left to select their leaders for training, the persons chosen were usually existing leaders drawn from an educated élite.

The problem of deciding who was benefiting most from the NGO programme at Magarini was not, however, merely a question of differences between the poor and the well off. Throughout discussions in 1988 local NGO field staff raised questions about who the principal beneficiaries of the NGO programme really were. They were not raising perennial concerns over whether resources intended for the poorest were being captured by the élite. Rather, their questions stemmed from the realization that because the NGO programme was ameliorating problems created by the project, it was potentially blunting the edge of social protest. The field staff knew the Giriama had identified threats to their cultural identity and landlessness as their two greatest problems. The NGO, the local staff suggested, rather than being an agent of significant intervention into the circumstances which were creating the major fundamental disruption to Giriama life, was merely being a palliative. One event in particular illustrates their point.

The Joint Kenya–Australia Review Mission (JRM) of March 1987 endorsed the establishment of a Water and Food Security Consultative Group (WFSCG) combining Kenyan and Australian project staff, representatives from the NGO programme, the District Commissioner and senior officials from the Ministries of Water Development and Agriculture. For a twelve-month trial period, the NGO was encouraged to undertake water catchment development activities jointly with project water staff – the JRM had promoted surface water (dams, ponds, shallow wells and roof catchments) as a priority in light of the probable failure of the groundwater reticulation system. The NGO had lobbied for the WFSCG, a grouping that was to break down the control of the project over key decisions, and create a balance between headquarters, district and local interests, and an avenue for the NGO to assist local groups to gain access to project resources such as machinery, skills and materials.

For the first six months from July 1987, NGO staff worked with potential community water committees to identify sites for development, to explain and highlight how project resources could be drawn upon and to mobilize local contributions of labour and materials. But the expected 'coordination' with the project did not occur. Repeated community deputations to the project management, with NGO assistance, failed to secure the delivery of project resources. Faced with a credibility problem in the eyes of the community, the NGO converted funds from its own budget to purchase diesel, concrete blocks and cement, rather than lose momentum in an activity for which they had joint responsibility with the community.

This experience prompted local NGO staff to re-assess relationships between the NGO programme, the Magarini Project and the people. 'Here we are providing resources for the same water sources that have already been funded by the project budget', one argued. Another observed that the NGO activities now included activities which were really activities the project was obligated to carry out. Another made the point, 'The NGO is providing not so much an alternative infrastructure for aid delivery as a system for "looting the people" again.' Aid dollars, far in excess of what the community could command, were being raised in the name of the people, 'but the project doesn't deliver'. These staff argued that by helping to organize the mobilization of local contributions of labour and materials, the NGO was abetting 'the project double-dipping into the community's pocket'.

Kenyan NGO staff believe this type of situation is not well understood in the offices of Northern donor NGOs. The progressive debates among Northern development agencies contrast those who argue for palliative interventions and those who support transformational interventions. Palliative intervention is said to be what governments do. Many NGOs believe they deal with transformation and the root causes of social injustice. The Magarini experience suggests that this is a gross simplification. Enough has been said about the uncertainties of development practice and the host of unintended consequences, good and bad, which are promoted by transformational project interventions, to demand caution in using this dichotomy to judge the worth of field activities. As Elliot (1987: 58) cautions, 'There is clear evidence that welfare delivery, development, conscientisation and empowerment are much more subtly interrelated than is assumed by the simple spectrum.'

The exhortation to respond to real needs must be tempered with practical experience. At a general level Goran Hyden (1983: 111) argues,

> NGOs are not going to solve the problems of underdevelopment... nor will, as we now know from experience in post-colonial Africa, cataclysmic political changes. Material conditions in African countries, with very few exceptions, are not really congenial to revolutionary acts of change. To that extent, development in Africa is likely to come about only in a piecemeal fashion. In view of the popularity of the blueprint approach, this will be difficult for many to accept. Yet a mental reorientation on this point is likely to be a prerequisite to progress. What is needed is a longer time perspective on development, more patience with the inadequacies inherent in the contemporary situation, and greater tolerance with new institutions, formal as well as informal.

It is evident from long-running programmes that the rural poor can be mobilized for significant change. But it is worth noting that the more outstanding movements have not come out of explosions of discontent or direct confrontation. Experience suggests direct intervention to meet 'real interests' is less likely to be transformative than astutely organized tactics which recognize the often fuzzy and indeterminate relations between what Malindi NGO staff call 'entry points' and 'end points'. When we review the origins of activities which brought about significant changes at the local level at Magarini, we find that some were government initiatives, others NGO, some originated in national policy, while others were truly localized 'bottom-up' efforts; some dealt with palliative activities, like health training, some involved siding with the poor while others made no distinction between rural classes or the poorest and less poor.

Who bears the risk?

Serious ethical questions are raised for NGOs by the necessity for them to have two development agendas, one acceptable to governments and another which attempts to address the real needs of the people. NGOs face the real danger that they will make the very short journey from believing, in Tim Brodhead's words, that they have 'unique access to and knowledge of the real needs and aspirations of the people' to believing that they know better than the people, who, by virtue of poor education, lack of knowledge of the world outside the village, or their overwhelming concern with immediate survival, have distorted or wrong ideas about their situation or 'real needs'. If they reach this point, NGO workers are perilously close to being in the same position as many non-NGO development project staff who frequently quite openly, and often with the same humanitarian concerns, know what is best for the people.

Robert Chambers' remarks about risks in development practice are pertinent given the sharpening of political tensions often accompanying NGO programmes (1983: 164). Figure 5.3 shows how, as we move from essentially palliative interventions toward transformational changes, there is an accompanying shift in acceptability to élites and official gatekeepers who define what passes as legitimate development work. NGOs, generally speaking, can penetrate local communities, can establish excellent rapport with people and are flexible enough to take on whatever political hue is acceptable to people. NGO workers who think they know what is best for the people have, therefore, a far more insidious potential to manipulate community responses than non-NGO project staff who are clearly identifiable as outsiders and who are recognized by the community as posing a risk to them. Thus the bedrock of the NGO credibility is at once both their strongest and potentially their weakest, most vulnerable and dangerous feature.

At Magarini, perhaps because of the circumstances in which the NGO became involved in the project, the dangers of this situation were recognized early in the programme. This difficulty above all others is the reason why the NGO programme took so long to get going, in the views of AIDAB and the project, and why it has been so reluctant to become involved in funding 'participatory community projects'. The NGO has retained an element of self-doubt, has tried to remain as autonomous as possible, and has taken seriously its belief that effective participation depends on the development of analytical skills and articulacy among the people.

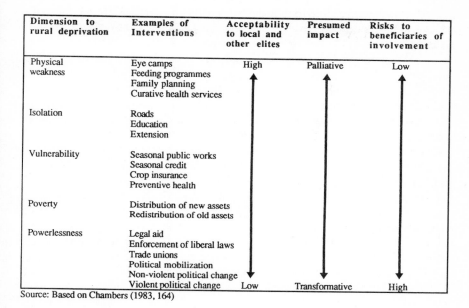

Dimension to rural deprivation	Examples of Interventions	Acceptability to local and other elites	Presumed impact	Risks to beneficiaries of involvement
Physical weakness	Eye camps Feeding programmes Family planning Curative health services	High	Palliative	Low
Isolation	Roads Education Extension			
Vulnerability	Seasonal public works Seasonal credit Crop insurance Preventive health			
Poverty	Distribution of new assets Redistribution of old assets			
Powerlessness	Legal aid Enforcement of liberal laws Trade unions Political mobilization Non-violent political change Violent political change	Low	Transformative	High

Source: Based on Chambers (1983, 164)

Figure 5.3 Acceptability and risks of rural development approaches.

FRAGMENTARY AND ISOLATED?

Sustainability?

It is fair to ask, if the NGO has been so intent on swimming against the stream of events at Magarini, what is the sustainability of its stroke and the scale of its splash?

When people ask about sustainability, it is the products of development interventions, the entry points, they most often have in mind. Are the shallow wells constructed being maintained by the user community? Does the government system provide enough back-up to ensure that the improved health systems are maintained? Does the women's bakery group set aside funds to cover maintenance costs of the ovens and equipment? Alongside product sustainability, it should be evident from discussion of the longer term strategic objectives of the Malindi NGO programme that what might be called 'process' sustainability is important too. Has the experience gained through participation in water projects, or in the group-based credit programme, led to a wider capacity within the community to tackle other concerns, whether these be additional wells, or activities outside the scope of the NGO programme, from which political sensitivities precluded direct NGO attention?

NGOs do not have a particularly good record on the first measure. Robert Cassen's study concludes that even though 65–76 per cent of projects do achieve their stated objectives, something of the order of two-thirds are not sustained (1986: 111). The documentary record on NGOs shows somewhat disappointing results too. In 1980 a study commissioned by the EEC found that only five of twenty-six projects they examined were sustainable in the economic or financial sense (CEC 1981). More recently, Tim Brodhead's study of NGOs concludes that less than half had little chance of surviving without longer term infusions of foreign human or financial resources (Brodhead *et al.* 1988).

It is too early to assess whether the efforts of KFFHC at Magarini will fare any better. We have more to say about process sustainability below, but whether the products of the development interventions are sustainable will depend on many factors, including how well they fit with community needs, whether the task, maintaining a well for example, is suited to the character of the group assembled by the community, and whether the basic skills necessary to collect revenue, install spare parts, and organize labour to perform these tasks, have been acquired. These matters will, in turn, have been determined by the quality of the participation by the community in the programme. Benefit sustainability is not dependent on participation in every case, but participation in each stage, from the time an idea is first expressed by the community, through to getting a new venture running, is a reliable indicator of long term sustainability.

Marginal in marginal environments

NGOs worldwide are re-examining the question of sustainability in relation to the scale of impact. NGOs have recognized that by acting on their own they can never hope to benefit more than a few isolated communities. They are aware of evidence that success or failure in terms of sustainability depends frequently on how well local activities promoted by NGOs are linked with the government, the banking system, or with mercantile interests. There are widely differing views amongst Third World and donor NGOs about this problem. Some acknowledge that NGOs are indeed marginal but argue that they should avoid incorporation into larger structures, and should discard idealistic dreams that they can organize an alternative future on a large scale. This argument associates increased scale with a corresponding loss of independence and autonomy, and a detachment from the interests of constituent local groups and individuals.

The NGO programme at Magarini is marginal in a geographic sense, as a glance at the map of Kenya shows. But it is worth considering other aspects of the NGO's marginality which illustrate relatively neglected issues. Much has been said about the environments in which NGOs are considered to be most effective. The first refers to physically marginal environments, which in Africa refs to areas occupied by pastoralists or semi-nomadic communities, and to people devastated by climatic disturbance, degraded lands, and under threat of displacement by sedentary agriculture, which the state is either too heavy-handed or inflexible to assist effectively. The historical record of state intervention with such populations supports this case (see, for example, Walker 1987).

The second kind of marginal environment in which NGOs are said to be more effective is in sectors where the state system is ineffective or inoperative. This recognition acknowledges that the policy reach of the African state is typically beyond its operational grasp, a remark which will have increasingly greater pertinence as IMF-conditioned public sector spending cuts take hold. NGOs are said to provide an alternative institutional structure for the delivery of services in this environment. Although it is questionable whether governments will ever be able to resume their responsibilities, a growing proportion of NGO assistance is directed into stop-gap activities as a substitute for services which were previously the responsibility of Third World governments.

These two kinds of marginal environment often coincide. It is argued that with larger geographic scales of operation, NGOs can expect to reduce their institutional marginality, according to the recipe that the bigger their purse and scale of operations, the bigger the institutional and political clout they can mobilize in the interests of their beneficiaries. But geographical scale and institutional clout can be related in quite perverse ways. Magarini is classically marginal in the physical sense, but institutionally the opposite is true. Magarini is a politically contested area, and has been since the 1890s. It is a land settlement frontier, and most important, it has been the location of high levels of government expenditure and donor investment for over a decade. While the NGO programme is marginal in terms of its geographic scale, despite the formidable vested interests rallied against it, it has survived and enlarged both the resources accessible by the community and the institutional space in which these resources can be used by the particular sections of the community in their own interests. The NGO consciously chose not to attempt to capture a larger part of the project budget, or to gain direct control over project plant and equipment. Partly this choice reflected the inability of the NGO to amass the staff, managerial and logistical requirements in the time required. But while there would have been support from the Australian government for the NGO to follow this path (and from other donor agencies which had expressed interest in providing additional funds), there were also clear signals from senior Kenyan officials that there would be immediate political repercussions if the NGO tried to make a claim on the project. NGO staff were warned by at least one official, 'If you do this, it will be the death knell for us, and we just can't let you do it'.

Many of the significant changes occurring at Magarini since 1985 were promoted by the NGO, through anonymous lobbying in a very circuitous manner

through networks of alliances with government officials created for this express purpose. The tactical entry points of the problems with water,
settlement and agriculture on the Magarini Project, were reviewed and publicized by the NGO staff during 1985. These issues had been raised in the early
stages of the project, but were obstinately excluded from the agenda for years.
Where efforts by NGO staff to tackle such issues through community representation or direct consultations with project staff failed, from early 1987,
NGO persistence moved control over key project decisions from the project
to the District Development Committee, and it was the NGO which behind
the scenes drafted terms of reference for joint government missions, and provided the background briefings, verbal and written, for these missions.

As a result, the Water and Food Security Consultative Group (WFSCG),
inspired and briefed by the NGO, began to take the initiative from the project
management. The Australian managing agent found it increasingly difficult to
justify continued contracts for services since AIDAB now had an alternative
source of information about events in the field, and in 1987, a very significant
redirection of Australian resources occurred, away from the groundwater reticulation, roading and land clearing towards NGO concerns of water and
food security. The Australian government dispensed with the services of the
managing agent in the middle of Phase III, apparently the first time AIDAB
has removed a consultant from a large project. NGO staff increasingly gained
more influence over project activities in both management and field-level
operations. The intention in promoting the WFSCG, which was ratified by the
Joint Review Mission in March 1987, was to establish pilot areas where both
NGO and project staff would cooperate in developing land management areas
around water catchments where a combined water and food security strategy
could be tried on a pilot basis (Figure 5.2). The NGO legitimized their involvement through reference to their contacts with the community, to supportive
government policy (which was replete with references to community participation, mobilization of local resources and initiative, and the complementary
role of NGOs) and the genuine belief of AIDAB officials that the NGO had
something to offer beyond the prospect of the much sought after honourable
withdrawal from Magarini.

The NGO hoped this approach would give it and the community better
access to project resources, without the political risks which would have been
involved in a direct attempt to capture a share of these resources. Despite the
successes described above, this approach failed in the longer term to gain the
NGO or the community sustained access to project resources and further, was
partly responsible for the cynicism which began to develop among local NGO
staff, expressed in remarks about 'looting the people' and 'double-dipping'
into the community's pocket. As a result, since mid-1988, joint NGO–Project
operations and the WFSCG have ceased. Only in the area of health has the
NGO continued to maintain direct links with government services in the
Magarini Project area.

BENEFITS AND COSTS OF SCALING-UP: LOSING COHERENCE

During March 1988, just prior to the scheduled arrival of an AIDAB Review Mission to examine progress on joint NGO–Project water and food security activities, KFFHC arranged for an independent evaluation of the NGO programme (Wanyama 1988). The purpose was to assess the needs of and the need for, each programme component, in terms of responsiveness to community needs, the results of coordination with the project, and to recommend modifications in the NGO programme as required. The evaluator, a Kenyan with much rural development and NGO experience, concluded that the NGO programme had, over the previous nine months of cooperation with Magarini Project, rapidly lost coherence both in terms of field staff understanding of the relations between immediate tactical objectives and longer term strategic goals and more significantly, their association with community interests. The pace of field activities was no longer directed by the participating community groups, and the integration between the various components of water, health and income-generating had become severely disjointed.

These conclusions prompted a serious re-appraisal by all staff of their activities. The NGO programme at Magarini was facing the fundamental dilemma of NGOs which attempt to move to larger scale, sustainable development initiatives: how to sustain an activity which is largely informal, spontaneous and locally initiated and controlled, whilst benefiting from the economic and political advantages of increased geographic and administrative scale? We will examine only two features of this dilemma. The first concerns the political consequences of incorporating local initiatives into large projects with regional and national objectives. The second again raises the matter of a control-orientation in development practice, discussed in Chapter Four.

Incorporation

The NGO literature contains increasing calls for NGOs to scale-up, either by capturing the ever-frequent multilateral and bilateral agency offers of larger budgets and agendas, or by closely integrating with wider government development activities. Whether the justifications are couched in terms of helping the state to reach down to the people, or helping the people to reach up to the state, the intention is the same. The scale of the Third World rural problem is so immense that NGOs must move in from the margins to the mainstream of development practice. This challenge to the NGOs has occurred coincidentally with a recent dusting off of long-shelved post-independence books about decentralization and local mobilization by many Third World governments. Kenya's District Focus for Rural Development policy, announced in 1984, is similar to policies throughout eastern and southern Africa. This policy speaks of making each district the focal point of rural development. It is intended to enhance coordination of resources and local efforts, and to motivate the

Plate 18 Selling their identity: ancestor memorial post in a tourist shop

people and incorporate the wishes and proposals of the people who are in close contact with the real problems.[9]

In Kenya, collective community action is a feature of indigenous ethnic group cultures. People of the Luo tribe call it *konyir kende*, the neighbouring Luhya call it *obwasio*, the Kikuyu people refer to similar labour and material exchanges as *ngwatio*. The Giriama know this form of exchange as *mweria*. The Kenyan national institution of *harambee*, popularized by the post-independence government of Jomo Kenyatta, is a now famous example of generalizing the practice of collective and cooperative participation. The manner in which *harambee* is now used in Kenya is probably a good indication of the local-level future of the new District Focus for Rural Development policy.[10]

Before the extension of the market economy and private ownership of land, *harambee* efforts were oriented to production of basic needs through an exchange of labour and forms of mutual assistance. They served educational purposes too, and are said to have reinforced group identity and fostered group morals and ethics (Orora and Spiegel 1979; Ngau 1987). *Harambee* remains a keystone of national policy on rural development, in the building of schools, health facilities, cattle dips, roads, bridges and water facilities. But incorporation into a national development programme has resulted in what

Ngau (1987: 523) calls 'disempowerment and departicipation' among local communities. Only the material ends of *harambee* have been appropriated and local people participate less and less in decision making, management and control of projects. Integration, says Ngau, has overwhelmed the ability of peasant farmers to control their activities, and contributions of materials and labour have become increasingly coerced and compulsory. According to Thomas, another recent observer of *harambee*, it has been 'used by all to justify the accumulation of wealth in an economic system which fosters great inequities. It is also used to legitimise the amassing of power because it serves as a key instrument whereby those who are most powerful can best aid their local communities' (1986: 477). Practically speaking, *harambee* has not led to long-term organizational efforts, the particular efforts are *ad hoc* and task oriented, the regulatory structures have created disincentives to locally based activities and '*pro forma* regulation, compliance, together with official inertia, [has] resulted in delays and idleness on projects' (Ngau 1987: 533).

This history of the consequences of incorporation of local initiatives into national development priorities underpinned the concern of KFFHC staff. Nor is the experience restricted to Kenya. From the Etawah Project in India in 1952, arguably the first of its type, through to Tanzania's *ujamaa* village resettlement programme, the consequences of state incorporation of local institutions and participation are well documented (Korten 1980: 482). *Ujamaa* was based on the principle of voluntarism which, after government efforts to dovetail local and national imperatives through the Villages Act of 1975, became 'part of a political project for gaining control of peasant production [and consequently] the new institutions created within the settlements should be considered as extensions of the state apparatus' (Thiele 1986: 541). What lessons does this experience hold for NGOs about to scale-up their operations?

The successful incorporation of local development into district or national programmes is predicated on a number of highly dubious assumptions. First, it is assumed that the issue in development is the delivery of a homogeneous service; second, that both government and NGO are in the same relationship to the recipients, and third, that the NGO has no valid reasons for suspecting the outcome of cooperation will be anything but positive (Elliott 1987: 64). The number of idealistic statements which abound in academic texts in particular, about how local action should dovetail with regional or national development plans suggests they have little real world experience and take these assumptions for granted. It is as though voracious state politicians and administrators, once prevailed upon by reason and overwhelming evidence that local people should have a say, or that they indeed have something to offer national development planning, will turn overnight into benevolent democrats and readily devolve their power to autonomous, territorially organized political associations and enterprises. In stark contrast to this view, the Magarini experience and experience from all over the Third World, suggests that politicians and administrators are not always benevolent, nor are states benignly pursuing policies which are always in the interests of local communities.[11]

The Magarini case offers insights into a more insidious and subtle problem than a hostile state in the relationships between small-scale local development issues and regional or national plans. Once again, it was local field staff who first brought the problem out into the open. During the March 1988 evaluation, a senior member of the NGO team remarked,

> The joint [NGO–MSP] programme schedules are a good thing because they keep the Australians away. If they come and see the three months work schedule covering our office wall, then they think everything's okay. But it's not.

This was not a flippant remark from someone who believed they had all the necessary management skills and considered the Australian interest to be patronizing. Indeed, most African NGOs agree they are marked by weak planning and management capacity.[12] Rather it was an expression of a growing realization that the programming and scheduling techniques required by the Joint Review Mission for cooperation with the Magarini Project which had been adopted by the NGO were an important part of the explanation why the NGO programme had lost coherence. Of why, too, the programme had begun to lose sight of the end points, the strategic objectives of meeting local people's needs and priorities, which the programme staff had striven to link with tactical or entry point activities over the previous two years.

It was always a possibility that the NGO, a small and weaker partner in the collaboration, would be overwhelmed by the procedural requirements of input–output scheduling and programme budgeting. According to AIDAB evaluations, they had met these requirements but the time and energy necessary to prepare and maintain these schedules had diverted staff attention away from the communities, and they had become absorbed in the frequent meetings, liaison and lobbying with the project and district authorities. But the most critical problem was the way in which programme activities became driven by the procedures and time lines of the schedules rather than the pace, capacities and peculiarities of each of the project communities the NGO was serving. Little by little, the NGO programme had begun to align itself to the priorities and criteria of the larger organizations it had become enmeshed with. The field priorities of staff had become tailored to suit the activity schedules designed in advance for the larger project. The peculiarities of each community group, their differing capacities to participate (by this time, reduced to a matter of labour and material contributions for water and catchment development), the pace at which they could make decisions, resolve difficulties and become involved, had quietly, but surely, been subsumed to the larger effort. NGO work schedules to assist local initiatives had become stringently conditional on their adoption of specific guidelines regarding the timing, quantity, and pace of community contributions.

The NGO was being afflicted with the control-oriented approach in its planning. The programme budgeting used by the NGO, developed during March 1987 with the JRM, involved the forecasting of expenditure, the allocation of resources and linkages, over twelve months, between different activities. This seemed entirely sensible at the time. These linkages were designed to bring community organizers, agriculturalists and technicians together at the right time, along with heavy plant and machinery and community involvement for development of particular dams, and catchment protection activities. These activities had been proposed up to twelve months in advance with no firm knowledge of the future, and yet they took on an aura of certainty. Moreover, once a particular future activity had been timetabled and written into the schedule, it became very difficult to change the overall programme when community members decided they were for some reason unable or unwilling to participate at that time.

In the event, of the six water catchments proposed for joint NGO–Project development during the twelve months, only one was completed, and this not at all according to plan. After November 1987, when an AIDAB Implementation Report Mission visited Kenya to observe progress, the donors concluded that the NGO was not capable of performing as required and overall funding of the NGO programme was questioned. The knowledge that their future funding depended on evaluation of performance according to the annual joint NGO–Project works schedule, placed a great deal of stress on NGO staff. Concentration on the works schedule meant that their ability to respond to various community activities which lay outside the schedule had to be neglected ('Hold on, we'll get to you later'), or simply censored ('Sorry, that's outside our scope of activities for this quarter').

An exchange between two good friends on the NGO staff, one responsible for the programme expenditure schedule and the other a community organizer, typifies the malaise which was setting in. Some months previously a water committee had agreed that following construction they would plant the embankments of a dam and the surrounding catchment with grasses and trees for erosion protection. However, at the programmed time, the rains had begun early and committee members were hastily preparing their fields for planting and unavailable for communal work. The NGO programmer, stressed with the demands of negotiating with project staff, of keeping the works schedule together in the light of funding imperatives, and aware that heavy rains could destroy the unplanted embankments, heatedly demanded in a meeting that the organizer 'Get the committee out to work. And if they don't come this time, I'll get the DO [District Officer] to order them out'.

The DO was not called on to coerce the committee to plant trees. But this encounter between two friends brought home to NGO staff that they were fast beginning to establish a bargaining relationship with the community. 'In this kind of relationship', one said, 'all we have to offer is the money. Follow our program and you will get our assistance.' Another observed that while the NGO had become more accepted as a partner by the project and AIDAB, it was in danger of becoming just another inflexible and rigid project-funding agent. Subsequently, NGO staff began to scale down their involvement in joint NGO–Project activities. The internal NGO evaluation in March 1988 found significant progress had been made with unscheduled activities. An external evaluation by the government of Kenya and AIDAB could not take account of these activities because they were not on the work schedule, and strictly speaking, did not count. During the NGO evaluation one Animator remarked,

> That kind of activity schedule which details who does what, when, and where, and with checks to see it was done, just doesn't make sense. Some of the projects we've been working on, the ones that seem to be working, aren't even on the work schedule. But we keep talking about that schedule. The good thing was that we didn't tell each other off. Our people don't work that way. The good thing is that we now can see the difference and importance of working to our people's schedule, even if the people who came here [the Review Mission] didn't really see it that way.

The NGO had experienced for a short time the very profound distancing that occurs between donors and beneficiaries as a result of increasingly fashionable programme management techniques. The Animator's remark about 'not working that way' recognizes that these techniques follow their own perilous logic. It is clear that our need to be in control of people or in the Australian parlance, 'to nail the bastards down', when taken as cornerstones of professional practice, is reinforcing this logic. Development agencies are told to be pragmatic and realistic. A host of synonyms exists for efficiency and accountability. Efficient agencies need to know what a project will do (the purpose), and in detail (the objectives), whom it will benefit, who is to carry it out (agency institutional capacity, track record) and whether they are participatory, have a vision, identify with the people, precisely how much money they require and when they need it (the programme budget), what are the performance indicators in the activity schedule, by what date it will be sustainable and with what prospects for replication.

It is ironic that this growing demand for certainty on the part of donor agencies is being placed on the very people who best know that even with the greatest foresight in the world, nothing can overcome the unpredictability and uncontrollability of rural development outcomes in reality. One consequence is the dressing up of proposals, packaging with a view to satisfying the buyer, the sort of activity we describe in relation to the water and agriculture proposals of Phase I at Magarini (Chapter Three). If everyone knows the rules of the development game the damage of that sort of behaviour is limited. Of greater concern are the detrimental effects the control-orientation approach is having on the desired outcomes. The KFFHC Field Director describes the problem from within Kenya, but he provides us with a vivid reminder of the sort of structures with which we are in danger of saddling development practice.

> The problem is that what we're really after is slipping between our fingers when we get involved with projects. We are being held hostage to the procedures and the people along with us. Normal procedures in Kenya, and what is normal here in Magarini is just a shade off what [a European donor] requires, don't take account of our need to pick opportunities that just come and go, and have to be picked up at the time or they're lost. What's normal for village people here to gain assistance? Now they have the District Focus policy [with procedures established by another donor] and have to get assistance from the RDF [Rural Development Fund held by the District Development Committee]. First, the people have to get an idea of what they know will be saleable. For some things there are funds, like a women's group poultry project, or bakeries, so long as they are group and not individual projects – and for some things not, a revolving credit scheme run by the women would not even make it onto the agenda, neither would a proposal to cover the costs of bringing women from another group to assist overcoming management problems. The people might make contact with a local extension worker, if they can find him. Or the Assistant Chief might be approached, but most are reluctant to get him involved because of the later costs. However, the proposal would have to go to the Sub-locational Development Committee, and be considered there. Then, if it ranks among the favoured projects, and it's prepared the right way, it can go up to the Divisional Development Committee. And the vetting continues. Is this project consistent with District objectives, and all the questions about schedules, targets and so on that you ask, are asked but in a different way. Have the people approached the KANU rep [Kenyan African National Union], or the MP, is the group registered with the Ministry of Culture and Social Services? And at each stage the file could go back to the extension worker for clarification – by now it's his project. Finally, they might get to the District Development Committee where all the heads of ministries sit, along with all the political leaders, and divide up the RDF. This might take years, and by then what's left has nothing to do with what the people wanted or now want to do.[13]

People become instruments in the larger scheme, passive bystanders in a process which has become institutionalized by design. Development is a process internal to the people and their communities. It can be externally stimulated, but it cannot be externally controlled – except by force. NGO workers, like the man quoted above, do not expect development agencies to adopt the 'anything goes' or 'everything's open' attitude. While the turnkey mentality, which is the archetype of control-orientation, can work for efficient implementation of some capital works, rural development practice must be geared to reflect, as the Animator said, 'the way our people work' and recognize the powerful urge by local people to take greater control over their affairs. Control-oriented programming, paradoxically, increases the uncertainty from the viewpoint of local people. Situations will change, often rapidly, and it is local people who are best placed to anticipate change, and reduce uncertainty.

Unless this is recognized at the procedural level, the intended beneficiaries of development frequently have no option but to resist, most often by passive withdrawal. Bernard Lecomte (1986: 24) puts the result well,

> Any fresh project will fit into their history as one more unfortunate episode of outside influence on a rural community. It will be accepted not as something radically new but as one more trial to be undergone, with the need yet again to safeguard the group's own existence as far as possible.

We have seen that there is scope for increasing the scale of impact of what critics of NGO projects say are fragmentary, isolated bits-and-pieces. Certainly, powerful political impediments exist to increasing scale, and it is true that NGOs have hardly begun to examine the economic logic and structures of self-financing and sustainability which increased scale imply. The experience at Magarini has caused the NGO staff to adopt views about what is essential to make a project successful and self-sustaining, which fly in the face of what is understood in professional development circles today as essential to achieve the same goal. The Magarini experience is that practices of increased control, insisted upon by the major donor agencies in the name of greater certainty of outcomes, in fact constrain local people's capacity to cope with uncertainty, and directly contribute to increased levels of ineffectiveness and non-sustainability of development assistance.

Chapter 6

Against whose odds?
Constructing certainty Giriama style

Several hundred people are gathering around the homestead in the hot afternoon sun. They are here to witness a diviner name the witch responsible for
Kabibi's death. Kabibi was the wife of a Marafa shopkeeper. She died in child-
birth yesterday. Their son also died only a few weeks ago. Everyone wants to
know who is responsible for the deaths, for two sudden deaths in the one family within such a short time cannot have occurred by chance. The relatives have
been gathering throughout the day and some from Malindi and further away
have spent the night here. Family interests in the outcome have drawn
together settlers from within the project area, and their relations from outside. Many other people from all over the area are also here. Kaviha Mutama
is the only officially recognized witch-identifier north of the Sabaki River and
he is renowned for his ritual performances. The people want to be enter-
tained, but they also want to know what changes in neighbourly alliances will
be created by the naming of the witch.[1]

The crowd is gathered in a large circle around an open area of hard-beaten
clay. The government-appointed chiefs of Marafa and Magarini are seated to
one side and behind them stand four administration policemen. The chiefs
and police are here to prevent revengeful violence against the witch, if and
when he or she is exposed. Their presence is paradoxical, however. While on
the one hand if sufficient material evidence is found after the naming, the
witch may be tried in a court of law for murder, in Kenya, there is no legal
recognition of the existence of witchcraft. Through the presence of the chiefs
and the policemen the state is recognizing that witchcraft causes death, but it
officially denies the existence of the causal phenomenon itself (Mutungi 1977:
4). For the people in the crowd no such semantic problems exist. The chiefs
are local men, and everyone knows the first wife of one of them is also a diviner
who regularly identifies witchcraft as a cause of misfortune as part of her work.
The crowd knows someone present will probably be identified as the witch. A
neighbour, a relative, a policeman, a mother, a wife, it could be anyone. The
family have been for some time uncertain about the causes of the illness and

minor misfortunes which have afflicted them. The deaths make it impossible to avoid the conclusion that witchcraft is the cause.

The babble of the crowd is suddenly hushed as the diviner's assistant moves into the centre of the circle. He speaks, 'We are gathered here today to catch witches. The government is here too, but only to watch. What we must know is, is it because of our ancestors, is it flesh-eating spirits, or is it witchcraft. Kaviha will tell us! He is our diviner. If witchcraft is indicated and the witch is found, then the witch will be sent on to the ordeal oath, where Kaviha's truth will be proven.'

All possible causes are to be considered, ancestral and evil spirits, as well as witchcraft. If witchcraft is discovered the witch will be sought and identified. A secondary ritual ordeal will prove the correctness of the identification.

Now the witch-hunter Kaviha moves to the centre of the crowd. All eyes are on him. He is praying to the spiritual hosts, appealing for benevolence for the people, blessings to enrich their fecundity, and the fertility of the land for the production of food to sustain them. Kaviha's assistants have begun beating drums. Kaviha is singing a spirit-evoking song encouraging his familiar spirits to possess him. At last he has fallen into a trance possessed by a favourable spirit. The crowd is encouraging him with loud cheering and clapping. Only snatches of his words can be heard above the drumming and cheering. People are beginning to become completely engrossed in the event. They are laughing at Kaviha's repartee, and urging him to seek justice. They are calling, 'Find the witch. Find the witch and let him pay blood-money!' Kaviha is seeking to identify the symptoms of the disorder. He is divining general causes. Now he is beginning to focus on individuals who may be to blame. He is dancing among the people, exaggeratedly sniffing out the acrid stench of witchcraft, offering his hand to be shaken so he can feel the evil embodied in the guilty person. To refuse implies guilt. People are becoming more and more excited. Kaviha now draws out a man to stand in the centre of the crowd, and now a woman, another man, and another. There are now ten people standing facing the crowd.

There is a break in the ritual. The drummers are resting and Kaviha has gone to change his clothes. The suspects stand, eyes downcast and the crowd murmurs in anticipation. Wives or husbands of the suspects are shocked and anxious. Kaviha is returning, wearing the costume of his familiar spirits, with bells strapped to his ankles. The drumming begins again. Kaviha is displaying his power over witchcraft, dousing a burning stick in his oracle, an earthenware pot of water, stamping his feet to the drum beat, adding to the cacophony. Again he is working to gain the confidence of the crowd, drawing them into the ritual with him, for it is only when they show their total support that he can pronounce his judgement on their behalf. Kaviha is now eliminating the ten suspects, one by one. The crowd's excitement is now tangible and the drumming and cheering deafening. At last, one man is left standing alone before the crowd. Kaviha can now make the final accusation without fear of challenge. He names the man as a witch.

The crowd has fallen suddenly silent. People are moving away and hurrying off into the late afternoon. Within a few minutes they have dispersed as if repelled by the knowledge that this evil person has existed within their community without their knowledge.

CREATING CERTAINTY: A RITUAL EVENT IN MAGARINI

This was not the first attempt by Kabibi's family to find the cause of their misfortune. The elders had sought a number of lesser divinations in connection with previous incidents suspected to be linked to a witch's activities. A young woodcutter had had a narrow escape from death when he fell from a tree. Then, following a spate of children's illnesses that failed to respond to treatment at the local government dispensary and the hospital in Malindi, Kabibi, the shopkeeper's wife had died in labour. Earlier divinations had revealed a range of possible causes. But since the death of Kabibi, divinations sought by the elders indicated witchcraft had been the cause all along. The divinations sought before Kaviha's had been private affairs, with diviner and client meeting alone in a secluded place. Private divinations can only reveal general areas of causality and offer socially accepted remedies. In cases involving deaths, chronic illness or misfortune, or situations affecting a great number of people, only when a sufficient degree of certainty has been generated by agreement between more than one divination, can a predominating cause be transformed into a concrete reality and a witch identified. The naming was a self-validating confirmation of people's suspicions and of the methods of investigation exposure.

The pressing need to find a witch to blame for the deaths was partially responsible for the unquestioning acceptance of Kaviha's final indicting pronouncement. But previous experience of this ritual made everyone aware from the beginning of the inevitable ambivalence of its outcome. Although people felt a compulsion to participate, to chant this destiny closer, their emotional fervour of support for the diviner belied the ambiguity of the consequences of his words and actions.

The divination was about marginality. A new social identity was created in a dangerously indeterminate context. Even though the diviner was not himself in his state of trance, he deliberately urged the spirits to work for him, and he cleverly gained the support of the crowd in his role as a medium for judgemental spirits. The elaborate construction of an image for himself of a morally just leader successfully deflected attention from the ambivalence of his role and the contradictions generated by the event. Throughout the ritual, familiarity was used to overcome contradictions, so that the audience could enthusiastically support old ideas which they no longer practise in a day-to-day sense. The ritual generated a commitment in everyone to deny the existence of uncertainties. The diviner created the circumstances in which this could occur.

The diviner's role

Kaviha made much of his control over the spirit world. His considerable theatrical skills orchestrated the ritual; he carefully managed the activities of the drummers, the mood of the audience, and ultimately the identity of the accused witch. His identification of the man as a witch conferred on him a new lifelong identity. To minimalize challenges to his pronouncements, Kaviha drew strongly on the words of the ancestors, an idiom of tradition uniquely available to him as the translator of wishes and views of his spirit familiars. As tradition incarnate, he legitimately took the disorder and uncertainty in the community, and using his knowledge of attitudes and of individuals, re-established order and certainty.

Kaviha's credibility was drawn from the unquestionable authority of the traditional social system and the powers vested in the ancestors of leading elders. Although Kaviha himself is not an elder, his access to their status gave him the right to use their traditional authority and their role of upholding society's moral values.

Kaviha was also responding pragmatically to people's immediate needs, a factor which lent considerable weight to his legitimacy. His public exposure of the witch who had caused suffering within the community was a welcome relief. However, he exposed a new 'witch' who would become available to those with bitterness or jealousy in their hearts to consort with, or to purchase the knowledge of witchcraft from. Kaviha perpetuated the belief in witchcraft by providing the conditions for the reproduction of witches, who would in turn generate more fear and uncertainty. However, most importantly for him, he also ensured the continuation of the need for the institution of diviners to find and expose witches.

The wider context: themes of interest

An examination of Giriama beliefs about witches raises questions about the way in which beliefs about causes of misfortune are created and recreated. Like many other tribal and peasant peoples across the world, the Giriama conceive of their world in a holistic way,[2] where physical and less tangible spiritual elements are interdependent. This explains a great deal about Giriama strategies for controlling uncertainty. In the face of persisting misfortune the Giriama rely on this complex cosmology for explanation and reassurance that the world can be morally re-ordered and levels of uncertainty reduced. But coincidental with the use of traditional means of explanation and alleviation, the Giriama are also willing to try more modern solutions to the same problems.

Critics of the Giriama have pointed out their lack of commitment to a 'progressive' way of life. But it is precisely because the Giriama do not rely wholeheartedly on any one particular institution for minimizing uncertainty about the causes and outcomes of their misfortunes that they survived the rapid and sometimes traumatic impacts they have suffered since the 1880s. Parkin (1970: 217–33) has described, for example, how the adoption of Islam by young entrepreneurial Giriama men in the progressive coastal palm belt during the 1960s gave them freedom from customary obligations to share their income. Their conversion, however, was frequently nominal and allowed them to continue to be involved in many traditional rituals.

Arguably, the low rates of attendance of Giriama at hospitals, clinics and mosques is less evidence for a lack of commitment to change, than it is for their use of strategies which maximize their chances of gaining particular benefits. Similarly, for many years, they have survived in a harsh environment by not relying exclusively on subsistence agriculture or the cash economy. By straddling both economies and incorporating small new changes into their basic traditional repertoire, risks are minimized.

A number of parallels can be drawn between the role of Giriama diviners and their rituals for the creation of certainty, and development practice. As latter-day diviners, development workers have their rituals too. They also seek to identify causes of disorder and misfortune. Early in the Magarini Project we saw a variety of predesign divinations. Technical studies of problems and causes were undertaken, which, when sufficient agreement between them had been established, a predominating cause like 'the ineffectiveness of traditional agriculture' was given a concrete reality in the form of specific remedial prescriptions for intervention. Somewhat like Kaviha, Magarini's development workers used their considerable theatrical skills to orchestrate the ritual. The NGO development workers too, in responding to people's needs, confirmed with each step the need for a continuation of their involvement and the institutions they represented.

But between Giriama rituals and the world of development workers there is a fundamental difference. Development practice, at least as seen in control-orientation, involves exclusive secular rituals. Whereas Giriama are eclectic and draw on a diverse range of strategies for minimizing uncertainty, conventional development practice seeks a linear and single-minded chain of cause and effect reasoning, and demands wholehearted adherence to this. Where these ritual predictions fail there are dire consequences for powerless so-called beneficiaries involved, who are left without alternatives.

MAGARINI SIXTY YEARS ON: RESETTLEMENT IN THE 'DISPOSSESSED TERRITORY'

The well-intentioned aims of the Magarini Settlement Project to encourage fundamental organizational and attitudinal changes among the Giriama assumed that these outcomes would be integral to their relationships with the land. The Giriama were to be settled, and given a better chance than ever before to increase their security of tenure, food output, standards of living, and well-being. But to the Giriama, land they had originally paid the Galla for, and fought the British for in 1914, was to be paid for again. The project invoked deep feelings of insecurity and uncertainty about the land. The plan was to compensate those who were already living on the land before dividing it and returning it to them as plots for resettlement. The concept of compensation for permanent tree crops and other assets was familiar to the Giriama, though there were two aspects of the actual implementation of this plan which caused a great deal of uncertainty and tension.

First, on acquiring a plot, settlers were required to begin repayments to the government according to the terms defined by the obligatory land-loan. Many settlers saw this as a form of deceit which trapped them into a financial commitment they had never asked for nor wanted. In the event, and reminiscent of tax evasion during the early colonial years, it has taken the project over eight years to extract even the initial deposits on their land-loans from most settlers. This is despite considerable pressure from project management to pay. Everything was tried, from the threat of eviction and the use of force, to the linking of payments with access to development loan packages. The additional lure of a tied loan package deal only served to confirm the settlers' suspicions that the loan repayment was a dubious means of gaining access to support services that appeared otherwise unforthcoming. Second, because the compensation process took place at a much faster rate than the plot allocation process, many former occupants of Magarini technically became landless. Through the mechanism of compensation they were relieved of their rights of occupation and for all intents and purposes, became squatters. The project fostered the antithesis of its primary aims of settlement, and contributed in no small measure to people's overall uncertainty about their future.

Land is central to Kenyan politics, but the experience of land-grabbing at Magarini provoked such protest at all levels that no plots were allocated from 1983 to 1989. In 1983 the first allocations of blocks to non-Giriama occurred, project policy at this time was that 10 per cent of all settlers allocated plots would be landless people from other parts of Kenya, a move which had widespread repercussions at Magarini. The covert transactions that resulted in land being acquired by some of the wealthier landless Kenyans from upcountry to the disadvantage of Giriama claimants created deep mistrust between the settlers and the Kenyan project staff, particularly as the great majority of project staff were themselves non-Giriama. Strong expressions of antagonistic ethnicity abounded on the project. These tended to reinforce Giriama feelings of ethnic group unity, and enhanced their desire for autonomy. Giriama perceptions of the project are understandably inconsistent, because of their eclectic approach to life and the uneven nature of contacts people have had with the project. The accessible southern part of Magarini has drawn the greatest political attention. This is the area where plots were initially allocated and resettled, and where the major effort at installing project infrastructure was first concentrated. It was here that Giriama claims to plots were contested and some settlers experienced violent confrontations with armed police.

Neither plot nor project boundaries take account of soil type or land capability. Crops suited to different soils, therefore, are still, in the traditional fashion, planted in appropriate locations, wherever swidden rights can be bought both inside and outside the project. Similarly, Giriama family networks of dependency and support also cross the project's boundaries. If maps were drawn showing the distribution of agricultural extension contacts, loan beneficiaries, reticulated water points, plots occupied by squatters, plots that have been resurveyed up to three different times for unspecified reasons, plots with contested claims, the intensity of use of fertile and infertile soil types, and extended family network distributions of settlers and non-settlers, they would depict the polarities of project and Giriama interests. The majority of settlers perceive their alienation from the project in terms of their exclusion from the channels down which the project benefits flow. Interactions of the project staff with settlers have tended to further emphasize biases which already benefit the progressive minority of settlers. Most agricultural assistance services, for example, were unfavourably granted primarily to non-Giriama, or only to those Giriama who had money or important local political positions. Only by paying over the odds for everything could ordinary settlers gain access to project-funded assistance. Because the Giriama settlers were reluctant to pay for anything, they were labelled by project staff as conservative, stubborn and resistant to change.

IMPACT: GIRIAMA REACTIONS TO ENCLOSURE

> Magarini is like a child born out of the adulterous relationship of a woman whose husband is away. On his return he finds himself burdened with a child that he never asked for, that he never even had a part in creating. But what man would not also welcome another child to his family? Children are our wealth and hope for the future.

Giriama ambivalence in the face of the development imperative is forcefully expressed in this analogy recorded at Magarini. The 'illegitimacy' of Magarini has been one of the principal reasons why it has not been accepted by the Giriama. The first disclaimers were recorded in Chilungu's sociological study in the 1978 Project Report on Magarini (McGowan 1977e). In this, the majority of the residents in the area expressed in different ways their opposition to the idea of a project for their resettlement. But all development projects have their lures, their visions and promises of a better future, and Magarini was no different. Local people saw the arrival of a project which promised gifts of money and food, security of title to land, and income from learning new and better ways of production. Outside of the formally settled areas of Magarini, on its borders and beyond, many people were envious of what they saw as the big amounts of money (compensation) given to those who live on the project. Additionally, many women from outside the project particularly, noted their failure to benefit from gifts from Magarini, such as the distribution of large quantities of maize, cooking oil, beans and other necessary foods at the beginning of the project, which came from the food-for-work programmes. The sustained expectations that more of this would come from the same source has preoccupied some people ever since. It is not difficult to understand people's disenchantment with the eroding promise of a bountiful future which the project had initially brought with it. Disenchantment and the need for survival in a harsh environment where conditions were exacerbated by enclosure, fuelled the persistence of several illegal activities which undermined the basic principles of the project. Settlers continued to hunt, cut and sell timber, burn charcoal for sale, cultivate forest reserves and brew local liquor. Simply to survive, settlers continued to pursue activities which were either not supported by government services or were officially discouraged.

Undeniably Magarini has affected the material basis of Giriama life. Settlers' relationships to the land have been severely altered by restrictions to their movements within a fixed plot of land, and by fragmentation of families in the allocation of plots. Many settlers, for reasons such as depleted soil fertility or water-logging on their plots, have shifted away from the project onto the more productive bushland in the northwest of the project to cultivate cleared forest areas. This Giriama tradition has far more limited horizons nowadays, however. The impact of Magarini has been uneven. For example, farmer Johnson Kalume settled on his plot in 1982. Six years later, having hired oxen to assist in cultivation for two years, because of repeatedly unfavourable rainfall and a bizarre imbalance of soil resources, he unhappily only harvested enough food to last his family for up to eight months of the year. Before he moved to his plot in Magarini, his family had maintained two maize fields, and had income from cashew nuts to pay for extra hand labour for weeding, the most pressing task. The family had been self-sufficient throughout the year. With the move onto the project, they were now living too far away to send one of the family to protect the cashew fruits from theft up to harvest time, because of the unexpected and overriding demand in the new home for labour resources. Kalume therefore sold the cashew trees and invested his hopes and money in high expectations of farming assistance from the project. He knew the sandy soils of his plot favoured permanent tree crops, and he wanted to grow these on his land, but the common species known by the Giriama to be successful on these soils were not in any of the loan packages offered by the project. He was forced therefore to plant only general subsistence crops. His accumulated savings became eroded by the outlays involved in his subsistence farming. Soon his family found themselves reduced to the status of casual labourers, working on other people's farms on better soils in exchange for food. Kalume's capital resources were reduced to the point where in his own words, 'we are unable to be progressive at all. Never before have we been so poor and penniless'. These sentiments are repeated by many settlers on Magarini, many of whom started with less than Kalume.

But there are some for whom the political and physical conditions have been more favourable. A large casual labour force was employed by the project. Over 400 people, mainly young men who would probably have migrated elsewhere in search of work, instead formed a significant client group dependent on the project's employment favours. In response to the greater overall cash flow and increased demand in the area, many new small traders, women selling tea from little kiosks and marketing vegetables, and men with small shops, set up in business. Many more shops offered credit facilities and the increased cash flow also allowed a number of Giriama to pay seasonal casual labour to work on their plots.

It is significant, however, that although the project affected the material base of Giriama society it has not so far managed more than a superficial penetration of Giriama culture. The staff showed little interest in the world views of the Giriama and many of the most meaningful reference points in tradition were not challenged. Their brush with the project did not challenge their beliefs, evidenced, for example, by the extensive support for continued witch-hunting dances, but actually fuelled their sense of group identity by propagating ethnic rivalry. To their great advantage, Giriama strategies for survival have never been clearly visible, and interventionists from outside their world have been left to speculate about their apparent resistance and opposition to development. But while Magarini probably reinforced existing feelings of alienation, it must also be asked how much the project has accelerated the momentum towards the inevitable submission of the Giriama to 'capture' by the state.

NGO–GIRIAMA RELATIONS: AIMING FOR THE HEAD

One of the earliest challenges faced by the Kenya Freedom From Hunger Council (KFFHC) staff at Magarini was the questioning of its objectives and motives by the Giriama. The insidious legacy from Magarini defined community expectations of what the NGO had to offer. 'One never licks an empty hand', they said hopefully. Different groups converged in curiosity asking what was in this hand. Would it threaten or support, what about local leaders' interests? Everyone watched closely. Project staff feared the undisclosed power of the NGO. Was the hand holding enough political influence and money to lose them their jobs and monopoly on resources in the area? They verbally prodded and poked Animators and other staff; 'Show us what you have done, we want to see what you are doing!'

From the start the NGO never intended its work to be a very visible exercise. Despite the expectations of the Giriama community and other agents of development in the area, the NGO never claimed to be able to benefit the

Giriama materially, or in any other substantive way. Its strategic objectives were aimed expressly at strengthening the capacities of those people who were benefiting least from current project development activities. The NGO sought to encourage people to define their own needs and general interests, and 'undertake sustainable strategies through which they can manage their own affairs'.[3]

At the field level it was expressly hoped that the sustainability of the programme would grow out of its close identification with the people. It aimed to be a Giriama programme, run for and by Giriama people. The programme used an approach specifically designed to penetrate Giriama culture, identify with the positive aspects of it and build on these features, with the long-term objective of bringing about change in the culture. The NGO was deliberately aiming for the heads of the Giriama. Giriama people were assisted by Giriama Animators to define their own interests and needs through a problem-solving participatory approach, and to devise sustainable affordable solutions, such as projects to undertake and attitudes to change. The participatory approach identified by the NGO advocated the popular notion of 'starting from where the people are'. Participation in the NGO programme, was on the one hand considered to be the means towards achieving sustainable material development ends. But on the other hand, participation was also more importantly seen as a subtly crucial end in itself. Thus in the sense that participation is politically all about people taking charge of their own affairs, assessing their interests and devising strategies to protect themselves from outside control, and in so doing, reducing their dependence and enhancing their autonomy,[4] the NGO intended to facilitate the people's political development.

The legitimacy of the NGO's approach in the eyes of the government was based on their nominal conformity to government policies for development. The NGO programme appeared to address people's needs related to their water problems and general poverty and was seen to allocate some material benefits to its projects. The Giriama welcomed this familiar line, but when a dialogue quite new to them was initiated with the NGO development workers, the interactive basis of sharing an understanding of the local social, cultural and political welfare gained the programme its own special legitimacy.

The NGO, through its Giriama Animators, used the local people's own language and symbols. The local legitimacy of the programme was expected to emerge from this close identification with the people, where it would gain its specifically 'Giriama' identity. Ostensibly it sought no external legitimacy, except in its mandate for development. In this respect the fieldworkers aimed to raise awareness among people of their own personal role in effecting future changes, and encouraged them to take responsibility for these.

NGO Animators had to perform their work with a critical awareness of the double-faced legitimacy which defined their acceptability. On the one hand their identification with Giriama-ness and traditional ways of doing things supported a strong internal legitimacy. This had to be carefully balanced with their externally designated mandate defining their pre-planned development objectives. Only with skilful manipulation and controlled commitment could this critical balance be maintained. Success in achieving this balance would produce the crucially marginal status required for the Animators to be most effective. As local insiders bearing a development imperative, the Animators' unique mediating position was expected to give them the chance to influence deeply rooted attitudes and concepts. Like all people assuming leadership roles in the political process, however, a very slick kind of manipulation was required and the moment that this became exposed would be the moment the Animator's legitimacy was going to be questioned by the Giriama participants.

Ideally Animators had not only to convince the people they worked with of their own legitimacy, but also of the validity and acceptability of their propositions. While playing on their shared Giriama identity, Animators objectified their words to present them as legitimate messages from outside which would be seen to serve the people's interests and not their own personal gain. Following from this, it was hoped that when the people became mobilized into action they would be aware that, since the Animator had absolved him or herself of personal involvement during the facilitation process, it was their own efforts which were responsible for immediate and longer term outcomes. That is, an awareness of their defining role in dealing with their own circumstances, and their ability to cope with newly perceived problems. The potential for achieving great good, personal and communal, was readily evident in this approach, and it was hoped that the widely popular appeal of this would be one of the key factors influencing the commitment and energy of all who became involved in it.

The NGO deliberately aimed for the head, with the good intention of using a promisingly popularist approach to development. They were unaware, however, that their methods of acting upon the world of development practice were being practised equally, if not more popularly among the Giriama already. The remarkable similarity of the approach employed by the NGO Animators to bring about change, and the methods used by Giriama diviners are impossible to overlook. Side by side, we see practitioners who provide meaningful explanations in problematic situations, and who offer guidance to people's actions. Importantly, both recognize that their role is to define socially relevant prescriptions which 'allow intervention and determine social action'. For example, as anthropologist Evans-Pritchard (1937: 73) observed, belief in witchcraft among the Zande does not preclude empirical knowledge of cause and effect, but in 'every case witchcraft is the socially relevant cause, since it is the only one which allows intervention and determines social behaviour'.

DEPARTURES AND DESTINATIONS: DEFINING LEADERS AND FOLLOWERS

The key role of the diviner in the maintenance of people's belief in the truths of the Giriama cosmos, has historically resulted in their becoming leaders of collective responses to critically threatening insurgencies. Giriama responses to major threats to their fundamental epistemological beliefs in the form of evangelical Christianity and Islam, capitalism, secular politics of domination, and closer to home, the fears of social disruption brought about by the uncertainty generated by witchcraft, have varied considerably over the last hundred years. Where diviners have played a role in leading the collective responses to any of these threats, they have done so in their traditional capacity as healers, and there has been a notion that they were repairing or healing an illness, and a sick society.

For example, widespread disturbances occurred throughout the hinterland in the years immediately preceding Kenya's independence. The uncertain politics of nationalism were accompanied by increasing internal disorder expressed in escalating witchcraft attacks. Unrestricted, these powerful self-generating spirals of fear and uncertainty increased tensions on a wide scale.[5] There was a general atmosphere of uncertainty in almost all domains at this time. Two prophetic diviners, Kagombo wa Kalu and Kajiwe, known as 'Little Rock', rallied the hopes of many Giriama for a re-establishment of peace and predictability. In their unique positions as mediators with the divine, both of these men in different ways, attempted to use their special legitimacy to deliver their people from the oppressive social and political disarray surrounding them. Their visions of a new and secure, world they stressed, could only be achieved by routing out the evil among them, whether they were referring in the one case to the Arabs, or in the other to the witches. Through Kagombo's initial public meetings and covert rituals, and later through the witchcraft eradication movement led by Kajiwe, the divinely sanctioned purposes of these efforts generated a fervour of widespread support for their activities.

Both men succeeded in gaining large Giriama followings. By being seen to answer the obvious needs of their people for relief from uncertainty, their legitimacy was at the time unquestionable. But the movements were short-lived. In order to sustain the existence of their own institution for problem-solving, diviners must actually ensure that their impact is transient. There are exceptions, however.

A millenarian movement initiated by Kenga wa Kasiwa, a diviner who led a traditional healing crusade among the Giriama, divinely curing all illnesses brought to him, appeared around fifteen years ago, and has survived to the present. Followers of this diviner, in order to achieve a long-term cure, had also to be baptised and join his syncretic 'Christian' church. Since the movement began, its millenarian energies have dissipated, but the church still

attracts a large following. The geographical spread of congregations throughout the hinterland and coast today are a testimony to the sustainability of this
movement. The acceptance by its members of its unique divinely inspired
dogma as a legitimate alternative basis for organizing their beliefs and activities, together with its powerful healing role, have both been effective in
maintaining their commitment to it in the long term.

The visionary or prophetic qualities and healing roles of the diviners who
led these movements made them ideal leaders. Since the loss of traditional
centralized *kaya* leadership resulted in a politically loose sense of authority
among the Giriama, these conditions have fostered innovative redefinitions
of leadership positions by diviners. Giriama encounters with colonialism, and
later with nationalism, and their experiences with evangelical religions have
caused many among them to seek a new security, and reaffirm predictability
in their worlds by supporting the leadership roles of the diviners.

If we now generalize we find that these movements not only generated
unity against new threats from outside, but at the same time drew elements
from them, giving rise to syncretic characteristics in the Giriama cosmology.
The contents of these new views were increasingly mixed with Christianity and
other secular development imperatives. Interventions by leading prophetic
diviners have involved far-reaching innovation, and they are important
indigenous mediators of change, both at the neighbourhood level and on a
wider scale.[6]

DIVINING DEVELOPMENT: A GENERATIVE METAPHOR?

The methods used by NGO fieldworkers at Magarini to establish legitimacy
are in many ways similar to those of the witch-hunter Kaviha. At one level we
can see Animators armed with the skills of 'facipulation',[7] a subtle blend of
facilitation and manipulation, combined with the powerful secrets of development, as the ones who make the whole thing work, who orchestrate the ritual.
Using their Giriama identity they claim special access to the traditional system to realign the two worlds, subtly, with skills they have learned as part of
the NGO's participatory training. They facilitate redefinitions of reality,
which are seen as responses to the discontent generated by the raised critical
awareness of the Giriama participants.

In parallel to Kaviha's witch-exposing ritual, Animators become our 'new
diviners'. Drawing on linguistic and other traditional symbols they skilfully
'facipulate' events. Would-be bystanders become participants as the new
diviners penetrate their worlds and gain their support. Even though people
are aware of the fundamental contradictions for their sense of identity implied
in development outcomes, they join in wholeheartedly. At the point of divinatory revelation, however, these new diviners must be much more subtle than
conventional diviners. Although the revelation of ways to deal with the conditions of this discontent are expected to fuel people's desire to do something

constructive about rectifying the situation, diviner–development workers must disclaim any role in the authorship of such prescriptions, in other words the people must feel that they did it all themselves.

Does the application of such a metaphor mean that NGO fieldworkers might also facilitate large-scale social movements and fundamental changes, in the same sense as the diviners have in the past? Their patterns of creating an enshrined or 'divine' legitimacy are strikingly similar, and their methods of working merge in the common 'facipulation' process. Both are interventionists, both aim to remedy or heal situations and relationships that are perceived to be pathological.

The answer is 'potentially, yes'. The NGO can indeed facilitate the articulation of grievances, and the speaking of truth to power. This process can challenge the state, it can be used as a very effective means of 'advertising'[8] and can even articulate shifts in the balance of power. In practice, however, these tactics endanger its very existence, and in view of the Kenyan political context, we are forced in the short term to conclude that the answer is more likely 'no'. Direct challenges are self-destructive and cannot hope to succeed in the achievement of change in any sustainable way (see also Chapter Five). Animators, in the way of diviners, must take the longer, and more circuitous routes. They must dig into local Giriama worlds, encourage an identification with the most positive aspects of the revealed situations and then present another reality as being in the people's interests.

Animators use a very effective method of penetration into Giriama worlds. As Giriama insiders themselves, Animators use the outsiders' idiom of development. In practice, however, Animators as a group are unlikely to achieve the level of skill required to make them successful manipulators. Some individual Animators will doubtless penetrate and bring about significant changes in the attitudes and actions of the households and groups they are immediately associated with, but the scale of the impact is likely to remain localized and affect those people most receptive to change. These changes will show up in many unpredictable ways such as enhanced negotiating competence, or entrepreneurial skills, or perhaps in changed health practices or new patterns of leadership. Overall, this NGO intervention is just as likely to be absorbed within the highly diverse, eclectic mix of ideas, beliefs and commitments that typify the Giriama world view.

Materially and technologically oriented development programmes rarely penetrate the culture of the people for whom they are intended at a fundamental level, and, certainly in the case of Magarini, any changes in people's attitudes are likely to be incorporated into a plural and diverse world, making them difficult to fathom in a cause and effect way. The NGO approach, on the other hand, involves the most risky sort of meddling that can be done. The potential of this approach to inflict irreparable damage to the Giriama world view is, of course, the necessary obverse of its potential for beneficial change. For this reason the NGO must also be capable of presenting and then ensuring that workable alternatives are established. We should not forget that Giriama belief systems have enabled them to cope with adversity, and organize their own and other plural interventions together without debilitating conflict, for many years.

The relevance of Giriama experience

In certain respects Giriama historical experience, and their means of explaining existential and practical problems, are unique. However, despite the complexities, the idea that all facets of experience are connected in a holistic way is one common to most African and other traditional peoples. The organizing principle of explanatory holism is widespread in the Third World. The NGO's participatory approach is not unique either, and it is used in the areas of the world occupied by traditional people specifically because of its greater potential for successful communication and persuasion. However, in the case of the NGO, caution must be the password, for the approach incongruously uses a Western model of intervention to fasten selectively onto bits of a holistically integrated traditional system so that those bits may be improved on in some way.

Much is said nowadays of the need to incorporate indigenous knowledge into all aspects of development practice. The NGO has attempted to do this in ways that are not superficial but are central to the character of its programme of interventions. But in doing so, the NGO is unable to escape the fundamental problem of Western technical rationality, the rationality on which the whole idea of development practice is based. This holds that all aspects of life can be isolated into bits, whether they be complex agro-ecosystems or traditional knowledge systems. Following on from this it assumes that these bits may be removed, manipulated, and then sometimes re-inserted into the culture, in order to bring about desirable outcomes in a controlled manner. However, far from these outcomes occurring as part of a unilinear cause and effect process, the practical operations of the environment, or social and political life are inconsistent and multi-stranded. In order to gain greater insights into the unpredictable, non-linear character of knowledge systems in peasant societies (Tambiah 1985: 84) and perhaps also take some lessons for development practice, we take a closer look at the Giriama world.

Managing non-linear causality Giriama style

Most Giriama people today live in a morally defined world, in the sense that they perceive a divine or spiritual force as being an integral part of their lives. In Chapter Two, based on figures available for 1972, we estimated that between 75 and 80 per cent of the Giriama still have not adopted any of the major world religions, or joined recognized independent churches. In 1972

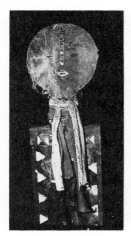

The moral order: *Plate 19* Speaking to an ancestor (top middle) *Plate 20* A decorated wooden ancestor memorial post (top left) *Plate 21* Performing a divining dance (top right) *Plate 22* A sorcery 'trap' (bottom)

the Giriama were the largest ethnic group in Kenya with the greatest number unconverted. Their population comprised the third highest percentage of traditionalists in Kenya (Barrett 1973: 181). It is unlikely that these ratios have radically changed since 1972, given that there have been no major evangelical campaigns at the coast since then that have not also had counterparts in other parts of the country.

This is most evident in the vicinity of Marafa where, despite the establishment of eight different Christian denominations with their own churches, Christians actually form less than 15 per cent of the locality's total number of residents. In this area very few Giriama have become Muslims. None of these converts ever attend prayers in the mosque built in the trading centre by men associated with the project. Although the Giriama have been in close contact with the coastal Muslims for several hundreds of years, on the whole they have independently maintained their own religious ideas. Those who were forced by adverse circumstances to live on the coast, often as clients, servants, or dependants of other kinds, of the Islamic coastal people, were more likely to take up Islam. David Parkin (1970) also shows how, when the beneficial effects of capitalism began to be felt by many young entrepreneurial Giriama in the southern hinterland, they used their conversion to Islam as a means of escaping their traditional obligations of reciprocity and sharing, in favour of accumulating their wealth.

Let us look more closely at what it means for a Giriama to be traditional. The moral ordering of most Giriama lives is expressed in their relationship with the spirit world or divinity, of the ancestors and god. Within this framework we find their socio-political domain located within an overall environment composed of both physical elements, and spiritual forces.

The different domains are recognized as existing as loosely bounded entities while at the same time being part of an interlinking matrix that makes them responsive to one another. The concept of environment, for example, incorporates not only physical elements such as the land, animals, other humans, and plant life as well as rain and wind, but it also encompasses transcendent divinity and less tangible Giriama social and political institutions. For the Giriama their experience of the spirit world acknowledges its transcendence, while at the same time they perceive its inhabitants as firmly anchored in the physical world. Spirits pervade their lives, some existing in their bodies, at times causing them to become possessed or suffer spirit-caused sickness; and others also exist outside, and inhabit trees, caves, and ancestor memorials and shrines.

If we schematically separate the three domains of people in their socio-political and economic organization, the divinity of ancestors, possession-spirits and god, from the physical environment, we can view the interventionist role of diviners more clearly (Figure 6.1). When anything goes wrong in these domains, or between them, diviners are the ones who have the legitimate right to interpret the disorder, and who ultimately are the ones to intervene, and

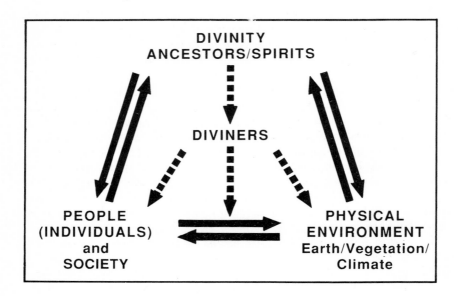

Figure 6.1 The mediating interventionist role of Giriama diviners.

establish a redefined order. Their privileged position is rooted in their unique channels of communication with the ancestors, other possession-spirits, and ultimately, through these intermediaries, with god. Quite simply, they mediate between the divine world and the physical world.

Famines or deaths, or even mild illnesses, for example, may be interpreted in a number of ways. They may be 'the will of god', the result of crumbling or ignored relationships between people and their ancestors, or personal possession-spirits, witchcraft, or curses which defile the land. All these cases presuppose remedial intervention by diviners is possible, initially to interpret the causes, and then subsequently, to facilitate a ritual reconciliation of the appropriate divine entity with their human miscreants.

Until this century, ritual reconciliation of humans with the most important spirits of all, the ancestors, was a role taken by the *kaya* elders. Traditionally, the *kaya* elders expressed most of their political and mystical powers in their control of the productive and reproductive spheres of Giriama life. The persistent erosion of their overall authority after dispersal out of the *kaya*, and subsequent political decentralization severely curtailed their practice of rituals of intervention with the spirit world. Nowadays this power is defined by diviners. They mediate and articulate the supreme authority of the ancestors.

It is important to understand at this stage that knowledge of the use of 'medicines' is a principal organizing factor in all spheres of Giriama political, economic, social and cultural life. Giriama medicines are usually herbal concoctions which may be prepared in a variety of ways, but which in the great majority, only become 'medicines' when they are used in conjunction with rituals. Many of the rituals are secret or are the exclusive knowledge of specialist practitioners. Beliefs in the efficacy of medicines in all these spheres means that they can be influenced by healers. Today it is healer–diviners who mediate to reconcile disordered relations between the three spheres of influence, the divinity, the human social world and the physical environment. These imbalances cause socially recognized illnesses, suffering, and other misfortunes.

Diviners respond to ills suffered by individuals caused by spiritual caprice or the sufferer having wronged members of the spiritual domain in some way. They also respond to ills felt on a corporate scale by society, such as the widespread fear of witchcraft, or the effects of defiling curses on families and communities. Additionally diviners respond as healers of ills of the land or the physical environment which may be caused by capricious spirits, defiling curses, or spoiled relationships between the people and the spiritual world. To do all this, they have a unique knowledge of medicines used for healing.[9] In tackling the ills of people and communities, regardless of the potency of herbal and other treatments diviners may prescribe as remedies, it is only when they have performed the appropriate reconciliatory rituals that these may become effective. The key importance of sacred rituals is to legitimize the practical uses of these medicines.

As agriculturalists, the Giriama epistemology is devoted in great part to dealing with ills affecting the land and its produce. In *kaya* times it was the male elders who were responsible for controlling the rain while the women were responsible for controlling the fertility of the soil and the health of its crops and plant-life in general. Senior women healers cooled and purified their human world of its accumulated defilement, in order to increase the probability of growing healthy crops and reaping good harvests. These rituals also affected the health of the population generally, for it was assumed that the people's general immorality and specific social transgressions caused the ills in the first place.[10]

The 'owners of the land', the men who formed the supreme ruling council in the *kaya*, were the inner circle of a secret society whose hidden knowledge of the most powerful medicines was used to maintain social control. It was also, importantly, used to try to ensure peaceful relations with outsiders. During initiation to this supreme rank, the elders learned the secrets of rainmaking and rain-prevention. Their control over the rain could be used either

Alternative explanations: *Plate 23* Diviner casting a divination (top) *Plate 24* A popular local Pentecostal church (bottom)

to benefit their people, or coercively as a threat to gain their cooperation if necessary. The high value of this knowledge was reflected in the limited number of men who possessed it and their high rank in society. Today, diviners have redefined the ancient rituals for purification of the land and its people, incorporating them into a single ceremony aimed primarily to increase the certainty that rain will fall. Diviners are the rain-makers nowadays.[11]

Diviners' efforts to establish the formal coherence of their image and ideology has resulted in their creation of the most elaborate assemblage of ideas describing the Giriama belief system in existence today. Nowadays it is diviners who are ambassadors for Giriama tradition and the professional dispensers of the modifications of 'traditional' knowledge. All their efforts are aimed at increasing the predictability of the outcomes of the shifting and potentially chaotic situations in everyday life.

DEVELOPMENT ECONOMISTS AS DIVINERS

It is obvious that diviners' interventions do not always work. The rain does not fall, people die, contagious diseases defy spiritual rationalities, and the land's fertility continues to decline in areas where fallow cycles are no longer long enough to allow for its natural regeneration. These sorts of outcomes do not falsify Giriama beliefs in their system of divination, however, or contradict the truths that the diviners claim to reveal. Instead, these outcomes are perceived as being the results of either the incorrect performance of the prescribed remedial ritual activities, or the influences of particular conditions or circumstances in the social context which were overlooked and thus not accounted for in the remedial rituals. The use of systems of secondary explanations allow people to sustain their faith in the validity of the belief system and the diviners who articulate it. In this way, people can seek more than one divination concerning a single problem and all redefinitions of the problem are held to be equally valid individually, but importantly, become increasingly credible, if they conform with one another. Additionally, where divinations are sought throughout an illness and diviners' interpretations of the conditions change with the changing face of the illness, secondary explanations play a fundamental role in sustaining peoples' faith in divinatory prescriptions in the face of apparently deviant outcomes.

All this should be familiar to the reader who has followed our description of events which occurred during the Magarini Settlement Project. Whereas the superficial analogy of development workers and diviners has startling parallels at the levels of legitimation and 'facipulation', it is limited by their fundamentally different working environments, in other words, their respective professional commitments to scientific and mystical explanations. But what of development practitioners' rituals? The rituals for establishing certainty within development practice, cost–benefit analysis for example, like those of diviners, are explicitly concerned with prescription and even prophesy.

Plate 25 The diviner's apprentices

Giriama divination has the object of providing prescriptive outcomes which will remedy pathological situations, usually illness or misfortune of one kind or another. The cost–benefit analysis conducted as part of AIDAB's Phase III Appraisal of Magarini was carried out to the mandate set by a higher authority, and claimed the unquestionable objectivity of the empirical facts gathered for, and presented at its completion. Neither divination nor cost–benefit analysis acknowledge the role of the personal or political preferences of their authors, nor is the reality of the ephemeral nature of their 'facts' or 'truths' ever admitted. Our analyses of both rituals have described the mystification of the stylized ritual performances, manipulations of the facts or truths within a limited range of options in a standardized format, their orientation towards generating an acceptable final pronouncement, and the clients' foregone acceptance of the predictive value of these prescriptions. Should either prescription fail in practice, the techniques are not falsified. Rather the fault is seen to lie in the incorrect performance of the ritual, perhaps where the cost–benefit analysis was not done properly, or due to inadequate and insufficient primary data. The principal value of the cost–benefit analysis to AIDAB was, after all, in its cathartic value rather than the actual results. Indeed with the possibility for self-examination in any ritual being virtually impossible, the diviner's pragmatic manipulations and the economic analyst's professional hegemony over the definition of an adequate appraisal protect their authenticity.

We do not intend to undermine the professionalism of economists by comparing them with Giriama diviners, instead we agree that in both belief systems their work has a vital predictive value. The point is that both practices undoubtedly share similar characteristics at the level of their role in their respective political–economic contexts. Conventionally the tendency to underline the differences between development practice and the practices of its beneficiaries justifies the very mandate for development. But by highlighting the similarities between them we gain insights which urge us in no uncertain terms to look as hard at ourselves and our own assumptions, as we purport to do when appraising others. It is, after all, in the spirit of diversity that new views of the control-orientation will reveal more about its insidious penetration. Our analogy is not as far off the point as economists and their fellow professionals might want to believe. Anthropologists Sally Moore and Barbara Myerhoff (1977: 24) explain,

> Since ritual is a good form for conveying a message as if it were unquestionable, it is often used to communicate those things which are most in doubt. Thus where there is conflict, or danger, or political opposition, where there is made-upness and cultural invention, ritual may carry the opposite message in form as well as content. ... Ritual can assert that what is man-made is as undoubtable as physical reality.

THE PLURAL ENVIRONMENT: EVADING CAPTURE FOR SURVIVAL

It was a cool morning in Gongoni trading centre, and a tea room was filling with labourers on their way to the salt works. A lively conversation focused the attention of everyone in the room, and participants were quickly drawn in from all sides. The argument was about birth control. All the conversers were men, and tensions were rising. Two women entered and sat down in the throng of men to wait for their sweet tea and bread. One of the women, overcoming her timidity in front of the men, broke her silence and exclaimed, 'Pills from hospital are rubbish, children are given by God! Who are we to compete with His decisions? He plans how many, where and when we bear children. Even a woman who is dirty, if people say to her, "Your children will become ill". Her answer is that illness is brought by God.'

An elderly man who had been the one to raise the issue in the first place, solemnly retorted, 'Giving birth is not easy, like shitting. I pray to my God for our safety in this world'. A young man jibed the older man, 'Do you really know what God is?' Provoked into declaring his beliefs, the old man replied contentiously, 'Islam or Christian, I have never seen a preacher yet who can bring the rain. Witches can control the rain though. Witches they pray to God, and then, well, witness for yourselves in the fields ... .'

Outraged by this, the first woman interjected, 'Witches pray to God? How can that be so? How can such evil people reach to the Holy Spirit of God?' The old man, unimpressed with such naivety, stood up and declared, 'God is responsible for everything. Whether you believe in hospitals or believe in Giriama healers, one sun shines on us all'. Then he delivered his parting shot, 'We use roots as our medicines and none of you can deny we are cured!' Not waiting to hear a response he turned on his heel, strode outside into the sunshine, and was gone.

This tea shop conversation is rich with allusions about the nature of the moral and social order facing the Giriama today. Bouncing up against one another are secular ideas about institutions for healing, traditionalist thoughts defining the causes of misfortune and their healing remedies, and facets of the dogmatic religiosity of the fundamentalist Pentecostals. The validity and legitimacy of these apparently conflicting ideas were once more being hotly contested, in spite of their usually more liberally tolerated pluralistic co-existence in everyday life

In terms of sacred or religious beliefs and the morality that conceptually orders individuals' lives and their social interactions, most Giriama traditionalists contest the exclusiveness of the Western-originated Christian denominational alternatives. The old man emphasized that all humans live under the same sun, as servants of one God. His opinion is a familiar one. It is an objection to the exclusiveness of Western beliefs and to the tendency for these to smother all other contending ways of life and world views.

Shifts by increasing numbers of people out of the older orthodox Anglican and Catholic church congregations into the more dynamic fundamentalist groups in northern Giriamaland coincided with the awakening of the nationalist movement. It was the beginning of an unsteady flow of people between churches, and also sometimes out of them altogether. Today the shifting

populations are mainly women. Locally, popular views argue that a major reason why women do not join Christian congregations more permanently is
because they come in search of healing for emotional or physical ills, and not
to learn about Christianity. The majority of women also agree that they join
to seek divine healing.

Giriama women's strategies are an important concern of the church
leaders, for it is women who usually make up most of their Christian congregations, particularly among the prolific Pentecostal churches. If they view
alternative Christian denominations as differently organized sources of relief
from illness, then the success or failure of the church to cure illness tends to
exert a considerable influence on their degree of commitment and length of
stay in the congregation. In seeking treatment these women, and some men
too, also seriously consider secular healing options offered by dispensaries
and hospitals as relevant alternatives.[12]

Giriama women and their children, it is widely agreed locally and profes-
sionally, suffer more illnesses than men, and spend more time seeking
treatment for their conditions. Commonly their strategies for seeking help are
eclectic. Advice and treatment sought first from diviners may be followed by
the health centre, and in certain cases even the church, all during the one
illness episode. Here we see three apparently contradictory belief systems
being used at once. In practice, contradictions tend to be suppressed when it
is necessary to seek alternative explanations and treatments for persistent illnesses. Contrarily, however, traditionalists still tend to attribute the healthy
outcomes of their various treatment strategies to Giriama existential explanations, thereby maintaining the long-term validity of their own belief system.

It is not only health problems which cause people to use different offerings
in their plural environment to reduce the risk of failure to solve problems.
Giriama people on the whole tend to hedge their bets in all domains where
there are plural options available. An anecdotal example of this comes from
the strategies of a progressive farmer in Magarini. Silas Katana planted all his
maize seeds in straight lines according to the prescriptions of his agricultural
extension agent. After the first failure of the seeds to germinate, he returned
to his field and replanted in the traditional random or broadcast style. He
explained this seemingly irrational decision, saying, 'It is always the same,
when I plant in straight lines, if there are mice, they start eating at one end and
move on swiftly straight down the line, and I quickly lose the whole crop. I
always replant randomly because there is a greater chance that less seeds will
be found by the mice this way.'

He later highlighted the secondary and tertiary benefits of another customary strategy he used to avoid excessive risk by explaining his use of hired
labour. Instead of accumulating debt to cover the cost of acquiring oxen or the
regular services of a tractor he used a traditional method which benefited all
concerned. He retained a poor woman neighbour to do his farm work, his wife
worked around the homestead and in other fields, while he himself went out

to earn money for the family and to cover the cost of hiring labour, by teaching at the local primary school. In this way, he argued, he had labour for his fields, his wife had help in the home with the children when necessary, and his neighbour earned money, ate with the family, and strengthened her network of reciprocal support.

Critics of the Giriama focus on their resistance to change, but the situation is obviously not so straightforward. They are not isolated from the project's overall interventions delivered by the state or other agencies. But their reactions to these agencies' assumptions of a linear view of history and their presumption of an exclusive right to define the future, should be seen less as direct resistance, and more as a complex eclectic acceptance of change and accommodation of their uncertain future.

Chapter 7

More diversity for more certainty

The Magarini Settlement Project was afflicted with two closely related problems widely reported from rural development projects elsewhere. First, many of the interventions worked against the real interests of the intended beneficiaries, and the project staff were unable to hear the warnings of specialists and protests from the people themselves that this would occur. Second, the interventions were not sustainable, partly because they did not meet people's needs and partly because the project ignored environmental and economic realities or approached them with a totally unrealistic optimism. We attribute these very common features of rural development projects to what we have called control-orientation. In Chapter Four we acknowledge that this is an unpopular and hazardous position to adopt. It is unpopular because many of the solutions now being enthusiastically proposed by donor agency staff to correct these problems are, in fact, refinements of control-orientation. We believe these 'solutions' will exacerbate the problems. It is hazardous because in a debate in which extreme positions are commonly adopted, there is a chance that those in control will accuse us of simply fuelling flames of criticism and, ignoring the point, will conclude that rural development is just too hard.

Nevertheless let us try to summarize our concerns about present development practice.

Development projects are not the products of immaculate conceptions. At least one Giriama settler saw Magarini as a bastard child. Projects are born of an amalgam of international diplomacy and vested interests, humanitarian concern and optimistic good intentions. It is no wonder that the early stages of project aid assume common objectives can be established and held to weather a relationship of convenience for five or more years duration. Yet, in such a fertile field, it is astonishing that the repertoire of objectives produced by the architects of projects is so limited. Available information about Magarini does not suggest a single credible or coherent picture of the problems that would yield common objectives. A seething mass of contending perceptions, divergent personal and institutional strategies, and polarized interests, yes. But a common medium- to long-term statement of objectives or targets that could make sense outside the confines of a project document, no. Perhaps it is that the goal statements which today must be listed in logical frameworks in order to have any standing, are designed solely to attract fashion-conscious buyers? Not entirely. As we have learned in our study of Magarini, some objectives can be explicit, some can be implied and some, as the NGO learned when it tried to raise awareness of Giriama people's interests, cannot be mentioned at all.

The majority of development projects begin with a diplomatic commitment and then the first mission sets out to find a problem to deal with. In September 1975 SMEC asked AIDAB how much money they were prepared to spend and were told $10 million over 5–7 years. SMEC then designed a project and this design, undertaken in Cooma, New South Wales, Australia, set the direction taken at Magarini for the next fourteen years, despite a number of attempts at redesign.

Two things commonly happen at this stage of a project. First, the die is cast in the form of the Project Cycle. Ranging between nine and fifteen stages of pre-feasibility, feasibility, planning, design, appraisal, and monitoring, a process is set in train that effectively ensures that the designers are seldom around to share the risks when their plan is implemented, the implementers are not involved in shaping what is possible, and the beneficiaries' obligations, detailed on their behalf, are slotted into an overall scheme. In focusing attention on itself, this approach effectively conceals problems and approaches that lie outside the narrow confines of 'the project'.

The second occurrence is the development of a comprehensive and systematic framework for problem analysis. Here development agencies are in tune with academic advisers who challenge them to be more holistic, more conscious of the human system–ecosystem interface, and to take all things into account. The systems approach is eminently scientific in intent. Beginning with the 'facts', all the components of the system are to be identified. A qualitative tool of enormous proportions is created, as Paul McGowan realized within a year of unleashing a dozen specialists to define the components and produce the thirteen Technical Annexes for the Magarini Phase I resource investigation. To fathom in which direction the system is moving, being transformed or sustained, the relative rates of change in the relationships between each component need to be known. Uncertainty can enter at many points, in the assessment of how the rates of change are affected by functional relationships between components elsewhere in the system, by having inadvertently omitted some of the boxes, or by not having identified all the dynamic processes. The result in situations like Magarini is that uncertainty is greatly increased.

The fundamental logic of this activity is that once everything is known about the area and the people, the fine detail of the design can be manipulated to meet the already decided project goals. There are now literally piles of books on what the 'right' information is and how to collect it. Since the 1970s, to the list of soil, water, plants, animals, markets and transport, have been added health, nutrition, women and the environment.

At this stage at Magarini, McGowan was confronted with a mass of contradictory advice and a leap in the level of uncertainty. He took the course followed by the positive practitioner, to 'push on', to 'fly by the seat of the pants', to 'crash through or crash'. The resource investigation at Magarini virtually ignored the Giriama, but even if it had taken them into account, it would still not have been able to reduce greatly the level of uncertainty which increased relative to the amount of information being generated. We are not suggesting no information be collected. But we make the point that development must be an on going, adaptive and therefore diverse process and any cycle which attempts to dictate that most of the learning should occur in one stage and that most of the application of that learning should occur in another stage, is deeply flawed.

Many development practitioners are paid large amounts of money to solve conundrums, not to put them back onto their clients' desks, even if that is where many of them originate. So despite the uncertainties and contradictions, the donor's consultant produces implementation schedules, logical frameworks, critical path analyses, input–output statements and programme budgets; all right and proper ways to manage and control projects when the initial assumptions are firmly based in reality. But in contemporary rural development practice, the preceding stages have already replaced reality with a ritualized behaviour, not unlike the excessive boot polishing and cleaning of equipment which army recruits carry out and which British sergeant-majors know affectionately as 'bullshit'. The unreality is perhaps best reflected in what are euphemistically called Memoranda of Understanding (MOU). When the recipient government inevitably begins to fall behind the scheduled commitments in money and personnel, the MOU is referred to by the donor government with mutterings about 'a lack of political will' and the 'need for a demonstration of commitment to the project'. Donor efforts to lean on the recipient and, in essence, get the recipient government to wrap their institutions around the donor's definition of the problem are futile, because the recipient government seldom has the authoritative capacity to make the system work according to the plan. The donor finds that the impressive array of policy levers they thought could be used to influence the outcome of the project are not attached to anything.

But by this stage the project has gained a life of its own. Institutional responsibilities are defined and agreed upon, coordinating committees assembled, and almost without exception, local institutions are by-passed in the interests of efficient and effective use of resources. We have seen most examples of by-passing at Magarini. The dependence on expatriate development workers and technique peddlers (Hyden 1983: 150) is assured some stages before: during the heady days when medium- to long-term targets are decided; when sophisticated rituals of appraisal are introduced; when 'the problem' is systematically compartmentalized; when the human resource implications of implementation rates are determined; in sum, when the donor agency is persuaded that despite good intentions, the recipient institutions are not up to the task. Institutional weaknesses are created by this approach. Despite the now obligatory institution strengthening components in projects, the approach reproduces this state of affairs in paradoxical ways. By-passing is not the result of a lack of knowledge about institutional capacity; the aggregated human resource implications of alternative project designs are a simple accounting exercise. Rather, by-passing is the result of looking the other way, toward economically viable implementation rates of similarly viable scales of investment, and inevitably, the imperative to control what is increasingly an uncertain commitment of aid monies.

The efficacy of participation by this stage is well established; indeed, this fundamental concern of development workers covers the pages of project documents and literature. The records and files of the Magarini project are no exception. But unfortunately, with the above edifice in place, participation can only be rhetorical, regardless of the number of times the need is confirmed by hard-pressed exclamation marks in the margins of project evaluation reports. There is little an NGO can do to meet the expectations of this conventional approach. The NGO limitations of institutional scale, management skills and scope of operations are not to be underestimated. But more significant issues were raised by the Magarini case. The dilemma is put well by Martin Buber when he says, 'One cannot, in the nature of things, expect a little tree that has been turned into a club to put forth leaves' (cited in Chomsky 1970).

PRACTICE MAKES PERFECT?

The objective of this book has not been to design an alternative approach to development practice. Rather, we set out with the intention of recounting how Magarini was created and sustained for over fourteen years. In the face of so many books on project practice, our task was simply to write one about development practice. But as we moved into the story, and compared it with contemporary donor practices elsewhere, it became obvious that we must also try to clear away some misconceptions about an unnervingly prevalent form of development practice. Most often it seems, decisions to refine the control-orientation are made by anxious people unaware of the paradoxical effects this has on practice. This is another way of noting that policies and procedures are inadequately informed by reality. It is not our purpose to criticize particular individuals or institutions, although it has been difficult not to be critical of both in reaching our objective. Those criticized may well argue that the events which we have described occurred in the past, and present practice has improved. Perhaps, but present practice is the legacy of the development fashions of the 1970s and 1980s. For the Giriama and thousands of other Third World peoples, these fashions proved almost fatal. We are uncertain whether increasing the efficiency of such a deadly weapon can be viewed as an improvement.

It has also been suggested to us that Magarini is unique, one bad apple in a barrel of quite good apples. We doubt this. It is an exaggeration to suggest that contemporary development practice always gives rise to outcomes of Magarini-type proportions, but it is not misleading to generalize from Magarini to contemporary development practice, to the problems of farming in resource-poor, marginal environments, of political tensions related to the occupation of land, of myriad institutional difficulties, of food and water security, and of reluctant, if not resistant, project beneficiaries. Try buying a beer for the next hard-bitten professional practitioner you meet, and settle back to listen to the woes of Magarini echoing from all corners of the Third World. AIDAB's own Appraisals and Evaluation Section has recently concluded in a draft paper on AIDAB's involvement in Integrated Area Development Projects in Thailand, the Philippines, Indonesia, Sri Lanka, Papua New Guinea and Kenya that,

> In general, performance is disappointing, and targets established for raising income levels and improving livelihoods are unlikely to be met. Health, education and other community services were usually treated as add-ons to the infrastructural components and were of limited impact and sustainability. Economic returns are likely to be low.

> (AIDAB 1989: i)

More important, it is highly likely that the constellation of land–food–people problems faced at Magarini will challenge development practice in the future.

Our conclusions imply a fundamental re-orientation in development practice. We know, however, that less will have to do. The challenge seems to be to explore what could be, while tempering our enthusiasm with the knowledge of what the opportunities are in each situation. This is a crucial task. On the one hand, it is to avoid seeing development workers as unable to do anything but act out the various diplomatic, strategic and commercial imperatives which, with three broad strokes, are often used to paint a highly determined view of what happens in development practice. This approach leaves the development worker a frustrating and unwitting role as a dupe of the system. On the other hand, and this seems to mark many of the manuals enjoining development workers to do this or that, we need to avoid an unjustifiably voluntaristic view of what is possible.

We do not take the view that 'if only' the project had got the people's real interests represented firmly in the central objectives, or if only the people had participated fully in the implementation, then a happy ending would have been guaranteed. There are serious constraints on what Robert Chambers calls reversals (1983). 'Good' outcomes are not ensured merely by blindly following a prescriptive list of 'good' practices and eschewing 'bad' ones. For large public policy issues like population control or employment, participatory approaches in their present form are at best marginal and at worst irrelevant to the mobilization of power, rhetoric and bias characteristic of the international arena in which most of these issues will be decided.[1] We are not arguing that at the project level all of the trappings of control-orientation like cost–benefit analysis, log-frames or project appraisals, should be abandoned. But where the central objectives of an intervention require considerable participation of intended beneficiaries to ensure their appropriateness and sustainability, and where major gaps exist in knowledge about present conditions, needs, resources and institutional capabilities, with a consequent high risk of unforeseen and unintended outcomes, then the biases of control-orientation are pernicious and need to be strenuously countered by more pluralistic approaches.

'Recognizing no authority'

It is not by chance the story of the Giriama people of Magarini runs throughout the preceding chapters. Control-oriented and pluralist-oriented approaches to development both attempt to manipulate present resources to reach desired futures. But while a control-orientation tends to vest power with increasingly distant, higher authorities, from project managers to cabinet ministers, a pluralist-orientation relocates judgements about risk, uncertainty and options in the hands of the people most likely to bear the unforeseen consequences of such decisions. Where the former approach increases uncertainty and non-sustainability, the latter more closely imitates the diverse ways in which poor rural people reduce uncertainty and increase sustainability.

An understanding of Giriama life, even at a necessarily simple level, reveals ways of coping with uncertainty which are important metaphors for development practice. The apparently contradictory cosmologies expressed in the debate in the Gongoni tea shop or the chaotic order of the swidden garden, co-exist in a taken-for-granted everyday world. Men and women in poor health consult elders, diviners, herbalists, fundmentalist Christian church leaders and health centre staff. Giriama agriculture is similarly eclectic, employing multiple plots on a range of soils, a large number of species, staggered planting and as insurances against a bad year, a complex of off-farm employment, reciprocal networks of obligations and exchange within a community.

What the Giriama have to teach us is that the greater the uncertainty the greater the desirability of having the largest possible number of options available. This approach is the antithesis of what has been called the 'single, ready-made-idea-plus-feasibility-study approach' (P. Smith 1987: 21), represented, for example, by fashions like 'training-and-visit' in extension, or the 'integrated-area-development-project' approach to agriculture. Arthur Champion, the Assistant District Commissioner at Jilore in 1913 described the Giriama as anarchistic and recognizing no authority. Our support for more pluralist approaches contains elements of methodological anarchism, and a word on this may help redress any confusion which has arisen over the pluralist-orientation. From this point of view it can be argued that Giriama life is richer, not poorer, for its diversity, and that we should be deeply suspicious of interventions which attempt to reduce diversity. We should also be questioning institutionalized rules and procedures which, rather than ensuring success, give substance and permanence to errors. Successful development practice must be able to grasp the rich and diverse forms of social life and survival which typify rural people in the Third World.

Magarini and many other rural development projects of the last decade demonstrate that a determination to regularize and standardize development practice is not matched with success. There is not a single aspect of successful development practice that does not at some time violate a well-rehearsed approach. This is not because of insufficient knowledge, or inexpertness of practice; nor are these accidental lapses. Rather, it seems an entrepreneurial spirit of rule-breaking was a necessary condition for progress. We should be reminded of circumstances when it is advisable not only to ignore 'correct' procedures and all vestiges of control, but to adopt their opposite.

It is possible to enforce an approach that is bound together by comprehensive manuals of procedures, replete with segments for inputs–outputs, cross-impact matrices, strict timelines, budgets and enforceable performance contracts. That is how NASA put a man on the moon. But rural development is not about putting men on the moon. It is about less external control, less pretence that control creates certainty of outcomes, and more space for individual human creativity to react to circumstances and find lasting solutions, solutions which will lead to greater order not greater chaos. Anarchy does not mean 'out of control; it means out of their control' (Dodge 1981).

THE NEED FOR HUMILITY

We can already hear the snorts of derision from the positive practitioners and the cries of despair from the aid bureaucrats. Those who view rationality in strictly functional terms, classification, calculation and manipulation of variables, and who administer aid programmes in the capital cities of the First World will find pluralism hard to live with. We make two responses to these protests.

First, the pretence of control-orientation to certainty, apart from the stultifying effect it has on originality in development practice, actually increases the risk to the intended beneficiaries. In Robert Chambers' words,

> To take risks for oneself is one thing. To encourage others to do so is quite another. Even more, for any outsider to encourage vulnerable poor people to take risks raises ethical questions, especially when it is they and not the outsider, who will pay the price of failure.
>
> (Chambers 1983: 193)

Second, the conceptual origins of the control-orientation techniques are themselves questionable. The mathematical tools which economists use, for instance, owe a great deal to Newtonian physics and linear regression, but 'the economy cannot be analysed in terms of an organon which has been cast in the mould of mechanics that deals only with invariant phenomena endlessly repeating themselves' (Singh 1976: 111). The critics of so-called scientific practice, which control-oriented development practice mimics, question whether a single category 'science' exists at all (Chalmers 1976: 166). Albert Einstein once observed, 'The external conditions which are set by the facts of experience do not permit him [the scientist] to let himself be too much restricted ... he must appear to the systematic epistemologist as a type of unscrupulous opportunist' (Samuel and Einstein 1951: 683). The control-orientation is unrealistic and pernicious. Paul Feyerabend, a challenging and provocative critic of scientific practice, says,

> The idea that science can, and should be run according to fixed and universal rules, is both unrealistic and pernicious. It is unrealistic, for it takes too simple a view of the talents of man and of the circumstances which encourage or cause their development. And it is pernicious, for the attempt to enforce the rules is bound to increase our professional qualifications at the expense of our humanity. In addition the idea is detrimental to science, for it neglects the complex physical and historical conditions which influence scientific change. It makes our science less adaptable and more dogmatic: every methodological rule is associated with cosmological assumptions, so that using the rule we take it for granted that the assumptions are correct.
> (Feyerabend 1975: 295)

The word 'development' could be substituted for the word 'science' without substantially altering the statement's truth. The positive practitioner would observe that it is all very well for science to be based on multiple frames of reference, like wave and particle theories of light, but development practice requires decisions; choices must be narrowed, actions taken, targets reached. True, development practice is about choices, but good development practice is about widening, not narrowing choices. A pluralist-orientation acts as a stimulus to identify and approach problems from different directions and assists in defining alternatives. The economist would counter that cost–benefit analysis is all about choices. Again we agree, but maintain that cost–benefit analysis should be only one means of making choices, and point to the irrefutable evidence that cost–benefit analysis is too often employed not as an open, honest presentation of options, but as an obfuscatory, after-the-decision justification of a particular choice.

Readers of development theory might be surprised to learn that contemporary development practice is narrowing the range of choice. Despite the view that it has reached an impasse (Kitching 1982), a burgeoning development literature presents a wide range of viewpoints. But in practice, there is a striking concordance: the outcome of the belief, or perhaps the vain hope, that if all the components can be controlled and determined, eventually the right answer will be discovered. Our position is that it is better to come right out and consider the alternative: we must abandon the ambition to find one 'right' answer to every dilemma in development practice. Even if it exists, by the time we have groped our way towards it, the problem to which we have initially sought an answer, will have changed, or shifted somewhere else. We must recognize, as John Cool explains, 'There is an enormous need for humility both in our capacity to understand and intervene, in these processes' (quoted in Thompson *et al.* 1986: 101).

PLURALISM AND MAKING THE RIGHT DECISIONS

Positive practitioners are not known for their humility and even those imbued with less optimism have great difficulty in resisting the almost pathological temptation, to 'have a go' at solving a development problem.[2] A pluralist-orientation does not absolve us of the responsibility to get it right. However, until such time as the plural frameworks which are represented in the Gongoni tea shop debate can be integrated at a theoretical level and then wrestled down to the level of practice, we will have to show greater humility in the way we make decisions in practice.

Three types of decision are presently made in development practice, all of which are amply illustrated by the Magarini experience. The first are the numerous decisions which are forced by the unintended consequences of a single earlier decision. The decision to use the bulldozer blade to clear scrub to enable the land development programme to keep up with settlement, or the decision to provide food-for-work are examples. We have called this type of decision 'knock-ons' and they tend to carry the practitioner further and further away from original objectives, with the likelihood of ever reaching those objectives decreasing with each step.

A second type of decision is made because the proper decision, the one which logically should have been made, is blocked by factors beyond the influence of the decision maker. When the 1980 review team gathered at Magarini, it became clear that unless radical changes were made, the project was doomed. But there were extenuating circumstances, perceived to be diplomatic, political and commercial, which led team members to block logical decisions. The shifting constellations of interests, of the managing agents, the aid bureaucracy, the Kenyan patrons and clients, the Australian diplomatic push, mobilized and manipulated the rules and resources, so that the decisions reached were consistently not in the interests of the Giriama beneficiaries.

A third type are the objective decisions, where the techniques provide the answers, and the 'facts' are said to speak for themselves. In 1983 and 1984, within a matter of weeks the project went from having 'major unresolved difficulties' to possessing the 'financial and economic viability' to justify

Plate 26 Who leads?

Note: From left to right: Australian advisers, Kenyan project staff, Giriama and the ancestors (memorial posts)

further Australian commitment. This decision, it was argued, followed logically from the results of the economic analysis, independent of the ideological, personal or political preferences of the decision makers. Responsibility for the decision became vested in the technique. We chose to examine only one example of this; there are, we believe, increasing cases of decisions being made in development practice 'because it's in the log-frame', or which 'follow from the project budget', which avoid the difficult choices that logical thinking would require.

If the decisions made under existing practice are less than desirable, how would a pluralist-orientation result in better or more appropriate decisions? Chambers' reversal (1983), 'putting the last first' is, like most striking and resonant slogans, not easy to put into practice. Redclift (1987: 157) argues for a better balance in the present process in which 'we' do all the managing while 'they' operate within the space and the technology we have provided for them. There are, however, three cogent reasons why we should promote reversals. First, this exceedingly simple unequivocal message echoes the fundamental humanitarian concern expressed most consistently by NGOs, but which underlies the common citizen's support for a continuation of aid to poor and oppressed people.

Sentiments aside, reversals make sound operational sense. The Magarini case provides numerous examples of problems which could have been partly or wholly avoided if knowledgeable Giriama had been consulted. The principles of farming systems research and a growing literature on indigenous knowledge argues the indispensability of consulting with local people. Consultation and participation of local people in decision making demonstrably improves the mobilization of resources and the energy of people who are too often left out of the development process.

Our third point about a pluralist-orientation to reversals in development practice reaches further than moral or operational needs. Pluralism contains an important ethical component noticeably missing from present practice. It explicitly recognizes that knowledge is always and everywhere incomplete, that many of the conditions bearing on decisions will be unknown at the time the decision is made and that decisions made under these conditions will have unforeseen and unintended consequences. Everyone knows there can be no social change, no development without costs. The question is determining what those costs are likely to be, who is likely to bear them, and whether they are capable and willing to do so. Participation is not merely a utilitarian incorporation of the views or knowledge of the people into the project plan. It is a matter also of ethics, one that is unavoidable given the tendency for rural development to leave people, as many Giriama were left, 'worse off now than before the project started'.

The pluralist-orientation requires, therefore, that development practice incorporate a process, call it what you wish, organizing, training, empowerment, whereby those most likely to be adversely affected when things do not go according to plan, are better able to judge, decide and influence political events which in most cases once set in train are beyond their control. The adoption of this approach will not of itself reverse the knock-ons, blocked or technique-driven decision making, but it will reduce the likelihood of them happening and will raise the general quality of decision making. Cost–benefit analysis, for instance, when correctly managed could reverse the adverse development outcomes to which it now frequently contributes. Cost–benefit analysis is a means of 'systematically using organised human rationality to identify and evaluate the consequences of proposed collective decisions' (Campen 1986: 185) and to value all costs and benefits, social as well as financial or economic. This potential will only be realized if the assessments of benefits and costs, the discounting of future gains and risks, and the determination of rates of return, normally mystified and left in the hands of the spreadsheet technician, are flushed out into the public gaze.

This is not the same as saying that the people's view must always prevail. It is true that no development workers should fool themselves into thinking they know, as a matter of course, the people's real interests better than the people themselves, but it is also true that the people can be wrong about their best interests. Their knowledge may be incomplete and their choices may be as easily subject to political manipulation as the development workers'. The development workers will still be faced with choices, and by a function of their position in the decision-making hierarchy, their decisions will always have the potential to supersede those of the people. This paradoxical situation can be alleviated by participation, but ultimately, the paradox is inescapable.

THE LIMITS OF THE PLURALIST-ORIENTATION

Thus far we have discussed difficulties with the application of a pluralist-orientation to development at the level of the project. But a number of constraints exist which go well beyond these limits. We examine these constraints under three headings. The first, which we call institutional fashions and imperatives, refers to the distinctive, conservative economic orthodoxy which results in an inappropriately single-minded focus on efficiency and fiscal measures of project viability. The second set of constraints, which we call intellectual baggage, relate to the prejudiced generalities about Third World rural situations and the way rural people deal with threats to their food, land, water and political security. Finally, we consider what we call institutional egos and contests, institutional and individual practices which appear to prevent major agencies and their staff from learning the lessons of present practice.

International fashions and imperatives

It is clear that the early designers of development in the Third World went to great lengths to connect international, national and local project level activities by a universal set of procedures. Today, at a time of unprecedented international debt, development strategies down to the level of institutional priorities on the project are increasingly dictated by the imperatives of the international financial community. It is these agencies which by and large define the rules and resources, and create the fashions which are dutifully incorporated into the aid practices of smaller donor agencies like AIDAB.

It should be no surprise that the control-orientation imposed at Magarini and described in Chapter Four, originates in the international lending agencies. Their capital is at risk and they have maintained, since the late 1970s, a consistent conservative political outlook, backed by monetarist economic theories. Members of this economic orthodoxy, well represented, despite their differences, in the writings of Peter Bauer, Ian Little, Bela Balassa and Deepak Lal, believe that development problems can only be solved by the imposition of an economic system and a set of controls on government activities, which do little else but foster outward looking policies in favour of free market economies.

We are not here going to match slogan with counter-slogan, characteristic of the debate over the orthodox approach. It is obvious, however, that diversity and the last-shall-be-first reversals of the pluralist-orientation cannot prosper where development assistance is determined by an international economic system which perpetuates the manipulation of the weak by the strong. Despite recent and popularized questioning of the empirical validity of monetarist development policy (e.g. George 1988), we are daunted by the vacuum created in discussions on development practice by those who insist that their view of the solution to the problems of the Third World is the one true, reasonable and rational argument.

Intellectual baggage

Control-orientation is reaffirmed as the one reasonable way by the intellectual prejudice and ignorance about Third World development which prevails across the political spectrum in the First World. We restrict our comments to Africa. The view of Africa from outside is one of crisis. There is obvious poverty and nobody can but be distressed at the 1984–85 famine in Ethiopia, or the conflicts in places like the Sudan and Ethiopia, or the slaughter of Mozambicans by Renamo thugs funded by South Africa. Nor is it easy to ignore the suffering, much of it to come, inflicted on the poor majority by IMF-manufactured economic 'stabilization' and 'adjustment'. It is this sense of crisis which gives legitimacy to the orthodox view that Africa's economic problems come from within.

Yet we must be suspicious of crisis and acutely aware of the adverse effects this kind of outlook has in practice. When the evidence is sought for a justification of this view it is hard to find and according to Michael Watts, is largely 'incapable of supporting the weight of continental generalizations'. It is, argues Watts, 'not a case of theory shaping fact; it is fiction masquerading as fact' (Watts 1989: 3).[3] This concept of crisis in Africa illustrates three common characteristics of intellectual baggage which constrains the pluralist approach.

A generic sense of crisis leads too readily to the identification of particular local events as instances of predefined larger factors. Directionless agricultural extension services and the impossibility of procuring spare parts quickly, may be the result of inefficient government management, but the constant abstraction of local events to fit prejudices about generic problems which are believed to exist, can foster a blindness. The outcome can lead to a neglect of local social processes and the misjudgement of these processes. At Magarini, prejudices about Giriama agriculture were soon linked with ideas about the generic weaknesses of African agriculture which led to the conclusion that the whole system should be replaced. In another instance, what was perceived as Giriama conservativism, was quickly associated with cultural backwardness, and not with a historically developed local ability to evade external threats.

Crisis is also frequently taken as the precursor of acute catastrophic collapse. At Magarini, despite sympathetic observations that people were worse off than before the project began, we must conclude that most of those affected, except perhaps the old and infirm and the very young, have weathered the storm. They have demonstrated a remarkable resilience based on an ability to withdraw and sit out the crisis. The foreigners' propensity to carry their perceptions of crisis into every situation, leads them to neglect the contingent and contradictory ways in which people can often incorporate and translate external interventions into new, innovative and unexpected outcomes.

The overbearing sense of crisis also leads to attendant images of local people as weak, powerless and dependent, and unable to create their own futures. The sympathetic development workers, and this is a not an uncommon position of some NGOs, find themselves in the weak-kneed position of trying to soften the impact of a project on people, rather than looking for the people's strengths and building upon them. People are capable of resisting and they are adaptable. At Magarini, the Giriama had a long history of resisting intervention and surviving droughts of crisis proportions. They were survivors and they have survived the project, as a people.

Institutional egos and individual contests

Despite their diversity, the organizations involved in rural development display a number of points in common. They often have difficulty in dealing with error, have short institutional memories, tend to be hierarchical, authoritarian and punitive, and are oriented away from the field towards the rewards, and the punishments, which are dispensed from above. Bureaucratic systems of this nature have great difficulty handling diverse or apparently contradictory ideas. Attempts during 1982 and 1983 to introduce a greater degree of pluralism to the Magarini Project failed because neither AIDAB nor the managing agent could handle it.

One attitude of aid institutions which is particularly damaging to the introduction of a pluralist-orientation is the sense of heteronomy, the idea that development is something which is done by 'us' to 'them'. The major difficulties in project practice are seldom a question of money and 'doing things' to others, but rather that most of the recipients of aid are 'government institutions that have minimal or adversarial relations with the intended beneficiaries and have either no experience in, or commitment to, channelling aid funds for their use' (Hellinger *et al.* 1988: 5). The conclusions of this are hard to avoid. As Goran Hyden remarks, 'As long as foreign aid is being channelled through recipient governments its chances of reaching the poor or stimulating popular participation are pre-empted by the structural constraints prevailing on the continent' (Hyden 1983: 182). A recent report on the US aid programme observed,

> Every aid project officer knows the shortcomings of these institutions. But everyone also knows the institutional pressures back home to move funds. The effort to identify an institution that can design and implement a successful project may bring considerable benefits to the local poor, but it may not be as valuable to the donor organisation seeking to justify a larger budget for the next fiscal year as is larger-scale quicker funding through a far less appropriate institution.
>
> (Hellinger *et al.* 1988: 5)

At a level below that of the large institutions, vested interests are always at play. In relation to a settlement project in Papua New Guinea, Hulme notes,

> Those handling the progress of the project proposals through the procedures that culminated in approval and allocation were not impartial technical specialists, but individuals with personal interests and concerns about the pressures their agencies placed upon them.
>
> (Hulme 1989: 10)

This is not to say that desk officers and consultants, along with their Kenyan counterparts equally keen to see funding approved, were acting irresponsibly. Most lessons and warnings were not ignored, and in many cases the individuals involved could have influenced choices made. But there were overriding imperatives. All institutions have a tendency to shoot the messenger carrying the bad news and AIDAB is no exception. There was therefore a greater need to appear confident and certain about outcomes in official communications, particularly those that went outside an institution. A fine line exists between knowing the facts and pretending all is well to others, and the adoption of a misplaced sense of credibility and effectiveness.

Managing agents will always have commercial interests. As one of the consultants we interviewed about Magarini said, 'You always try and do your best for the local people, but when it comes right down to it, you're there to make money'. But the pernicious effects of the commercial interest are sometimes overplayed. More significant is the need to exude a confident sense of certainty and of being in control. This is not merely a matter of individual ego but has become horribly confused by aid institutions with credibility, accountability and a macho sense of effectiveness. At Magarini it can be traced from the bulldozer driver rolling up his sleeves for action, right through each link in a bureaucratic chain that landed not problems, but the 'next logical step', on the desk of the Australian Minister for Foreign Affairs. The usual remedy announced for this is more evaluation, more training in sophisticated appraisal, and increasingly, screwing the recipient counterpart down through performance indicators and quasi-legal conditions on aid. The Magarini experience, where each evaluation recited the concerns of its predecessor, questions this approach. Some evaluation is better than none; we would be hard-pressed to argue otherwise. But more thought needs to go into what is being evaluated, by whom, and especially, with what effect.

Some of these outcomes have to do with the 'cool' political climate in which aid is offered and received (Fowler 1982: 3). Amongst donors, aid is an instrument of foreign policy and since this is usually bipartisan, it is reasonably well insulated from debate. The Australian Parliamentary Hansard from 1972 to 1989 mentions Magarini only three times, and only once in a sense which could be construed as even slightly critical. The CAA Newsletter and a later article in *Time* magazine caused great anguish in AIDAB but raised very little interest in the community at large.[4] The constituency for lobbying and serious scrutiny is smaller than for domestic policies and programmes which may draw less revenue from the public purse. In the recipient countries foreign consultants are sometimes brought to heel, and charges of donor imperialism and embezzlement of aid funds are heard now and again, but any serious critique of aid-receiving policy is taboo. The pecuniary opportunities for revenue-hungry governments and politicians and public servants with big pockets are so great that the avenues for scrutiny are few. The 1987 Australian Review Team to Magarini discovered this to their embarrassment. When they attempted to trace wheat aid and other project funds through the Kenyan accounting system they were met with an exceedingly polite and skilfully manoeuvred smokescreen. For these reasons and by these means, the business of development practice is kept well out the hands of its consumers and the public 'shareholders'.

NO PRESCRIPTIONS

We have used the Magarini Settlement Project in Coast Province, Kenya to illustrate the course taken by development practice in the 1970s and 1980s. Our conclusions are that in this period development practice has become increasingly control-oriented in a futile effort to reduce the level of uncertainty which accompanies any rural development intervention. Futile, because increased control-orientation leads inevitably to a denial of reality and greater, not lesser uncertainty. We have argued that contemporary development practice must become more pluralist-oriented, accept the uncertainty and welcome the diversity, and face up to the realities.

If we are to be realistic ourselves, we must acknowledge the major constraints which the large aid institutions, orthodox monetarist economics and Third World politics present to the adoption of a greater pluralist-orientation in contemporary development practice. Nor would we be true to our argument if we offered the reader a glib and easy prescriptive answer. If we have anything quick and easy to offer, it is that there is no answer. The problem is a moving, evolving multi-faceted thing, and if it was possible to offer an answer today, it would be inappropriate by tomorrow.

We are not happy with the 'if only' prescriptions about how development practice can create appropriate, sustainable and equitable interventions. Nevertheless, our analysis of Magarini leaves us with a belief in the capacity of people to make a difference. In a workshop which presented some of what we have written to an audience of academics, development professionals and consultants, Peter Robertson reminded us that 'we are part of the problem, as well as part of the solution'. Some people, particularly those in the comfortable confines of large development agencies, take the view that Magarini-type outcomes are inevitable given the constraints we have identified. But what is characteristic of our contemporary situation is not just the playing out of powerful forces in which we are helpless to intervene, or the spread of techniques which hold promises that are always just beyond our grasp, but a paradoxical situation in which attempts to increase control are matched by resistance. This reveals the vulnerability of control and power. Questioning and reflection can enlarge these opportunities; but only if the so-called target population, development workers and a more vigilant public, refuse to be fobbed off with a 'Don't you worry about that'.[5] If this story of the Magarini Project causes us all to pause and question present development practice, and persuades us to try in some small way to be a little more pluralist it will have served its purpose.

Appendix A: Documentary and Giriama Record of Famines, 1836–1980

1836 Wakamba settlement at Mariakani due to famine (Giriama still in Kaya Fungo).

1850s Famine (*ndzala*) among the Duruma.

1876 *Ndzala ya kingo*. People were starving so they ate *kingo* (skin).

1882 *Ndzala ya mwakisenge*. The time people were forced to move on after a single planting and harvesting.

1884 Letter, Kirk to Glanville: 'There was a transient revival of slave-selling in Malindi District in 1884, when owing to drought and famine the Giriama people began to sell their slaves and their children'.

1889–90 *Ndzala ya mukufu*. People made *mukufu* (wire chain) to sell in return for food (5 arms' length for 1 *pishi*).

1894–96 *Ndzala ya fungayo*. A time of abstention. Famine of *bombom* in 1895, refers to the sound of guns used by the British against Arab 'rebels' and their Giriama allies.

1898– *Ndzala ya magunia*. Giriama brought *magunia* (hessian sacks) from
1900 their homes to sell to Arabs. Hardinge mentions selling of children for grain. Champion and Macdougall report partial migration of Giriama to Pokomo on the Tana River due to famine.

1901 *Ndzala ya kodi kwanza*. First Hut Tax Ordinance, introduced in August (tax of 1 rupee, or 2 shillings per person, 1 shilling per hut).

1909 *Ndzala ya kurima ngira ya Mwahera*. People worked on the road from Mariakani to Mwahera for a quarter of a *pishi* of maize.

1913 *Ndzala ya thupa*. People sold *thupa* (empty bottles) in Mombasa for food.

1914 *Ndzala ya kondo ya Muzungu*. Famine of the war with the Europeans.

1915   *Atu makwenda faini*. When the young men were taken (after the British defeated the Giriama). During the famine (June), labourers left Magarini estates for Malindi because of acute shortage of food. They would not work on the plantations.

1917–18   Return to the north bank of the Sabaki. The short rains failed and the migrants became short of food and returned to the reserve. Large numbers moved onto Arab plots where food was available.

1918   *Ndzala ya pishi mwenga, ndzala ya pishi rupia* (inflation from 1 *rupia* for 1 *pishi* to 15 *pishi*). Food shortages in January. The Giriama provided casual labour for the Arabs until all the food was gone, then moved to live at the coast. Arabs and Swahilis were 'very sympathetic, even charitable'.

1919   *Ndzala ya ukongo wa kipanya. Ukongo wa kipanya* (influenza) killed a lot of people, first time this illness had come as an epidemic. It came from *mwaka* (the southerly monsoon). The influenza pandemic prevented Giriama planting in the short rains. 'There was difficulty procuring food and water ... the natives being too sick to go and get it' (Senior Medical Officer, Mombasa).

1922   *Ndzala ya makopa*. Famine of the *makopa* (loans).

1928–29   (November–January) Locusts wiped out crops in the west until February. No Giriama maize is allowed to be sold or leave the district.

1932   *Ndzala ya kabushu tsi*. People ignored visitors to their home because there was not enough food to offer, so they just looked down and ignored them. *Ndzala ya ndugu si mutu* (when even your brother would not help you). *Ndzala ya mashini* (on the coast people were eating *unga* (flour) from *muhambo* (the mill).

1933   *Ndzala ya ndugu si mutu*. Western locations suffered hunger and partial failure of long rains.

1934   *Ndzala ya mashine*. Introduction of buying milled flour from the shops (£1 for 10 cwt). Short rains failed. Locusts (3 plantings and none successful). Cotton badly damaged by rain.

1935   Long rains poor and badly distributed. Acute food shortage in central and western parts of district.

1939   *Ndzala ya kondo ya Aitaliani viha ya Aengereza*. The famine of the war between the Italians and the English. Locusts. The failure of the short rains was almost universal.

1940   *Aitaliani kugwirana na Adachi*. The Italians are joined by the Dutch (?Germans). Partial failure of the short rains. Native Foodstuffs Ordinance applied.

1943   (May) Very short rains and 'a distinct though not yet serious shortage of food'. Locust problems in December.

1944   *Ndzala ya foleni hedu mugazidya*. The famine of the *foleni* (queue) or the *mugazidya* (cassava). The end of 1943 saw serious food shortages throughout the district, long and short rains failed. 32,642 bags of famine relief food distributed January to August.

1946   A fairly acute famine for 8 months of the year, 9,000 bags of maize meal and 600 bags of maize distributed throughout the district. The highest month of distribution was April. Heavy rainfall in September washed away approaches to Sabaki bridge.

1947   District had to import maize meal on payment for 9 months of the year because long rains too heavy and short rains failed.

1953   (May) Famine relief at Magarini.

1957   Very heavy rain. Food imported first half of year.

1960   *Ngowa kukota kiraho*. The diviner Ngowa cast an oath against witchcraft.

1971–72 *Ndzala cha ngilo*. One had to be patient and enduring to get food, one shop and many people in the queue.

1973   *Dzuwa kugwirwa mara ya hiri*. The second eclipse of the sun.

1980   *Dzuwa kugwirwa mara ya hahu*. The third eclipse of the sun.

Sources: PC/Coast/1/9/30, KNA; Malindi District Annual Report 1917/18; District Officer's Safari Diary, Malindi, 1928; Kilifi and Malindi District Annual Report 1934; District Officer's Safari Report, Malindi, 1943; Kilifi District Annual Report 1957; Spear 1976; Thompson, fieldwork 1985–88.

Notes

CHAPTER ONE: A PROJECT SOMEWHERE IN AFRICA

1 Throughout this book, for convenience, we write of the Giriama as though they were and are an undifferentiated group of people. Although all Giriama maintain links with their origins in the Kaya Giriama, inland of Mombasa, since World War II the northern Giriama, inland of Malindi, have become steadily poorer and more isolated from the mainstream Kenyan political and economic development, in comparison to their southern Kinsmen.

CHAPTER TWO: SETTING THE SCENE

1 'Mijikenda' is a term coined in 1947 to strengthen the political identity of the people of the Coast Province hinterland. It replaces the older name 'Wanyika' or 'bush dwellers' which was used perjoratively by Swahili and Arabs and later by the British.
2 Coast Province/Kilifi District Annual Report 1959: 18, KNA.
3 Champion, A., Coast Province 4/375; Memo 'Labour supply and the Giriama', 1914; Dundas, C., DC/KFI/3/1 1915; Giriama District Annual Report 1927, DC/MAL/2/1, KNA.
4 Kilifi District Health Education Officer, 1987.
5 Champion, A., October Report on the Present Condition of the WaGiriama, October 1913, CP5/336–I, KNA. Quoted in Brantley (1981: 93).
6 Hobley to Pearson, 17 December 1913. CP5/336–II, KNA. Quoted in Brantley (1981: 103).
7 DC/MAL/3/1 Political Record, 1914.
8 Hawthorne to Commander, Troops in British East Africa and Uganda, 31 August 1914, CP5/336–IV, KNA. Quoted in Brantley (1981: 116).
9 Hobley had confused information given to him of 5,000 families living north of the Sabaki, with 5,000 individuals.
10 'Poverty' refers to internationally agreed indices based on the ILO definition of four basic needs: (1) the minimum requirements of a family for personal consumption: food, shelter, clothing; (2) access to essential services such as safe drinking water, sanitation, transport, health care and education; (3) each person available for and willing to work should have an adequately remunerated job; (4) the satisfaction of needs of a more qualitative nature: a healthy, humane and satisfying environment, with popular participation in the making of decisions that affect the lives and livelihood of the people and individual freedoms (ILO 1977).
11 Kenyatta's famous dictum was *hakuna cha bure*, 'you can't get something for nothing', which became a central proposition of the individualist ideology. The Million

Acre Scheme was funded from CDC and IBRD, with shortfalls made up by the UK government.

12 *Australian Foreign Affairs Record* 1973, 44(7): 471.

13 This description of the steps leading to Australian involvement in Phase I at Magarini was assembled from AIDAB files.

14 Remarks in single quotation marks are excerpted from transcripts of interviews. In most cases the text makes it evident who the author of the remark is, but on occasion attribution is deliberately vague in order to protect the anonymity of the interviewee.

CHAPTER THREE: AGRICULTURE CHANGE AND UNCERTAINTY

1 Fermented coconut sap, called palm wine by Parkin (1972) and known as toddy in the Pacific and Asia.

2 Report on Malindi, 1913. DC/KFI/3/1, KNA.

3 Malindi District Annual Report 1920/21. DC/MAL/1/1, KNA.

4 Annual Report Malindi 1925. PC/Coast/1/1/411B, KNA.

5 Malindi District Annual Report 1936. DC/MAL/1/3, KNA.

6 Annual Report Kilifi and Malindi District 1934/35. DC/MAL/1/3, KNA.

7 Malindi Subdistrict Annual Report 1939. DC/MAL/1/3, KNA.

8 Tisdall, E.G.St.C. Coast Province/Kilifi District Annual Report 1937, KNA.

9 Safari Diaries, Malindi 1943. DC/KFI/4/2 KNA.

10 Annual Report Kilifi District 1944. PC/Coast/2/1/67, KNA.

11 Annual Report Kilifi and Malindi Districts 1935–36. DC/MAL/1/3, KNA.

12 In 1947 in Kilifi and Malindi Districts alone 1,856 unadjudicated claims existed and only one licensed surveyor was working in the Province. Kilifi District Annual Report 1947. PC/Coast/2/1/77, KNA.

13 Kilifi District Annual Report 1943. PC/Coast/2/1/63, KNA.

14 The Marafa bore was 45 m deep with rest level of 10.5 m and a safe yield of 1,818 litres per hour and the Adu bore 108 m with a rest level of 73 m and a safe yield of 445 litres per hour. Both bores were equipped with diesel motor-driven pumps in 1953. 903/KEL 83–417, KNA.

15 An examination of many of these dams in 1987 showed them to have been constructed without adequate overflow channels and almost all failed when water flowed over the dam and cut a vertical channel through the dam wall.

16 DC Kilifi to DO Malindi, 3 April 1950. DC/KFI/4/2, KNA.

17 Annex 6 is based on a survey of 190 households resident in the proposed project area in 1977. The report presents, as simple tables, the responses to 94 questions about family size, ethnicity, labour patterns, movement in and out of the area, land ownership, attitudes towards the proposed settlement scheme, water usage, the use of services and hopes for the future, administered by three female and two male Giriama-speaking university students. In addition less formal interviews were conducted with chiefs, assistant chiefs, tribal elders, health officers, head teachers, shop keepers, a cooperative chairman, the local chairmen of the KANU party, a priest and a basket maker. The survey offered people a number of qualified choices for future development and it is likely that some confusion ensued over exactly what each particular choice entailed. It is also likely a proportion of those questioned were suspicious of the motives of the survey and gave responses they thought were least likely to result in difficulties with the district administration. For these reasons some of the findings are difficult to interpret. Thus even though only 43 per cent said they did not favour a settlement scheme, 60 per cent of the people at Magarini in 1977 said they would prefer to maintain their present residential patterns and 70 per cent said they would prefer to live with their relatives.

18 These consequences of a breakdown in shifting cultivation systems are described by Clarke (1976).

19 In reply to a request from local British officers to extend the boundary of the Nyika reserve to include Adu the Commission found, 'There would clearly be no justice in extending the reserve boundaries to include every petty settlement of this nature and so secure large tracts of intervening land to the use and benefit of the tribe for ever, to the exclusion of all other interests'.

20 Evidence that tribesmen and women in pre-capitalist society can bring about soil erosion through what Brookfield calls 'social production' can be found in Allen and Crittenden (1987). On the relationship between colonialism and erosion, Beinart (1984: 84) observes, 'although there is considerable evidence of self-regulatory practices in land use in pre-colonial African societies, it cannot necessarily be assumed that peasant communities in the colonial period, their old systems of authority eroded, and faced with a shortage of land, increasing population densities, new opportunities and new constraints in their battle for survival, had the capacity to regulate themselves'.

21 Matthews questioned the project's economic viability, the evident lack of Kenyan commitment, over-ambitious physical targets for clearing, ploughing and road construction and incorrect estimates of settler labour inputs (pers. comm., A. Vale).

22 Entries in AIDAB files describe similar attitudes of the Kenyan staff towards the Giriama. For example, April 1982, 'the Kenyans on the Review Mission ... took a hardnosed attitude to social issues and showing respect for Giriama culture', and June 1982, 'the prospect of the Giriama being involved is nil. The Kenyans will block and inhibit any Giriama involvement'.

23 During 1977 two high-quality Bomag drilling rigs supplied by West German aid were discovered in Nairobi and were shipped to the project and the Kenyan teams were trained in their use. Enquiries after spare parts in Germany revealed they were prototypes and as such were the only two rigs exactly like that in the world. Parts were eventually manufactured for them by the members of a Swedish engineering aid team. A number of other problems caused the Australians great frustration. Kenyan financial regulations prevented the drilling teams' pay being administered through the project, and for some months they were not paid at all, and after some time refused to work. Finally every fortnight the drilling crews' supervisor drove to Nairobi and picked up the pay, which took him up to four days, during which the teams were idle because they had no vehicle to travel to and from their camp. On one trip the supervisor was held up and robbed of the cash. On another occasion a swarm of wild bees attacked a drilling crew, who fled the rig. The drilling stem fell down the well and was never recovered. The bore had to be abandoned.

24 See also Moris (1981: 73).

25 Food requirements were estimated for a family based on a daily energy and protein requirement for 3 adults and 5 children as 18,500 calories and 535 g protein. To produce this food in an 'average' year, given prevailing yields and taking storage losses into account would require 2.2 ha of maize and 1.25 ha of pulses. With a target cash income of K.sh3,000 and an estimated return of K.sh1,200/ha, 2.5 ha of cash crop, probably cotton, would be required, a total area of 5.95 ha.

26 The problems with tractor hire services listed in the Project Report include: poor maintenance, low work output (estimated at 20 per cent of capacity), high costs, increased demand on foreign exchange, administrative difficulties in sharing the tractor among farmers, technical problems with different soil types, disruption of customary work patterns and the loss of power and control over resources by women (McGowan 1978a: 94–5).

27 N-Butyl esters of 2,4-D and 2,4-T, which contain the chemical dioxin, were used in the infamous Agent Orange (and Agents Purple and White) employed as defoliants

in Vietnam. Dioxin has been implicated in causing crippling injuries in American and Australian war veterans and birth defects in their children, and for causing similar diseases among the Vietnamese.

28 G.P. McGowan & Associates Pty Ltd, QPR 24, December 1982.

29 Not all Kenyan project staff agreed with these policies, and some extension workers who gained the confidence of settlers developed sympathy for their plight. Over a couple of beers in 1987 an extension worker offered to introduce one of the Australian review team to his 'best farmer'. The offer was accepted in the expectation that it would involve a visit to a plot at Magarini. Instead, the extension officer led the Australian to the bar and with a broad grin introduced the barman as 'Settler number 128'. He later described how the settlers could not survive on the project without off-farm work but that it was not possible to convince the district administration of this, and they continued to try to force settlers to stay on their blocks with threats. (This officer has since left the project and the settler number is imaginary.)

30 G.P. McGowan & Associates Pty Ltd, QPR 17, February 1981.

31 Interview, R. McCown, Nairobi, 1988.

32 Most prominent has been Richards (1986), Brokensha et al. 1980.

33 The species which gave problems at Magarini was *Manilkara mochista*. Almost identical problems as those met at Magarini were met on a number of large Australian land-clearing schemes in the mallee and the brigalow areas. Soil moisture and plant moisture conditions determine whether scrub will bend, uproot or snap off under the pressure of the chain and least-cost clearing is restricted to times of optimum moisture conditions. The severe woody regrowth problem which occurred at Magarini also occurred in the brigalow areas where the ultimate solution was the widespread aerial spraying of herbicides and heavy repeated cultivation which increased soil erosion problems (Anderson 1982: 183–92).

34 G.P. McGowan & Associates Pty Ltd, QPR 14, May 1980.

35 Interview, R. McCown, Nairobi, March, 1988.

36 See, for example, Gow and Morss (1988: 1399–418), who identify political, economic and environmental constraints, institutional realities, personnel constraints, technical assistance shortcomings, decentralization and participation, timing, information systems, differing agendas and sustainability as serious difficulties facing all large development projects.

37 Nix observes that a study of climate in India, West Africa, Brazil and northern Australia by S.J. Reddy, a student at CRES, found that based on mean data, all these areas in the semi-arid tropics looked similar, but critical differences appeared when crop models were run on actual data.

38 We are particularly obligated to Bob McCown, CSIRO Division of Tropical Crops and Pastures, Davies Laboratory, Townsville and Brian Keating, ACIAR/CSIRO Dryland Project, PO Box 41567, Nairobi, for lengthy discussions on this matter and for their considerable efforts in running the model using Magarini data.

39 The simulation used actual rainfall at Marafa from 1936 to 1986 cycled through the simulation two-and-half times. Hence the repetitive patterns in the figure.

40 Support for this option comes from analysis of data from two farm efficiency surveys in Kenya, one conducted at the end of the 1960s and the other, the Integrated Rural Survey, conducted in two rounds, 1974/5 and 1976/7. Ian Livingstone's ILO report showed that smallest sized farms (below 10 ha) have substantially higher output per hectare, higher cropping intensity, more intensive use of grazing lands and greater operating surplus per area than larger farms. On this basis both Livingstone, and a later more radical assessment by Diana Hunt, favoured land redistribution to combine both efficiency and equity objectives.

CHAPTER FOUR: INSTITUTIONS FOR MANAGING UNCERTAINTY

1 The urgent task of development was, according to Truman, to 'create the conditions that will lead eventually to personal freedom and happiness for all mankind'.

2 The Second Communist International of 1920 had called the colonial world to arms and revolutionary fervour, drawing distinctions between 'oppressing' and 'oppressed' nations and by pointing out that these countries need not pass through capitalism before they could enjoy the fruits of communism. Gavin Kitching reminds us that 'Although a great deal of modern development studies literature states or implies that the main aim of development should be the relief of poverty and/or the reduction of inequality, it is doubtful whether this has ever been the main aim of the politicians and statesmen who endeavoured to stimulate development (Kitching 1982: 3). See also d'Encausse and Schramm (1969).

3 There is some debate on the precise nature of the changes and when they took place. Differing views, not of great moment here, are found in Noble (1977), Nelson (1975) and Palmer (1975).

4 See also Javits (1950), Espy (1950), Rosenthal (1957) and Escobar (1985: 384) for views of the period.

5 Hoselitz (1952: 15), Wohl (1952: 4), Clark (1957) and Lewis (1955) are representative of the times. They indicate the importance of economic theories such as those of W. A. Lewis, backed by the national accounting insights of people like Colin Clark. This glosses over a number of dissenting views that existed at the time in economics (such as between 'capital-shortage', 'vicious-circle' and Harrod-Domar theory). See also Brookfield (1975), Preston (1982), Livingstone (1981) and Arndt (1980). The views of policy makers and politicians were not always single-minded. But to review exhaustively the range would imply an equivocation in what was believed to be required in practice but did not exist. For instance, one only need read reviews by World Bank staff, of Bank thinking at the time, to see this. Morawetz (1977: 10) remarks 'What was needed was a grand simplification; and it was W. Arthur Lewis who provided it.... . Lewis set the tone for the next fifteen years'.

6 In all three Bank Group agencies (IBRD, IDA, IFC) the United States wields considerable power. It holds over 20 per cent of IBRD voting power, 37 per cent in the IFC and over 20 per cent in the IDA. See Williams (1981: 17).

7 With post-War decolonization, a strong feeling against Western capital emerged in the Third World. In 1948, one observer remarked, 'the height of feeling against Western capitalism is today so great that it is unlikely ... private assistance from the West in the building up of the underdeveloped world will ever again play a major role' (Gregory 1948: 54–5). On the non-political image of the Bank, Susan George observes, 'This, politely put, is rubbish' (1988: 53). It is precisely those countries which have been trying to maintain a commitment to social equity, health services, education and so on, that have had the greatest difficulties coming to terms with the IMF.

8 See also Bello et al. (1982) and Moss (1978). Early Bank promotion of this thinking spread through most other agencies, e.g. FAO (1979); ILO (1977) and ODI (1978).

9 Questions of income distribution and employment generation began to be emphasized. But these had been previously expressed. The First National Development Plan of India in 1951 aimed at 'maximising production, full employment, the attainment of economic equality and social justice'. The first World Bank Mission to a developing country stated its objectives in terms of meeting basic human needs. Many other problems highlighted during the McNamara years were considered (however cursorily) earlier. The World Bank's 1948 Annual Report cited a range of obstacles to development not unlike those emphasized during the more enlightened 1970s. The 1949 Report stated, 'Mention must also be made of the difficulties arising from the social structure of the underdeveloped nations where there are wide extremes of

wealth and poverty. In such cases, strong vested interests often resist any changes which would alter their position. In particular, the maintenance in a number of countries of inefficient and oppressive systems of land tenure militates against increase in agricultural output and the general standard of living.' (Quoted in Adler 1977: 32).

10 Reviews of integrated rural development projects in Africa (ODA and IBRD funded) indicated weaknesses in these terms: (a) insufficient knowledge of existing farming systems; (b) insufficient on-farm testing of recommended technology; (c) over-optimism regarding rate of adoption; (d) unrealistically low opportunity costs of labour; (e) inadequate financial incentives for farmers; (f) market and price policies inconsistent with project objectives; (g) inhospitable economic situation; (h) project management overburdened; (i) project management divorced from existing institutions; (j) inadequate consideration of sociological constraints; (k) inadequate monitoring.

11 See Steinfels (1979); Parboni (1981). The intellectual genesis is traced in Toye (1987: 22–46), and Keegan (1984: 33–104).

12 In classical definition terms, project aid applies to discrete projects, where it is believed inputs and outputs can be measured and subjected to cost-benefit appraisal; programme aid is general import financing, usually for intermediate goods; and sector aid is really a form of aid management, focusing on a package of assistance to a sector with a focus on institution strengthening.

13 See also the more general trend observed by Coverdale and Healey (1987: 99–105).

14 This information was released by AIDAB in response to a Freedom of Information request.

15 There are always at least two options in project appraisal. An implicit alternative is not to do the project – a careful analysis of the 'without' situation is needed if the incremental effects of the project are to be clear.

16 The World Bank (1978: 16) concludes 'Typically evaluation of new settlement projects 3–5 years after the start of implementation show economic rates of return at least 50 per cent below those in project appraisal documents.'

17 It is worth noting that the Appraisal saw considerable scope for collaboration between the Dryland Farming Research team and the project staff at Magarini. Yet at no time did the Appraisal authors approach the ACIAR researchers for the kind of information which we have presented.

18 The 1984 Appraisal states on page 87, 'the opportunity cost of 12.9 per cent used in conversion factors is not the relevant cut-off rate for ADAB projects. The relevant rate is that obtainable on similar Kenyan projects using the same IBRD shadow pricing assumptions.' Table 2.8 (p.19) compares other Kenyan projects and the maximum IRR reported is 12.3 per cent for the Hindi-Magongoni FRR.

19 'The focus must be less on the capital account and more on the recurrent account, where the main expenditure now occurs. In this context, investment appraisal techniques in their traditional form become less useful' (Coverdale and Healey 1987: 104).

20 Gerardo Sicat, former Philippines Minister of Economic Planning (1979: 192) provides an anecdote on this theme. 'There was a time when I was reviewing the work of a consulting group and I did a review of their analysis of the industrial sector of the Philippines. I was fascinated by some of the tables that were presented and upon cross-examination, I tried to rework the numbers. I discovered to my great surprise that the table was constructed out of a sheer belief that identification numbers for industries meant more than just identification numbers. The consultant had added up the ISIC known as International Standard Classification Numbers, got the percentage distribution and some nice information that government and other decision makers should be impressed with. Well, I was not as innocent as that.'

21 Blueprint planning is a generic term which refers to interventions where the central ingredient is the plan. According to Faludi (1973) blueprint planning consists of one or more goals or objective statements, and then specific policies, programmes and projects, all of which are related to various linking financial and activity budgets.

22 In AIDAB's case, this is called the Country Program Operations Guide, a two-volume *magnum opus* of 29 Activity Cycle Booklets specifying every aspect of the Project Cycle; small or large, short or long, environmentally and gender sensitive, fully integrated or component specific activity. AIDAB is not alone. The World Bank guide lists 266 issues that should be analysed in a pre-feasibility study of water and sanitation projects (Grover 1983).

23 Consistent with management fashions of the mid-1970s AIDAB was at the time involved in or initiating integrated rural development projects in Southeast Asia which adopted the 'autonomous project mode'.

24 The consequences become evident when we consider that Kenya currently deals with about forty different official donor agencies with varying degrees of intensity and contact. It was reported in the early 1980s Tanzania had to cope with no fewer than 250-odd donor-planning missions (JCPA 1983: 358).

25 See also Arndt (1979: 40): 'The more conscientious the donor, the more careful its pre-investment surveys, its built-in safeguards for efficient procurements and implementation, the more the choice, and shape of the project will be influenced by the donor's experts and the longer will tend to be the delays and frustrations.'

26 Australia is no exception, as reviews of the Australian official aid programme have repeatedly shown. See, for example, Auditor General (1981); and JCPA (1982).

27 Oyugi (1981: 38–9) confirms this. SRDP was the brainchild of a few expatriates, 'it's they who knew what it meant. The Kenyan officials did not see it as their idea and failed to identify with it. Accordingly, they did not give it the attention it deserved'.

28 See also Quick (c. 1980: 57), who argues that the conflict of interests/objectives results in 'a simplification of the agency's operational goal structure, eliminating many of the non-measurable or long-run goals and focusing attention exclusively on activities that will yield short-run measurable results. Immediate results have a political utility *for the organization regardless of the contribution that activity makes to the long-run success of its programme*' (emphasis added).

CHAPTER FIVE: STRENGTHENING THE PEOPLE'S HAND?

1 'Mr Hayden ... Any time members of the Opposition want to have a little argument in this place about dud aid programs, I invite them to be my guest, because I have a small mountain of these sorts of projects which were introduced during the period of the Fraser Government.' (*Hansard*, 21 April 1988: 1975).

2 The World Bank review of NGOs begins, 'One of the main features of NGOs that seek to provide aid in one form or another is their great diversity' (World Bank 1988: 15). See also Brodhead *et al.* (1988).

3 In the case of AFFHC this influence has been charted by Graham Alliband, Director, during the initial years of involvement in MSP (Alliband 1983). See also Brodhead *et al.* (1988); Kobia (1985); Twose (1987); Minear (1987).

4 Elements of these ideas are found in Korten (1989); de Kadt (1985) and interestingly, also in Ward (1982: 43).

5 See, for example, Cohen and Uphoff (1980) for a review of the concept, and Lecomte (1986), on the distortions created by project aid.

6 Even as project funding from official sources increases, many NGOs are beginning to question whether their primary energies should be devoted to project aid at all. Some Northern donor NGOs, for instance, regard lobbying and policy advocacy

work, for example to deal with debt and World Bank–IMF conditionality on assistance, to be of greater importance in the long term. We restrict our discussion here to NGO activities at the project level.

7 It is hardly sensible to compare the impact of the NGO programme to the Magarini Settlement Project. The resources are not directly comparable, some 15 NGO staff alongside a project workforce sometimes numbering 500. Too few studies of actual NGO performances exist to compare the Malindi NGO programme alongside its peers. We do not disregard the views of NGO staff that they have made significant progress, especially in the light of initial hostilities and their own conservative appraisal of the odds against success.

8 For example, Bureau for Food for Peace and Voluntary Assistance, USAID (1986).

9 Kenyan President Daniel arap Moi describes the objectives of the District Focus Strategy as: (1) to make each district the focal point for the initiation, planning and management of rural development; (2) to enhance the coordination of resources and efforts available locally and from the National Treasury for district-specific projects; (3) to stimulate rapid and planned development as critically identified by field officers and the local people; (4) to motivate the people, and incorporate the wishes and proposals of the people and the united leadership corps of the nation; (5) to relocate the identification of suitable projects to the people and local leadership, who are in close contact with the real problems (Moi 1986: 60).

10 Many authors have examined *harambee* in practice. See for example, Bolnick (1974), Keller (1977) and Mutiso (1974).

11 This naivety in the academic literature of regional development is discussed in Sandner (1985). Soja (1980, 1988) presents a different approach to these issues.

12 It is also true that many Third World NGOs are not disposed to improve management skills. For instance, often for good reason, many are very sceptical about participating in the variety of management training courses offered to them by European and American agencies, such as those offered by the International Council for Voluntary Action (see Campbell 1988).

13 See Therkildsen (1988) on the morass developed by the Tanzanian government, with donor assistance, for community involvement in the rural water supply sector.

CHAPTER SIX: AGAINST WHOSE ODDS? CONSTRUCTING CERTAINTY GIRIAMA STYLE

1 Some readers may be concerned over a terminological looseness here. What is known officially as 'witchcraft' in Kenya would probably be defined as 'sorcery' in other places. The Giriama remain ambivalent, however. They recognize that the witch, so-called, controls external powers of evil which is an act anthropologists know as sorcery, but they wonder if people who indulge in such wickedness must not also be possessed of some uncontrollable evil power. Anthropology calls the latter individuals witches.

2 Holism is the theory which makes the existence of 'wholes' a fundamental feature of the perceived world. It regards natural objects, both animate and inanimate, as wholes, not ready assemblages of elements or parts. The so-called parts are not real, but are abstract analytical distances and do not properly or adequately express what has gone to the making of the object as a whole. Although the theory of holism accepts the material basis of the world and recognizes the reality of order, it also fully justifies the claims of the spirit in the interpretation of the whole. Holism shows wholes and parts as aspects of each other. The finite is identified with the infinite, the particular with the universal. The whole is both the source and the principal explanation of all ideas.

3 Joint Review Report MSP/NGO June 1988: 48.

4 Malindi NGO programme, 'Design Report, Phase I', 1985 draft.

5 Most Giriama argue that it was jealousies caused by recent differences in wealth created by their participation in the cash economy that heralded the massive increases in numbers of victims of witchcraft attack.

6 For further details of these movements see Brantley (1979), Parkin (1968, 1972, 1985), and Thompson (1990).

7 This term was first coined by Constantino-David (1982).

8 Parkin (1968: 424–39), describes the innovatory aspects of anti-witchcraft movements among the Giriama, in the form of 'advertising' new power shifts away from the traditional leaders, the elders, towards younger, often entrepreneurial men.

9 Whereas all other Giriama healers purchase their knowledge of medicines and their uses, diviners acquire divinely inspired knowledge about medicines from their familiar spirits. This authenticates their knowledge to a much greater extent, since it is not subject to the vagaries and manipulations of human transactions, and is considered not only secret, but also sacred.

10 Women controlled this domain in an importantly ambivalent way, and are remembered primarily for their fearful powers. Not only could they promote the health of the land and the people, but they also had the ritual powers to withhold or retract these benefits which they could use as a coercive threat, for instance, when others were not politically compliant with their wishes.

11 In view of diviners' need to preserve their image of moral integrity, however, they actively oppose any association of themselves with rituals for withholding the rain. Preventing rainfall is an anti-social activity, which in today's increasingly individualistic context is more closely associated with the practice of witchcraft.

12 Recall too, Parkin's 'therapeutic Muslims'. Here even entrepreneurs' socio-economic strategies were idiomatically framed in religious terms which offered an alternative path to health, and a change in identity (Parkin 1968, 1972).

CHAPTER SEVEN: MORE DIVERSITY FOR MORE CERTAINTY

1 This is not to say that locally rooted, participatory organizations have not, or will not have influence on the complexity of 'land–food–people' sketched in the closing stages of Chapter Three – but how this might occur is well beyond our purpose here.

2 This book is not restricted to Australian development practice, which largely mirrors that of the rest of the developed world, but it is possible that Australians, along with Americans, who have grown up in a culture still influenced by the frontier development of their own countries and the need of the pioneers to roll up their sleeves and tackle problems head on, are more prone than others to a failure to recognize their limitations.

3 See also Hill (1986) and Berry (1986).

4 The *Time* magazine article was entitled 'The Foreign Aid Fiasco: a massive bungling is uncovered in a billion-dollar program'. *Time*, 28 July 1986 (Australian edition).

5 For our non-Australian readers, 'Don't you worry about that' is a phrase used so frequently by the former Premier of Queensland, Sir Joh Bjelke-Petersen in reply to questioning journalists, that it has become an everyday aphorism in Australia. Sir Joh resigned from office during a Royal Commission into corruption in the police force and his government in 1989.

Bibliography

ADAA (1976) Project Appraisal, Magarini Land Settlement Scheme in Coast Province, Kenya, June 1976, Canberra.

ADAB (1984) Magarini Settlement Project Phase III Appraisal Report, October 1984, Canberra.

Adler, J.H. (1977) 'Development theory and the Bank's development strategy: a review', *Finance and Development*, 14: 31–4.

Ahmed, Y. (1975) 'Project identification, analysis, and preparation in developing countries: a discursive commentary', *Development and Change*, 6, 3: 83–90.

AIDAB (1989) Review of Integrated Area Development Projects (Draft), Appraisals, Evaluation and Sectoral Studies Branch, Canberra, August 1989.

Allen, B.J. and Crittenden, R. (1987) 'Degradation and a pre-capitalist political economy: the case of the New Guinea Highlands', in Blaikie, P. and Brookfield, H. with contributions by others, *Land Degradation and Society*, London: Methuen, 145–56.

Alliband, G. (1983) *The Role of Voluntary Agencies in Overseas Aid*, Canberra: AFFHC.

Anderson, E.R. (1982) 'The native woody weed problem following Brigalow development', in Bailey, A. (ed.) *The Brigalow Belt in Australia: the Proceedings of a Symposium held at the John Kindler Memorial Theatre, Queensland Institute of Technology, October 1982*, 183–92.

Annual Report, Malindi (1924) PC/Coast/1/1/411, KNA.

Anterson, G.W. (ed.) (1979) *Consult Australia*, Melbourne: The Australian Professional Consultants Council.

Arndt, H.W. (1979) 'Problems of the aid recipient country', in Shand, R.T. and Richter, H.V. (eds) *International aid: some political, administrative and technical realities*, Development Studies Centre Monograph No. 16, Canberra: ANU, 34–45.

Arndt, H.W. (1980) 'Economic development, a semantic history', *Economic Development and Cultural Change*, 29: 457–66.

Auditor General (1981) *Report of the Auditor-General on an Efficiency Audit, Administration of Australia's Bilateral Overseas Aid Program by the Australian Development Assistance Bureau*, Canberra: AGPS.

Australian Foreign Affairs Record (1973) 44.

Ayres, J. (1981) 'Clausen and the poor', *New York Times*, 1 July 1981.

Barrett, D. (1983) *Kenya Churches Handbook: the Development of Kenyan Christianity, 1945–1973*, Kisumu: Kenya Evangelical Publishing House.

Bauer, F. (ed.) (1977) *Cropping in North Australia: an Anatomy of Success and Failure*, North Australia Research Unit, Canberra: ANU Press.

Baum, W.C. (1978) 'The World Bank project cycle', *Finance and Development*, 15, 4: 10–17.

Beer, T. and Hills, R.C. (1982) 'Systems theory: uncertainty in the design and management of complex development projects', *Development Studies Centre Occasional Paper* No. 29, Canberra: ANU.

Beinart, W. (1984) 'Soil erosion, conservation and ideas about development: a Southern African exploration 1900–1960', *Journal of Southern African Studies*, 11, 1: 52–84.

Bell, M. (1987) Magarini Settlement Project: a review of the status of project documentation and comments on water resources development, Melbourne: Australian Hydrogeologists International Pty, Ltd.

Bello, W., Kinley, D. and Elinson, E. (1982) *Development Debacle: The World Bank in the Philippines*, San Francisco: Institute for Food and Development Policy, Philippine Solidarity Network.

Bennett, G. and Rosberg, C. (1961) *The Kenyatta Election: Kenya 1960–61*, London: Oxford University Press.

Berry, S. (1986) 'Social science perspectives on food in Africa', in Hansen, A. and McMillan, D. (eds) *Food in Sub-Saharan Africa*, Boulder: Lynne Reinner, 64–81.

Bienen, H. (1974) *Kenya: the Politics of Participation and Control*, Princeton, New Jersey: Princeton University Press.

Bolnick, B. (1974) 'Comparative harambee: history and theory of voluntary collective behaviour', *Institute for Development Studies Working Paper*, No. 139, Nairobi: University of Nairobi.

Boxer, A.H. (1969) *Experts in Asia: An Enquiry into Australian Technical Assistance*, Canberra: ANU Press.

Brantley, C. (1979) 'An historical perspective of the Giriama and witchcraft control', *Africa*, 49, 2: 112–33.

Brantley, C. (1981) *The Giriama and Colonial Resistance in Kenya, 1800–1920*, Berkeley: University of California Press.

Brodhead, T. and Herbert-Copley, B., with Lambert, A. (1988) *Bridges of Hope*, Ottawa: North–South Institute.

Brokensha, D., Warren, D. and Werner, O. (eds) (1980) *Indigenous Systems of Knowledge and Development*, Lanham: University Press of America.

Brookfield, H.C. (1975) *Interdependent Development*, London: Methuen.

Brookfield, H.C. (1988) 'Sustainable development and the environment: a review article', *Journal of Development Studies*, 25, 1: 126–35.

Brown, P. (1973) *Smallcreep's Day*, London: Pan Books.

Bureau for Food for Peace and Voluntary Assistance, USAID (1986) *Development Effectiveness of Private Voluntary Organisations*, Washington DC: USAID.

Campbell, P. (1988) 'Management development and development management for voluntary organisations', Background Paper 1, Geneva: ICVA.

Campen, J.T. (1986) *Benefit, Cost and Beyond: The Political Economy of Benefit–Cost Analysis*, Cambridge, Massachusetts: Ballinger.

Carey-Jones, N.S. (1966) *The Anatomy of Uhuru: an Essay on Kenya's Independence*, Manchester: Manchester University Press.

Cassen, R. and Associates (1986) *Does Aid Work? Report to an Intergovernmental Task Force*, Oxford: Clarendon Press.

CEC (Commission of the European Communities) (1981) *Comparative Evaluation of Projects Co-Financed with NGOs and Micro Projects: Indicative Synthesis*, Brussels: CEC.

Central Bureau of Statistics (1980) *Kenya Population Census 1979*, Vol. 1, Nairobi: Government of Kenya.

Chalmers, A.F. (1976) *What is This Thing Called Science? An Assessment of the Nature and Status of Science and Its Methods*, St. Lucia: University of Queensland Press.

Chambers, R. (1974) *Managing Rural Development: Ideas and Experience from East Africa*, Uppsala: Scandinavian Institute for African Studies.

Chambers, R. (1983) *Rural Development: Putting the Last First*, London: Longman.

Champion, A.M. (1967) 'The Agiriyama of Kenya', *Royal Anthropological Institute Occasional Paper* No. 25.

Chomsky, N. (1970) 'Introduction', in Guerin, D. (ed.) *Anarchism*, New York: Monthly Review Press: vii–xx.

Clark, C. (1957) *The Conditions of Economic Progress*, London: Macmillan.

Clarke, W.C. (1976) 'Maintenance of agriculture and human habitats within the tropical forest ecosystem', *Human Ecology*, 4, 3: 247–59.

Cochrane, G. and Noronha, R. (1973) *A Report with Recommendations on the Use of Anthropology in Project Operations of the World Bank Group*, Washington DC: World Bank.

Coffey and Partners (1978) Magarini Land Settlement Project – Supplementary report of groundwater investigations – covering period October 1977 to July 1978, Coffey and Partners Pty Ltd, July 1978.

Cohen, J.M. and Uphoff, N.T. (1980) 'Participation's place in rural development: seeking clarity through specificity', *World Development*, 8, 3: 213–35.

Collier, P. and Lal, D. (1980) *Poverty and Growth in Kenya*, Washington DC: International Bank for Reconstruction and Development.

Constantino-David, K. (1982) 'Issues in community organisation', *Community Development Journal*, 17, 3: 190–201.

Conway, G. (1984) 'Agro-ecosystem analysis', *Agricultural Administration*, 20: 31–55.

Cooper, F. (1983) *From Slaves to Squatters, Plantation Labour and Agriculture in Zanzibar and Coastal Kenya 1890–1925*, Nairobi: Kenya Literature Bureau.

Coverdale, A. and Healey, J. (1987) 'Project appraisal and project aid: a decade of experience in rural development', *Journal of Agricultural Economics*, 38, 1: 99–105.

Cracknell, B. (1988) 'Evaluating development assistance: a review of the literature', *Public Administration and Development*, 8: 75–83.

Cracknell, B. and Rednall, J. (1986) *Defining Objectives and Measuring Performance in Aid Projects and Programmes*, London: Overseas Development Administration.

Dasgupta, A. and Pearce, D. (1978) *Cost Benefit Analysis: Theory and Practice*, London: Macmillan.

Davidson, B.R. (1982) 'Economic aspects of the Ord River Project', in Davidson, B.R. and Graham-Taylor, S. (eds) *Lessons From the Ord*, Sydney: The Center for Independent Studies, 1–22.

de Crombrugghe, G., Howes. M. and Nieukerk, M. (1985) *An Evaluation of CEC Small Development Projects*, Brussels: CEC.

de Kadt, E. (1985) 'Of markets, might and mullahs: a case for equity, pluralism and tolerance in development', *World Development*, 3, 4: 549–56.

d'Encausse, H.C. and Schramm, S.R. (1969) *Marxism and Asia*, London: Penguin.

Dodge, J. (1981) 'Living by life: some bioregional theory and practice', *Co-Evolutionary Quarterly*, Winter: 6–12.

East Africa Royal Commission 1953–55, London: HMSO.

Elliott, C. (1987) 'Some aspects of relations between North and South in the NGO sector', *World Development*, 15: 57–86.

Escobar, A. (1985) 'Discourse and power in development: Michel Foucault and the relevance of his work to the Third World', *Alternatives*, 10: 377–400.

Espy, W.R. (1950) *Bold New Program*, New York: Bantam Books.

Evans-Pritchard, E. E. (1937) *Witchcraft, Oracles and Magic among the Azande*, Oxford: Clarendon.

Faludi, A. (1973) *Planning Theory*, Oxford: Pergamon.

FAO (Food and Agriculture Organization) (1979) *World Conference on Agrarian Reform and Rural Development*, Rome: FAO.

Feyerabend, P. (1975) *Against Method: Outline of an Anarchistic Theory of Knowledge*, London: Humanities Press.

Fowler, A. (1982) '"Temperatures" in development funding: the hot money model', *Development*, 2: 81–2.

Fransman, M. (1985) 'Conceptualising technical change in the Third World in the 1980s: an interpretive survey', *Journal of Development Studies*, 21, 4: 572–652.

Friedmann, J. and Weaver, C. (1979) *Territory and Function: the Evolution of Regional Planning*, London: Edward Arnold.

Gasper, D. (1987) 'Motivation and manipulations: some practices of project appraisal and evaluation', *Manchester Papers on Development*, 3, 1: 24–70.

George, S. (1988) *A Fate Worse than Debt*, London: Penguin.

Gittinger, J.P. (1982) *Economic Analysis of Agricultural Projects*, Baltimore: The Johns Hopkins University Press.

Gleick, J. (1988) *Chaos*, Harmondsworth: Penguin.

Gold, J. (1983) *The Non-political Character of the International Monetary Fund*, Washington DC: IMF.

Goodman, L.J. and Love, R.N. (eds) (1979) *Management of Development Projects: An International Case Study Approach*, New York: Pergamon Policy Studies, Pergamon.

Goulet, D. (1977) *The Uncertain Promise: Value Conflicts in Technology Transfer*, New York: IDOC.

Gow, D.D. and Morss, E.R. (1988) 'The notorious nine: critical problems in project implementation', *World Development*, 16, 12: 1399–418.

Graham-Taylor, S. (1982) 'A critical history of the Ord River Project', in Davidson, B.R. and Graham-Taylor, S. (eds) *Lessons From the Ord*, Sydney: The Center for Independent Studies, 23–55.

Gran, G. (1983) *Development by People: Citizen Construction of a Just World*, New York: Praeger.

Gregory, T.E. (1948) 'The problems of the underdeveloped world', *Lloyds Bank Review*, 10: 54–5.

Grindle, M.S. (ed.) (c1980) *Politics and Policy Implementation in the Third World*, Princeton, New Jersey: Princeton University Press.

Grover, B. (1983) Water supply and sanitation project preparation handbook guidelines, Vol. 1, *World Bank Staff Working Paper* No. 537, Washington DC: World Bank.

Harbeson, J.W. (1973) *Nation Building in Kenya: the Role of Land Reform*, Evanston: Northwestern University Press.

Harrell-Bond, B. (1986) *Imposing Aid: Emergency Assistance to Refugees*, New York: Oxford University Press.

Hartman, B. (1981) 'McNamara's legacy: basic needs without basic reforms', *South*, August: 31–4.

Hatch, J. (1976) 'The corn farmers of Motupe: a study of traditional farming practices in northern coastal Peru', *Land Tenure Center Monograph* No. 1, Madison: University of Wisconsin-Madison Land Tenure Center.

Hellinger, S., Hellinger, D. and O'Regan, F. (1988) *Aid for Just Development: Report on the Future of Foreign Assistance*, Boulder: Lynne Reinner.

Herlehy, T.J. (1985) 'An economic history of the Kenya Coast: the Mijikenda coconut palm economy, ca 1800–1980', PhD thesis, Boston University, Ann Arbor.

Higgott, R. (1981) 'Australia and Africa', in Boyce, P.J. and Angel, J.R. (eds) *Independence and Alliance: Australia in World Affairs, 1976–1980*, Sydney: Allen and Unwin, 245–60.

Higgott, R. (1986) 'Structural adjustment and the Jackson Report: the nexus between development theory and Australian foreign policy', in Eldridge, P., Forbes, D. and Porter, D. (eds) *Australian Aid: Future Directions*, Canberra: Croom Helm, 39–54.

Hill, P. (1986) *Development Economics on Trial: the Anthropological Case for the Pros-ecution*, Cambridge: Cambridge University Press.

Hirschman, A. (1967) *Development Projects Observed*, Washington DC: The Brookings Institute.

Hobley, C.W. (1929) *Kenya: From Chartered Company to Crown Colony, Thirty Years of Exploration and Administration in British East Africa*, London: H.F. and G. Witherby.

Honadle, G.H. and Klauss, R. (1979) *International Development Administration: Imple-mentation Analysis for Development Projects*, New York: Praeger.

Honadle, G.H. and Rosengard, J.K. (1983) 'Putting "projectised" development in per-spective', *Public Administration and Development*, 3: 299–305.

Hoselitz, B.F. (1952) 'Non-economic barriers to economic development', *Economic Development and Cultural Change*, 1: 8–21.

Huang, P. W. Jr. (1975) *The Asian Development Bank: Diplomacy and Development in Asia*, New York: Vantage Press.

Hulme, D. (1989) 'Learning and not learning from experience in rural project planning', *Public Administration and Development*, 9: 1–16.

Hunt, D. (1984) *The Impending Crisis in Kenya: The Case for Land Reform*, Gower: Aldershot.

Hunt, J. (1983) Submission to Aid Review Committee, Joint Parliamentary Committee for Public Accounts, Canberra: Parliament of Australia.

Huntington, S. (1968) *Political Order and Changing Societies*, New Haven: Yale Univer-sity Press.

Huxley, E. (1935) *White Man's Country: Lord Delamere and the Making of Kenya*, London: Chatto and Windus.

Hyden, G. (1980) *Beyond Ujamaa in Tanzania: Underdevelopment and an Uncaptured Peasantry*, Los Angeles: University of California Press.

Hyden, G. (1983) *No Shortcuts to Progress: African Development Management in Perspective*, Los Angeles: University of California Press.

ILO (International Labour Organization) (1977) *Employment, Growth, and Basic Needs: A One World Problem*, Geneva: ILO.

Irvin, G. (1979) *Modern Cost Benefit Methods: An Introduction to Financial, Economic and Social Appraisal of Development Projects*, London: Macmillan.

Islam, S. (1986) 'Introduction of draught power technology to the farmers of Magarini Settlement Project 1981–85' (mimeo).

Javits, B.A. (1950) *Peace by Investment*, New York: Hutchinson.

JCPA (Joint Committee on Public Accounts) (1982) *Efficiency Audit – Administration of Bilateral Overseas Aid*, Report 201, Canberra: Parliament of Australia.

JCPA (Joint Committee for Public Accounts) (1983) *Efficiency Audit – Administration of Bilateral Overseas Aid*, Canberra: Parliament of Australia.

Johnston, B. and Clark, W. (1982) *Redesigning Rural Development: A Strategic Perspec-tive*, Baltimore: The Johns Hopkins University Press.

Joint Review Report, Magarini Settlement Project NGO Component, June 1988.

Jones, R.K. and McCown, R.L. (1984) 'Research on a no-till, tropical legume-ley farm-ing strategy', *Proceedings of the Eastern Africa-ACIAR Consultation on Agricultural Research*, 18–22 July 1983, Nairobi, Kenya, 108–21.

Keegan, W. (1984) *Mrs Thatcher's Economic Experiment*, Harmondsworth: Penguin.

Keller, E. (1977) 'Harambee! Educational policy, inequality and the political economy of rural community self-help in Kenya', *Journal of African Studies*, 4, 1: 86–106.

Killick, T. (1984) *The Quest for Certainty*, New York: St Martin's Press.

Killick, T. (ed.) (1984) *The IMF and Stabilisation: Developing Country Experiences*, London: Heinemann.

Kitching, G. (1982) *Development and Underdevelopment in Historical Perspective*, London: Open University, Methuen.

Kobia, S. (1985) 'The old and the new NGOs: approaches to development', Institute of Development Studies, University of Nairobi, Nairobi (mimeo).

Kolko, G. (1968) *The Politics of War: US Foreign Policy 1943–45*, New York: Vintage.

Korten, D.C. (1980) 'Community organisation and rural development: a learning process approach', *Journal of Development Studies*, 20, 5: 480–511.

Korten, D.C. (1989) 'The US voluntary sector and global realities: issues for the 1990s', USAID, Massachusetts (mimeo).

Kramer, R.M. (1981) *Voluntary Agencies and the Welfare State*, Berkeley: University of California Press.

Krapf, J.L. (1860) *Travels, Researches and Missionary Labours during an Eighteen Years Residence in Eastern Africa, together with a Journey to Jappa, Unambara, Ihambani, Shea, Obessinia, and Khartun and a Coasting Voyage from Mombaz to Cape Delgoias*, London: F. Carson.

Lamb, G. and Muller, L. (1982) 'Control, accountability and incentives in a successful development institution: the Kenyan Tea Development Authority', *World Bank Staff Working Paper* No. 550, Washington DC: World Bank.

Lecomte, B. (1986) *Project Aid: Limitations and Alternatives*, Paris: Organisation for Economic Co-operation and Development.

Lele, U. (1975) *The Design of Rural Development*, Baltimore: The Johns Hopkins University Press.

Leo, C. (1984) *Land and Class in Kenya*, Toronto: University of Toronto Press.

Leonard, D.K. (1977) *Reaching the Peasant Farmer: Organisation, Theory and Practice in Kenya*, Chicago: University of Chicago Press.

Lewis, W.A. (1955) *The Theory of Economic Growth*, London: Allen and Unwin.

Leys, N.M. (1925) *Kenya*, London: L. and W. Woolf.

Livingstone, I. (1981) *Rural Development, Employment and Incomes in Kenya*, Addis Ababa: ILO/JASPA.

Livingstone, I. (1986) *Employment, Incomes and Equality: A Strategy for Increasing Productive Employment in Kenya*, Geneva: International Labour Office.

McCown, R.L. and Dimes, J.P. (1988) 'CERES-Maize: description, assessment and limitations for studies of long-term nitrogen fertilization', CSIRO Division of Tropical Crops and Pastures, Townsville (mimeo).

McCown, R.L., Jones, R.K. and Hammer, G.L. (1984) 'Agriculture in Australia's seasonally-dry tropics and subtropics: climate and soil constraints', *Proceedings of the Eastern Africa-ACIAR Consultation on Agricultural Research, 18–22 July 1983*, Nairobi, Kenya, 86–96.

McGarrity, J. (1980) Report on soils and soil management on the Magarini Land Settlement Scheme, McGowan International Pty Ltd, 4 January to 19 February 1980.

McGowan, G.P., & Associates Pty Ltd (1977a) Magarini Land Settlement Project, Technical Annex 1, Climate, December 1977.

McGowan, G.P., & Associates Pty Ltd (1977b) Magarini Land Settlement Project, Technical Annex 2, Surface water investigations, December 1977.

McGowan, G.P., & Associates Pty Ltd (1977c) Magarini Land Settlement Project, Technical Annex 3, Groundwater investigation – including geology, November 1977.

McGowan, G.P., & Associates Pty Ltd (1977d) Magarini Land Settlement Project, Technical Annex 5, Land inventory and capability, October 1977.

McGowan, G.P., & Associates Pty Ltd (1977e) Magarini Land Settlement Project, Technical Annex 6, Sociology, August 1977.

McGowan, G.P., & Associates Pty Ltd (1977f) Magarini Land Settlement Project, Technical Annex 9, Soil conservation and management, October 1977.

McGowan, G.P., & Associates Pty Ltd (1977g) Magarini Land Settlement Project, Technical Annex 10, Agronomy, November 1977.

McGowan, G.P., & Associates Pty Ltd (1978a) Magarini Land Settlement Project, Project Report, Volume II, April 1978.

McGowan, G.P., & Associates Pty Ltd (1978b) Magarini Land Settlement Project, Executive Summary, June 1978.

McGowan International Pty Ltd, (1983) Draft Phase III Project Design, May 1983.

McNamara, R.S. (1972) *Address to the Board of Governors, World Bank Group*, Washington DC: International Bank for Reconstruction and Development.

McNamara, R.S. (1973) *Address to the Board of Governors*, Washington DC: International Bank for Reconstruction and Development.

McNamara, R.S. (1975) *Address to the Board of Governors*, Washington DC: International Bank for Reconstruction and Development.

Malindi NGO Program (1985) Design Report, Phase I, AFFHC/KFFHC.

Malindi NGO Programme (1986) Project Files, KFFHC.

Malindi NGO Program (1988) Health/Nutrition Activity, KFFHC-DVBD Cooperation, Update, November 1988, Nairobi: KFFHC.

Martin, E.B. (1973) *The History of Malindi: a Geographical Analysis of an East African Coastal Town from the Portuguese Period to the Present*, Nairobi: East African Literature Bureau.

Maslow, G. (1970) *Motivation and Personality*, New York: Harper & Row.

Mbithi, P. M. and Rasmussen, R. (1977) *Self Reliance in Kenya: the Case of Harambee*, Uppsala: Scandinavian Institute of African Studies.

Memom, P.A. and Martin, E.B. (1976) 'The Kenya coast: an anomaly in the development of an "ideal type" colonial spatial system', *Kenya Historical Review*, 4, 2: 187–206.

Messer, J. (1987) 'The sociology and politics of land degradation in Australia', in Blaikie, P. and Brookfield, H., with contributions by others, *Land Degradation and Society*, London: Methuen, 232–8.

Minear, L. (1987) 'NGOs today: practitioners of development strategies and advocates for the poor', *Development: Seeds of Change*, 4: 96–9.

Ministry of Agriculture (1957) *African Land Development in Kenya 1956*, London: HMSO.

Moi, D. (1986) *Kenya African Nationalism: Nyayo Philosophy and Principles*, London: Macmillan.

Moore, S.F. and Myerhoff, B.G. (1977) *Secular Ritual*, Assen: Van Gorcum.

Morawetz, D. (1977) 'Twenty five years of economic development', *Finance and Development*, 14: 10–13.

Moris, J. (1981) *Managing Induced Rural Development*, Bloomington: Indiana University.

Morley, F.H.W. and Nix, H.A. (1975) Report on a technical mission on dry land farming in areas of medium potential in Kenya, Canberra: ADAB/CSIRO, September 1975.

Morss, E.R. and Gow, D.D. (eds) (1985) *Implementing Rural Development Projects*, Boulder: Westview Press.

Moss, L.A.G. (1978) 'Implementing site and services: the institutional environment of comprehensive development projects', PhD thesis, University of California, Berkeley.

Murphy, T.A. (1985) 'The Snowy Mountains Engineering Corporation as an instrument of Australian foreign policy', MA thesis, Department of International Relations, The Australian National University, Canberra.

Mutiso, G. (1974) *Socio-political Thought in African Literature: Weusi?*, London: Macmillan.

Mutoro H.W. (1987) 'An archeological study of the Mijikenda kaya settlements on hinterland Kenya Coast', PhD thesis, University of California, Los Angeles.

Mutungi, O.K. (1977) *Legal Aspects of Witchcraft in East Africa*, Nairobi: Kenya Literature Bureau.

Nekby, B. (1971) *CADU: An Ethiopian Experiment in Developing Peasant Farming*, Stockholm: Prisma Publishers.

Nelson, D. (1975) *Managers and Workers: Origins of the New Factory System in the United States, 1880–1970*, Madison: University of Wisconsin Press.

New, C. (1873) *Life, Wanderings and Labours in Eastern Africa: with an Account of the First Successful Ascent of the Equatorial Snow Mountain, Kilimanjaro*, London: F. Carson.

Ngau, P. (1987) 'Tensions in empowerment: the experience of the harambee (self-help) movement in Kenya', *Economic Development and Cultural Change*, 35, 3: 523–38.

Nix, H.A. (1980) 'Strategies for crop research', *Proceedings of the Agronomy Society of New Zealand*, 10: 107–10.

Noble, D.F. (1977) *America by Design: Science, Technology and the Rise of Corporate Capitalism*, New York: A.A. Knopf.

ODI (Overseas Development Institute) (1978) *Agricultural Development and Rural Poverty: the Need for Radical Policy Revision*, Declaration, London: ODI.

OECD (Organisation for Economic Cooperation and Development) (1988) *Aid Agency Cooperation with NGOs*, Development Assistance Committee, 85, 2, 8 January, Paris: OECD.

O'Riordan, T. (1981) *Environmentalism*, London: Pion.

Orora, J. and Spiegel, H. (1979) 'Harambee: Self-help development projects in Kenya', *International Journal of Comparative Sociology*, 21, 3–4: 243–53.

Overton, J. (1988) 'The origins of the Kikuyu land problem: land alienation and land use in Kiambu, Kenya, 1895–1920', *African Studies Review*, 31, 2: 109–26.

Oyugi, W. (1981) *Rural Development Administration: a Kenyan Experience*, New Delhi: Vikas.

Palmer, B. (1975) 'Class concept and conflict: the thrust for efficiency, managerial views of labor and the working class rebellion', *Review of Radical Political Economics*, 7: 31–49.

Parboni, R. (1981) *The Dollar and Its Rivals: Inflation and International Finance*, London: Verso Books.

Parkin, D.J. (1968) 'Medicines and men of influence', *Man*, 3: 424–39

Parkin, D.J. (1970) 'Politics of ritual syncretism: Islam among the non-Muslim Giriama of Kenya', *Africa*, 40: 217–33.

Parkin, D.J. (1972) *Palms, Wine and Witnesses: Public Spirit and Private Gain in an African Farming Community*, San Francisco: Chandler.

Parkin, D.J. (1985) 'Entitling evil: Muslims and non-Muslims in coastal Kenya', in Parkin, D.J. (ed.) *The Anthropology of Evil*, Oxford: Blackwell, 224–43.

Parrish, R.M. (1978) 'The scope of benefit-cost analysis', *The Economic Record*, September: 304–14.

Payer, C. (1985) 'The IMF in the 1980s: what has it learned? What have we learned about it?' *Third World Affairs 1985*, London: Third World Foundation for Social and Economic Studies.

Pearce, D.W. (1971) *Cost–benefit Analysis*, London: Macmillan.

Perrett, H. and Lethem, F.J. (1980) *Human Factors in Project Work*, Washington DC: World Bank.

Porter, D. (1986) 'Professionalism and technical sophistication in Australia's aid programme', in Eldridge, P., Forbes, D. and Porter, D. (eds) *Australian Aid, Future Directions*, Canberra: Croom Helm, 243–64.

Porter, D. and Clark, K. (1985) *Questioning Practice: NGOs and Project Evaluation*, Wellington: New Zealand Coalition for Trade and Development. (Also published as *Development Dossier*, Canberra: Australian Council for Overseas Aid).

Preston, P.W. (1982) *Theories of Development*, London: Routledge and Kegan Paul.

Public Accounts Committee (1982) *Administration of Bilateral Overseas Aid*, Canberra: AGPS.

Quick, S.A. (c. 1980) 'The paradox of popularity: "ideological" programme implementation in Zambia', in Grindle, M.S. (ed.) *Politics and Policy Implementation in the Third World*, Princeton, New Jersey: Princeton University Press, 40–63.

Rao, M.B. and Westley, S.B. (1989) 'Agroforestry for Africa's semi-arid zone', *Agroforestry Today*, 1: 1.

Redclift, M. (1987) *Sustainable Development: Exploring the Contradictions*, London: Methuen.

Reeves, T. (1979) 'Crop Production Handbook for Extension Workers', Magarini Land Settlement Scheme, November 1979 (mimeo).

Report of the Committee to Review the Australian Overseas Aid Program (Jackson Committee) (1984) Canberra: AGPS.

Report of the Kenyan Land Commission, September 1933 (1934) London: HMSO.

Republic of Kenya (1978) *Report of the Parliamentary Committee on Landlessness on the 10 Mile Coastal Strip*, Nairobi: Government Printer.

Richards, P. (1986) *Indigenous Agricultural Revolution*, London: Hutchinson.

Righter, R. (1982) 'The World Bank betrays poor says official', *Sunday Times*, 7 March, 10.

Roberts, J.S. (1967) *A Land Full of People: Life in Kenya Today*, New York: Praeger.

Robertson, A.F. (1984) *People and the State: An Anthropology of Planned Development*, Cambridge: Cambridge University Press.

Rohan, D. (1984) 'Elements of project appraisal: a study of social cost–benefit analysis and the adoption of innovations', MEc thesis, University of New England, Armidale.

Rondinelli, D.A. (1979) 'Planning development projects: lessons from developing countries', *Long Range Planning*, 12, 3: 48–56.

Rosenthal, A.A. (1957) 'I.F.C. and private foreign investments', *Economic Development and Cultural Change*, 5, 3: 227–85.

Rothchild, D.S. (1973) *Racial Bargaining in Independent Kenya – a Study of Minorities and Decolonisation*, London: OUP for the Institute of Race Relations.

Ruthenberg, H. (1980) *Farming Systems in the Tropics*, Oxford: Clarendon Press.

Salim, A.I. (1973) *The Swahili-Speaking Peoples of Zanzibar and the East African Coast (Arabs, Shirazi and Swahili)*, London: International African Institute/Prins.

Samuel, H.L.S. and Einstein, A. (1951) *Essays in Physics, with a Letter from Albert Einstein*, Oxford: Blackwell.

Sandner, G. (1985) 'Integrated planning as an agent of the state vis-à-vis the local community and the "patra chica" (homeland): a summary of Central American experiences', *Society and Space*, 3, 2: 169–74.

Schlipp, E. (ed.) (1951) *Albert Einstein: Philosopher Scientist*, New York: Tudor.

Segal, A. (1968) 'Politics of land in East Africa', *Economic Development and Cultural Change*, 16, 2: 290.

Shaner, W.W. (1979) *Project Planning for Developing Countries*, New York: Praeger.

Sharpley, J. and Lewis, S.R. (1988) 'Kenya's industrialisation, 1964–84', *Institute of Development Studies Discussion Paper* 242, Brighton: University of Sussex.

Sicat, G.P. (1979) 'The role of foreign consultants in development', in FIDIC, *The Role of the Consulting Engineer in Development Projects and the Transfer of Technology to Developing Countries, Report of the Seminar*, Manila, 20–1 February, Lausanne: Federation Internationale des Ingenieurs-Conseils.

Singh, N. (1976) *Economics and the Crisis of Ecology*, Delhi: Oxford University Press.

Slovic, P., Fischoff, B. and Lichtenstein, S. (1982) 'Facts versus fears: understanding perceived risk', in Kahneman, D., Slovic, P. and Tversky, A. (eds) *Judgement Under Uncertainty: Heuristics and Biases*, Cambridge: Cambridge University Press.

Smith, B. (1987) 'An agenda of future tasks for international and indigenous NGOs: views from the north', *World Development Supplement*, 15: 87–93.

Smith, P. (1987) 'Identifying better development projects: a systems approach', *Agricultural Administration and Extension*, 25: 13–23.

Smith, L.D. (1989) 'Structural adjustment, price reform and agricultural performance in sub-Saharan Africa', *Journal of Agricultural Economics*, 40, 1: 21–31.

Soja, E. (1980) 'The socio-spatial dialectic', *Annals of the Association of American Geographers*, 70, 2: 207–25.

Soja, E. (1988) 'Regions in context: spatiality, periodicity, and the historical geography of the regional question', *Society and Space*, 3, 2: 175–90.

Spear, T. (1974) *The Kaya Complex*, Nairobi: Kenya Literature Bureau.

Staples, R.J., Price, S. and Daw, B. (1980) Draft review, Magarini Land Settlement Project, July 1980, Canberra: ADAB.

Staples, R.J., Price, S., McCown, R., Cook, J. and Lawrence, S. (1981) Joint review: Magarini Settlement Scheme, On-going Evaluation Report, September 1981, Canberra: ADAB.

Steinfels, P. (1979) *The Neoconservatives*, New York: Touchstone Press.

Stewart, F. (1978) 'SCBA in Practice', *World Development*, 6: 153–65.

Sunkel, O. (1977) 'The development of development thinking', *Institute for Development Studies Bulletin*, 8, 3: 6–11.

Tambiah, S. J. (1985) *Culture, Thought and Social Action: an Anthropological Perspective*, Cambridge: Harvard University Press.

Therkildsen, O. (1988) *Watering White Elephants? Lessons from Donor Funded Planning and Implementation of Rural Water Supplies in Tanzania*, Uppsala: Scandinavian Institute of African Studies.

Thiele, G. (1986) 'The state and rural development in Tanzania: village administration as a political field', *Journal of Development Studies*, 22, 3: 540–57.

Thomas, B. (1986) 'Development through harambee: who wins and who loses? Rural self-help projects in Kenya', *World Development*, 15, 4: 463–81.

Thompson, M., Warbuton, M. and Hatley, T. (1986) *Uncertainty on a Himalayan Scale: an Institutional Theory of Environmental Perception and a Strategic Framework for the Sustainable Development of the Himalaya*, London: Milton Ash.

Thompson, S. G. (1990) PhD thesis 'Speaking "truth" to power: divination for the paradigm for facilitating change among the Giriama in the Kenyan hinterland', School of Oriental and African Studies, University of London.

Throup, D. (1987) *Economic and Social Origins of Mau Mau, 1945–53*, London: Currey.

Tidrick, G. (1979) *Kenya: Issues in Agricultural Development*, Nairobi: Ministry of Economic Development and Planning.

Tiffen, M. (1987) 'Dethroning the internal rate of return: the evidence from irrigation projects', *Development Policy Review*, 5: 361–77.

Toye, J. (1987) *Dilemmas in Development: Reflections on the Counter Revolution in Development Theory and Policy*, Oxford: Basil Blackwell.

Twose, N. (1987) 'European NGOs: growth or partnership?', *World Development*, 15: 7–10.

Udvardy, M. (1988) 'Women's groups near the Kenyan Coast: patron clientship in the development arena', in Brokensha, D. (ed.) *Anthropology of Development and Change in East Africa*, Boulder: Westview Press, 217–35.

United Nations (1971) *Integrated Approaches to Development in Africa: Social Welfare Services in Africa*, New York: UN.

Vale, A. and Gaston, G. (1983) Assessment of Magarini Settlement Project, Kenya, (2 vols), Mission Report, ADAB, February 1983.

Van Arkardie, B., Jansen K. and Wright, P. (1979) Structure, Policy and Distribution: A Comparative Study of Colombia, Sri Lanka and Kenya, Final Report to the ILO, The Hague: Institute of Social Studies.

van Houten, D.R. and Goldman, P. (1981) 'Contract consultings hidden agenda', *Pacific Sociological Review*, 24: 461–93.

van Nieuwenhuijze, C.A.O. (1982) *Development Begins at Home: Problems and Prospects of the Sociology of Development*, Oxford: Pergamon.

WCED (World Commission on Environment and Development) (1987) *Our Common Future: The World Commission on Environment and Development*, Oxford: Oxford University Press.

wa Thiongo, Ngugi (1982) 'The settlers under the skin', *Guardian Weekly*, Friday 19 November 19, 15.

Waaijenberg, H. (1985) 'An agro-economic history of the Mijikenda of Kenya, 1600–1985', Training Project in Pedology of the Agricultural University of Wageningen, Kaloleni, Kenya (mimeo).

Waaijenberg, H. and Salim, M. (1983) 'Land and farming systems in the Kilifi District, Kenya', Paper for a farming systems workshop, Magarini Land Settlement Scheme, Training Project in Pedology of the Agricultural University of Wageningen, Kaloleni, Kenya (mimeo).

Walker, P. (1987) *Food Monitoring and Targeting in Red Sea Province, Sudan 1985–87*, Oxford: Oxfam.

Wanyama, B. (1988) Program Review Report, Malindi NGO Program, March 1988, Nairobi: Kenya Freedom From Hunger Council.

Ward, C. (1982) *Anarchy in Action*, London: Freedom Press.

Waterson, A. (1965) *Development Planning: Lessons of Experience*, Baltimore: The Johns Hopkins University Press.

Watnick, M. (1952) 'The appeal of communism to the peoples of underdeveloped areas', *Economic Development and Cultural Change*, 1: 22–36.

Watts, M. (1989) 'Against: famine and ecology in the Sahel', in Tyler Miller, G. (ed.) *Resource Conservation and Management*, Belmont: Wadsworth, 1–23.

White, J. (1970) *Regional Development Banks: A Study of Institutional Style*, London: Overseas Development Institute.

White, J. (1976) 'The evaluation of aid offers', *Development and Change*, 7: 233–48.

Wiggins, S. (1985) 'The planning and management of integrated rural development in dry lands: early lessons from Kenya's arid and semi-arid lands programmes', *Public Administration and Development*, 5, 2: 91–108.

Williams, G. (1981) 'The World Bank and the peasant problem', in Hayer, J., Roberts, P. and Williams, G. (eds) *Rural Development in Tropical Africa*, New York: St Martin's Press, 16–51.

Wohl, R. (1952) 'Editorial', *Economic Development and Cultural Change*, 1: 3–7.

World Bank (1978) *Socio-cultural Aspects of Water Supply and Excreta Disposal*, Washington DC: Energy, Water and Telecommunications Department, World Bank.

World Bank (1983a) *Guidelines for the Use of Consultants by World Bank Borrowers and by the World Bank as Executing Agency*, Washington DC: World Bank

World Bank (1983b) *Toward Sustainable Development in Sub-Saharan Africa*, Washington DC: World Bank.

World Bank (1988) 'Collaboration with non-governmental organizations', *Operational Manual Statement* No. 5, 30 August, Washington DC: IBRD.

Name index

Subject index

agricultural extension: alienation of settlers 71, 76; Australians' opinions of themselves 79–80; competency of Australians in Africa 71; involvement in Phase III appraisal farm surveys 108

agriculture: and food security 53; Giriama 51–8, 195; intensification 87, 89; labour constraints in 66, 70, 74; shifting cultivation 51–4, 87; transformation models 65 *see also* dryland farming; drought; famine; fertilizers; General Investigation Station; green revolution; indigenous knowledge; Magarini Settlement Project; maize production; weedicides

agro-ecosystems 87 *see also* systems

agro-forestry 58

aid: Australian administration of 1973–6, 33; Australian 'comparative advantage' 84, 129; Bretton Woods (1944) 93; and communism 93; defensive modernization 96; effectiveness in Kenya 98; history of 93–8; an instrument of foreign policy 212; international trends 97–8; limitations of 133; and policy coherence 98; and State control 211; wheat 6, 105

animators: 10, 147, 180, 184; compared to Giriama diviners 175 *see also* NGO programme

Appraisal Report 1978: on agriculture 64–7; environmental constraints forseen 44; on groundwater 62–4; on land tenure problems 61–2

Arabs: conflict with British 14; conflict with Giriama 19; relations with Giriama 46, 48

Australian Centre for International Agricultural Research (ACIAR) 87, 89, 102

Australian Freedom From Hunger Campaign (AFFHC) 10, 136, 140

Australian High Commission (AHC): reports on IRR values acceptable in Kenya 91; support for continuation to Phase III 103; views of Magarini Settlement Project 142

Australian International Development Assistance Bureau (AIDAB) 33, 34, 36, 43, 50, 60, 61, 63, 67, 68, 70, 77, 84, 91, 100, 101, 102, 103, 104, 106, 125, 130, 131, 135, 141, 193, 198, 210, 211, 212: reorganization 1973–6, 33; Technical Advisory Panel 8

Australian Monitoring Review Mission 1986, 10

basic needs 97–8

Batt, E. 7, 35, 36

bilharzia (urinary schistosomiasis) 10, 70, 154, 155

Biwott, N. 9, 101

Blight, D. 7, 35

Bretton Woods conference (1944) 93

British Army East Africa Carrier Corps, 21

cassava 102

catchment communities 34–5; 70, 85

catchment management 70, 156, 167

CERES maize simulation model 87, 111

Champion, Arthur: 19, 57–8, 202

chaos and uncertainty in non-linear systems 85–6